REPORT ON THE RUSSIANS

Report on
the Russians

W. L. WHITE

NEW YORK

HARCOURT, BRACE AND COMPANY

21476
4/5/1945

A WARTIME BOOK

*This complete edition is produced in full
compliance with the government's regu-
lations for conserving paper and other
essential materials.*

PRINTED IN THE UNITED STATES OF AMERICA

Introduction

*T*HIS book is basically the story of a six-weeks trip to Russia which I took during the summer of 1944 in company with Eric Johnston, President of the United States Chamber of Commerce, and Joyce O'Hara, his assistant. They lived at the American Embassy during our stay in Moscow, while I moved down to the Hotel Metropole to be nearer the correspondents, most of whom lived there.

Although we traveled together, in fairness to them I wish to make it clear that the opinions expressed in this book are entirely my own.

Also a word about the Russian people: I liked them very much—in many ways they are like Americans. Actually, since we are all descended from Adam there is no such thing as a "young" nation; but they have a fresh and unspoiled outlook which is close to our own. They entertained us lavishly, but there was nothing sinister in this and I never felt it was intended to influence anything we wrote or said after we got back.

Finally I wish to thank the *Reader's Digest* for publishing an excellent condensation of this book. There are probably errors; I have corrected several since the *Digest* appeared. Some of these mistakes were favorable to the Russians; some were unfavorable, and these last of course I regret.

W. L. WHITE

January 1, 1945

REPORT ON THE RUSSIANS

One

THE SOVIET vice-consul spoke creaky, schoolbook English, but he was an agreeable young man. He was helping me fill out my visa application. His office was pleasant and airy, but I was uneasy. Maybe because the office of the consul, upstairs, had double doors. Not the kind you find in free countries. The kind with which, when you open one door, you are left staring at still another closed door, about six inches in front of your nose. If the knob of the first door is on your right, the knob of the second is on the left. So no one could possibly listen through both keyholes at once. Fumbling through them, and after carefully closing both, you feel dazed, like a rat emerging from a Yale University maze.

I was uneasy not because I had something to conceal, but something to proclaim. Because I had been with the Finnish army in the winter war of 1939-1940, which was bad news in connection with a Soviet visa. Now, of course, they knew I had been in Finland, but I wanted them to know I knew they knew it. So when I was told the Soviet consul would be pleased to see me, and after I had negotiated the consul's two whisper-proof doors, I began trying to work in my Finnish trip. The consul was an urbane, stocky little diplomat. It soon became clear that he was on a fishing trip for information. There is nothing sinister about this, for it is the avowed business of all diplomats, including our own, to report to their home governments on the state of the nation to which they are accredited. I had undergone, in 1940, a somewhat similar seance with the equally suave German consul in Copenhagen, when I was applying for a re-entry visa to Germany. Before it was refused me, the consul pumped me of all kinds of information on the state of affairs in Finland, from which I had just come. I knew he was doing it, and yet, because he was a pleasant diplomat and because he wielded the stomach pump with a skillful hand, I submitted gracefully to the operation, yielding to him freely all information about the Finnish situation which I was sure he already knew, and pretending an inscrutable ignorance on any matter which his government might pass on to their allies the Russians. The Russo-German pact was then only a few months old, and the totalitarian alliance in its honeymoon phase.

There was no need, however, in 1944, to withhold anything from this consul, as his questions did not concern military matters but were all in the sphere of politics. For instance, how was Mr. Roosevelt's health? There had been some dark stories that it was failing. When I had been in Washington last week it had been fine, I said, and these were only the usual rumors.

And who would the Republicans nominate? And if probably Mr. Dewey, who did I think would be elected? But if it were Mr. Dewey, what kind of president did I think he would make? All of which I answered freely and then, explaining that I was applying for a Soviet visa, gave him a short biographical sketch, including the fact that I had covered the Finnish war for the American press and radio, a fact that he did not appear to hear for, ignoring it, he fell to reminiscing. He also had been in Europe in that winter of 1939-1940, as Soviet consul in a great North German seaport. And although the pact was ostensibly in effect he had been practically a prisoner in his consulate, cut off by the Germans from all contact with the people. Twice more as we compared impressions of the Prussians, I managed a reference to my Finnish interlude; each time he apparently did not hear.

Just before I left the consul switched the conversation from politics to literature. I wished to go to the Soviet Union as assistant to Mr. Eric Johnston, but I was also connected with the *Reader's Digest?* Yes, I said, I was one of its editors. And perhaps I also knew Mr. Eugene Lyons? Here I thought the affable face of the consul darkened slightly, for Gene Lyons is hardly counted as one of the Soviet Union's fervent admirers.

Yes, I said, I knew Mr. Lyons quite well. And what, exactly, was the connection between Mr. Lyons and the *Reader's Digest?* There was none, I could answer truthfully.

This seemed to exhaust literature and since the conversation now paused, I bowed myself out the whisper-proof double doors and back to where Mr. Vavilov was waiting with the questionnaire.

It began with a large blank space for a brief autobiography, into which I inserted the fact that I had been with the Finnish army in 1939, a fact that Mr. Vavilov, reading at my shoulder, seemed again not to notice.

It continued with other questions, obviously designed for White Russians, about political affiliations. To what party did I belong? Of what other political parties had I previously been a member? When and why—giving dates and specific reasons—had I in each case changed my allegiance? I showed some dismay at all this, and Mr. Vavilov, smiling reassuringly, said there was no need, in my case, for detailed answers.

But at the end was a most curious question: I had hastily written "no" in its blank, but then I hesitated. Had I, they wanted to know, ever been associated with the armed forces of any government in opposition to the Soviet Union? Archly, I appealed to Mr. Vavilov. I explained—this time clearly so there could be no misunderstanding —that in 1939 I had been associated as a reporter with the armies of the Finnish Republic during its earlier war with Russia. So perhaps my answer should be yes?

Smiling broadly now, Mr. Vavilov shook his head.

"The proper answer there, Mr. White, as you have already written, is 'no.' Because in Finland in 1939, we understand that your opposition to the Soviet Union was purely verbal."

My visa came a week later.

All this had come about as the result of an impulsive letter I had written a few weeks before. Reading that Joseph Stalin had issued a special invitation to visit Russia to Eric Johnston, president of the United States Chamber of Commerce, I had sat down at my type-writer to tell Johnston I would like to go along.

Eric Johnston was to me a complete stranger, except that I had read a good deal of what he had written and liked most of it very much. He "believed in" this country; which is to say that he had been an eloquent voice preaching optimism and courage for the postwar period; a voice clearly saying that never again must we allow American business and industry to stagnate into a depression, but must continue to produce for peacetime needs and luxuries at almost wartime velocity: there would be free markets for everything if there were free jobs for all, and vice versa.

He seemed, in addition, to be a completely uninhibited extrovert, and in his so far brief career on the national scene, had approached its august and forbidding figures with friendly curiosity. He had opened his career as president of the National Chamber by calling at the White House—a precedent-breaking step, as American business had not hitherto accorded the New Deal official recognition. He had even sat down across a conference table from John L. Lewis.

For he has a theory, as simple as Columbus's egg trick, that before you begin to denounce an opponent, you should first go over with him the points on which you agree; you will both be surprised, Johnston points out, at how many of these there are and often the fight can be fairly compromised.

In somewhat this frame of mind he was approaching the Soviet Union; I wanted to go there for the very obvious reason that Russia is clearly the biggest and most unpredictable factor with which America must deal in the next few decades.

About a week after my impulsive letter I met Eric Johnston across his desk in Washington. The first thing you see is that Eric Johnston is handsome. At forty-seven he has all of his white even teeth, all of his wavy brown hair, and a clear, ruddy skin, and blue eyes. He has a longish, sensitive face and a Hollywood profile. Together, these make him unusually and conspicuously handsome and the fact that people turn to look at him when he walks down a street is as much beyond his control as though he were hunchbacked or had six fingers on each hand. It is the kind of striking male beauty which could easily become a handicap because it tends to annoy almost every other male. He counteracts this with a quick and completely disarming smile. I am sure he has done this for so long that he has forgotten just how and when he first discovered it was necessary.

Taken alone they might have made for him a successful career as an actor, were it not for his brain, which, considered as an organ, is uncommonly good. It starts with a phenomenal memory. He never forgets anything he thinks he will ever need, and his judgment on this point is good. He can read over three times the text of a twenty-minute speech, and then repeat it word for word. Or he can give you the year the Emperor Maximilian entered Mexico. It no more requires effort on his part than does his profile.

It is unfortunate that the word "opportunist" should have become a term of abuse, with the implication that one should be praised for daydreaming while chances go by. In any case, Eric Johnston is as constantly aware of the world around him as is a fox terrier who pricks up his ears at every creaking board. Walking down streets, he automatically locates corners for cigar stores. A crowd of idle, ragged Arabs becomes a potential labor supply and at the same time a potential consumer demand.

He is healthily competitive; he wants something like almost anything you have, or if possible, one just a little better. But he takes disappointments well. When I first met him he was being mentioned for the presidency; he had a small but definite chance. He watched it carefully, never overestimated or underestimated his boom. When it faltered, he pronounced it dead and instantly forgot it. This is mental health amounting almost to abnormality. Mention for the presidency is usually a catastrophe which requires years of painful convalescence. Eric Johnston was up, about, and interested in the outside world in a matter of minutes.

However, what with his keen mind he usually gets rather easily what he wants. Then he is able to think sympathetically about what other people need and is as eager to help them get it as though it were something for himself.

It wasn't just Eric Johnston going to Russia; he was American business appraising the whole Soviet show: and all of what we saw there should be available to any American who shared our curiosity. I was pleased when he told me that, because he wanted to feel free to write and say what he thought on our return, he was insisting to the Russians that we pay our expenses wherever possible. He was taking along money for that purpose, and suggested that I do likewise.

The other member of our party was Joyce O'Hara, Johnston's regular assistant in the Chamber of Commerce. He is a blue-eyed Irishman of fifty with regular features which, anywhere outside the radius of Johnston's dazzling profile, would be considered uncommonly handsome. Not too many years ago he exchanged a successful newspaper job for a career in the public relations division of the Chamber of Commerce in Washington.

Joyce and I were thrown together constantly from the beginning of the trip. The protocol of our entire voyage was that if the hotel or guesthouse boasted an Imperial Bridal Suite complete with sitting room, sitz bath, and breakfast nook, it would always be assigned to Johnston in solitary grandeur, in his capacity as President of the Chamber of Commerce, while Joyce and I would share twin beds in the second-best room. For a few days we watched each other shave and listened to each other snore with considerable reserve and some suspicion. He told me later that he suspected I was going to be a wild and unpredictable male Carrie Nation who would make trouble during the whole trip. At the outset I could see him only as an unnecessarily vivid character escaped from the pages of Sinclair Lewis.

Only slowly and after days of appraisal did we get down to a solid basis of friendly jibes at each other's weak spots, and he gave as good as he got. We ended up warm friends.

It developed that O'Hara's pet phobia was bacteria in any form, but this was only gradually revealed. We departed from Washington and our plane stopped for a meal in the Azores where we were met by staff officers of the American base and picked up sketchy information about these Portuguese islands. It seemed the British also have bases there and for a while there was ill-feeling because of differences in rates of pay. American soldiers get the most, the British considerably less, and the local Portuguese least of all. The American commandant sensibly eased the situation by permitting no soldier to cash more than $30 a month for spending money. But some disparity still existed and the local Portuguese girls, who have a keen sense of justice, had further eased it by charging Americans 80 milreis, His Majesty's troops 40, and the local Portuguese garrison 20.

The only entertainment, we were told, was the weekly bull fight, and here Portuguese customs differ from those of Spain.

The bull's horns are encased in leather and at the fight's end he is never killed. Instead his wounds are sprinkled with sulfa, sewed up, and he is thriftily saved for another day. These fights are attended en masse by the American G.I.'s, who cheer wildly for the bull.

Before breakfast at this base we washed up and shaved in an army tent. It was steaming hot and the staff captain suggested a shower bath in the next tent. Johnston followed him out.

"Where'd they go?" demanded Joyce. His ears and eyes had been full of lather.

"Out to get a shower."

"Hey, don't let him do that—go and stop him!"

"Why?"

Joyce looked around. We were alone. He leaned toward me. "Athlete's foot," he said in an ominous whisper. "Tell him not to bring it back—we'll all get it."

Yet Johnston somehow escaped this peril, only to fall victim to an infected sinus at Casablanca. We were all impatient to push on toward Russia, yet ahead of us lay high altitude flying which might spread the infection and lay him up for weeks, so we must wait until it healed.

We waited in considerable luxury in a spacious villa, once the property of Jean Maas who formerly owned a string of collaborationist newspapers and was known in the French-African colonies as the Hearst of North Africa. His San Simeon, which the Allied armies confiscated, is a beautiful blending of French Modern and Arabic. This spacious mass of elaborate bathrooms and penthouse terraces wanders down a hillside to trail off in a maze of tennis courts, gardens, and swimming pools. The Allied command were using it as an overnight hotel for high officers and distinguished guests, as we seem to be classified.

"Captain," demanded Joyce earnestly, "do you drink the water here?"

"Most people don't like the local beer. But I could get you some wine—"

"I mean can you drink the water—is it all right?"

"Oh, but the army runs Casablanca. We've been here since 1943. First thing they do is test the water."

"Oh. Well, how about mosquitoes?"

"We're too high up the hill to get many."

"Much malaria around here?"

"Some on the other side of the desert—about 700 miles away."

"Much in Casablanca?"

"Oh, none in Casablanca. Didn't you read that sign at the airport?"

"Just wanted to be sure. But you *do* have mosquitoes?"

"A few. Would you like a screened room?"

"Think we'd better."

Later we were taken through the old Arab city by the lieutenant in charge of American M.P.'s and finally the base hospital, a good distance out in the desert on the opposite side of the city. It was beautifully equipped, but we were far from the battle zone. The most interesting patient was a case of camel-bite.

"That screened tent over there," said Colonel Tinsman, who was showing us around, "is the malaria ward."

"They told us there wasn't any in Casablanca!" said Joyce, indignantly.

"There isn't. These three were brought in from way down the coast."

"Oh." But his voice still carried a note of triumph.

✦

It was about three in the morning. I had heard muffled thumps, sounds of a struggle, but I had been sleeping soundly and woke slowly. The servants at the Villa Maas were Italian prisoners of war, yet they seemed most respectful, even timid.

"Bill!"

The light was on. I opened my eyes. Joyce, clad in billowing B.V.D.'s down to his wrists and ankles and sagging at the crotch, was standing motionless in the middle of the room, brandishing what seemed to be a club.

"Wazzamatter?"

"Be quiet!" said Joyce in a tense whisper. "There's one in here."

The villa was very still. Outside not even a breeze rustled.

"I don't hear anything."

"I heard him. Woke me up. Listen! Flying around somewhere."

Joyce seemed to be staring fixedly at a corner next the door. The poised club turned out to be a folded copy of *Collier's*. It occurred to me that Joyce was having a stroke, and his enemy was the Angel of Death.

"It'll be all right," I said very evenly and quietly.

"Hell it will. Damn thing was buzzing right over my ear. Probably got in through that screen. There's always holes in 'em." *Collier's* poised, he had been slowly turning. Suddenly he froze. "There!" he hissed, and began gliding toward one wall. In its center was a tiny black spot. He let drive at this with *Collier's*. The spot was unchanged.

"Damn fly speck," he said disgustedly. "Where's my glasses?"

"Look, Joyce. Suppose there is a mosquito. There's no malaria in Casablanca."

"Three cases. Out at that hospital."

"All screened."

"Always have holes. How'd this mosquito get in here, if there wasn't always holes?"

"All right, now look. There might be one hole out there. But the mosquito's got to find it. Then he's got to bite a patient. Then he's got to find the same hole again to get out."

"Well, he could."

"And then, I suppose, without pausing, he pivots and flies over five miles of desert to Casablanca. And then you think he'd fly right over the bare backsides of 200,000 Arabs without pausing, just to get to the Villa Maas. And then, I suppose, he finds a hole in this particular screen, out of all the other screens on the house. And then, I suppose, he flies right over me, here by the window, in order to get to you. And then—"

"Here they are," said Joyce, picking up his glasses. "Now we'll see about this."

"Let me know how it comes out." I lay back on the pillow.

A quarter of an hour later there was a loud pop.

"Got him!" said Joyce, triumphantly. I raised up. He was advancing toward me, holding out *Collier's*. On its margin was a brownish smear. The Angel of Death.

"Blood," he said darkly, looking at me sternly and pointing to the smear.

"We can telephone Tinsman. He could come over and heat a needle and cauterize us."

Joyce pondered this. But then he glanced suspiciously at me and managed an unsteady grin.

"Oh, well," he said, and lumbered back to bed. He switched out the light. But presently I heard him stir. "One of us was bit, though; no doubt about that," he said grimly.

At Cairo a competent American nose and throat man peered into Johnston's ear and instantly forbade us to fly over the 16,000 foot pass between Iran and the Soviet Union, which meant a few days' delay. Anyway we would get a good look at ancient Cairo, which none of us had ever seen.

"And they say we can stay right here in the barracks at this airfield," said Joyce. "Good American food and water."

"But if we stay in town, we can really see Cairo," I argued. I wanted to avoid the boredom of three square G.I. meals a day in a desert mess hall. "At least we won't have all those corn flakes and hard pork chops and overcooked vegetables and powdered eggs."

"I'd just as soon stay here," said Joyce. "At least we'll know what we're eating. Maybe it's not the Statler but it's good American food."

"You're not going to get cat at Shepheard's. It's one of the best hotels in the world."

"How'll we know about the water?"

"This has been a military base for years. The army tests it."

"Yes, but what army?"

"The British. But probably we test it, too."

"We don't know that, though."

A stalemate; we both looked at Johnston. He never hesitates at decisions.

"I've never seen Cairo," he said. "I think we could try the hotel. Think we ought to see Cairo."

Shepheard's was full, so we stayed at its annex, the Continental, identical in every way, almost as large and just down the street. Yet it definitely was not a Statler. It had high tropical ceilings, dark, carved woodwork from the 1890's and the servants were raven-eyed Arabs in red fezzes, flowing white gowns, and noiseless slippers.

Our rooms were huge with spreading white marble washbasins and enormous brass beds, over which flowed mosquito bars. Joyce frowned at our room with measured approval. But then he got out his prized possession, the anti-mosquito bomb presented him by Colonel Tinsman just before we left Casablanca—a sinister black metal container about the size of a croquet ball with a nozzle which releases the compressed gas. A few puffs of it is supposed to rid any room of mosquitoes; it rids it even more rapidly of people. In Cairo it is hot almost to suffocation. Closing tightly the two tall French doors which lead out onto the tiny balcony, Joyce gets out his anti-insect bomb and, while I stand speechless, sprays our room with this noxious gas until the air is gray.

"Now," he says, slipping it back into his bag, "we'd better get down to dinner."

Still I have a little hope. Maybe when the Soviet border guards see this gadget, he won't be able to convince them his bomb is entirely non-political.

✦

Waiting for Johnston's ear to heal before we tackle Teheran pass, we fly up for half a day in Jerusalem, and on the return trip find the pilot of our plane has very sensibly filled its extra seats with about twenty soldiers on leave who have been waiting passage to Cairo. Americans, British, and colonials, officers and men—and two pretty English girls in ATS uniform.

We buckle our safety belts for the take-off. The rest of the plane is shyly eyeing the civilian clothes. The Cairo airport has provided a carton of sturdy G.I. sandwiches—more than three of us can eat. So Eric takes charge. He leans forward in his safety belt as we bump down the runway.

"Here, boys, want a sandwich?—Catch!" Without waiting for an answer he begins pitching cheese sandwiches, oranges, and hard-boiled eggs down the plane's corridor.

Baseball-trained Americans automatically put up their hands to anything whizzing through the air; soon a dozen are munching. But the British boys sit shyly in bewildered embarrassment.

At the airport they give me an army car to take me to my Cairo hotel and, discovering that the two English girls also want transportation to the Cairo Y.W.C.A., I offer them a ride.

They explain that they drive army lorries and their base is a tiny desert station on the Suez canal—about 150 girls. They get two weeks' leave a year. The plump sergeant is twenty-six and a robust cockney from east London. The slender private is prettier and finer-grained. She comes from Yorkshire, is twenty-one and left college to drive trucks in the Egyptian desert eighteen months ago. The sergeant has been out two years. Neither, of course, has been home since. Part of their company of girl truckdrivers is also from England, but they have Greeks from Cyprus and also girls from Palestine. The Palestinians, they say, are inclined to give themselves airs. Most of them are German refugees and the sergeant says that they like to boast, and not too quietly either, that they know more about English literature than do the English girls.

The Greek girls, they say, are at first inclined to be wild. They join up mostly because they are held down so tightly by their families at home, and want to see a bit of the world, but when they get freedom they can't handle themselves.

"It's our men they go for, too," said the private, gloomily. "Never their own."

"Cawn't say as we blime them," said the sergeant, "when you see what theirs are like."

Then they fell to talking about us. "We knew you were veddy important Ameddicans with your own plane," they said, "so when you got aboard we tried to decide which of you was the important one."

"I say," said the sergeant, "you Ameddicans do get on quickly, don't you? We English have to know people for quite a while, but you Ameddicans get on at once."

"And do you remember when the handsome one started throwing the food; we'd hardly got in the air!"

"It fair took our breath," said the sergeant, "throwing food at chaps you 'aven't met. All the other Ameddicans knew what to do, though. They caught it and began eating. We never saw anything like it."

"And did you notice that little English leftenant sitting down at the end of the plane?" said the pretty private. "He was very hungry but very bashful, and didn't know if it would be all right if he caught some or not. All the Ameddicans were picking it out of the air as your chap chucked it, but the English leftenant just sat there, holding up his hands shyly. Finally your handsome chap noticed it and threw him an egg. It was all so veddy like the Ameddicans we see in the music halls back home. We didn't really know all Ameddicans were like that."

"Were you at the Mena Conference?" asked the sergeant.

I said I wasn't.

"We first met Ameddicans there," said the pretty private. "We were driving staff cars. There were some veddy important Ameddicans at Mena. And some of them *were* odd—at least, quite different from us."

"What did they throw?"

"Nothing. They were veddy important Ameddicans, but they didn't throw anything."

"They worried about the water," said the sergeant. "All of them 'ad to 'ave special water. They were veddy important."

"And do you have little bottles?" asked the pretty private. "Each of them had dozens of little bottles, and they were always swallowing pills and nibbling medicines out of them."

I thought of Joyce who had in his grips, carefully wrapped in extra suits of underwear, antidotes for everything from snake bite to suffocation.

"'Ad to 'ave their own ice," said the sergeant gloomily. "Wouldn't trust our British ice."

"But they were veddy important Ameddicans," said the pretty private resignedly.

The next morning Eric, Joyce, and I continue our trip, and that afternoon at Teheran we see our first Russians. Their planes with the big red stars are on the field as we circle, and as we get out of our plane, the Russian Ambassador to Iran and half a dozen of his staff are there to welcome Eric Johnston. They are very solemn and do not smile as they shake hands. I suddenly remember that neither do Prussians; jump to the conclusion that there is little unnecessary smiling east of the Oder.

These solemn Russian diplomats are all in their thirties or early forties, and they wear curious, badly cut Soviet suits—somber in hue and of shoddy materials. You could take an American mail-order suit, boil it, press it lightly, and get the same effect.

Standing there in these single-breasted Sears, Roebuck models, they gravely ask us if we had a pleasant trip, soberly welcome us to Iran and solemnly wish us a pleasant trip through the Soviet Union.

The next morning Averell Harriman, American Ambassador to the Soviet Union, who has just arrived in Teheran, is taking us to Moscow in the official ambassadorial Liberator. Averell Harriman is one of the few ambassadors who actually looks like one. He is rich, tall, dark, handsome, pleasant-voiced and unimpulsive. His daughter, who is with him, is also all of these things.

As his official hostess in Moscow, she meets rather more than her share of important people and so is able to remain calm in the presence of the National Chamber of Commerce. After greeting us pleasantly in the plane, she returns to her novel. Immediately we begin to fight for altitude for the mountains are just ahead. Harriman as host and Johnston as the most honored guest dutifully chat in the best pair of seats. I look from my window. We are approaching a jagged divide. Snow gleams up at us from granite crevices.

Since the Liberator, unlike the Fortress, is a high-wing plane, and gas from a wing-tank leak might trickle down into the cabin, no smoking is allowed except up in the crew's compartments, which are forward of the wing. I presently stroll up here for a cigarette and chat with the crew. The American navigator and radioman stand idle, for at their tables sit two stony-faced Red Air Force men, wearing pistol belts from which hang forty-five's.

The American radioman notices my stare and grins.

"Never without 'em," he says. "Bet they wear 'em on their night shirts."

"How do you get along with them?"

"Okay. They don't speak any English. Far as we know they don't. They're strictly business aboard here."

I nod toward the Russian working at the navigator's table. "Does he know his business?"

"Seems to. Of course, our navigator checks everything he does."

"How do you boys like Russia?"

The boy grins. "Russia? Better let Ted tell you. We're in and out a good deal; Ted's there regular. He's just riding up with us now as a passenger back from Teheran. Oh, Ted!"

A master sergeant raises up from a bunk. "Yuh?"

"This guy wants to know how we like Russia."

The master sergeant sits up. "Want me to tell him?"

"Shoot."

"It's a hell of a place. Every time you get a girl in Moscow, she disappears. That is, unless she's working for the NKVD * herself."

* The Soviet secret police—formerly the GPU.

"Where does she go?"

"That's what you want to know. And if you go round to ask her family, that's what they want to know."

A red-headed boy had joined the group. "It gets so," he said, "that if you really like some babe, you don't want to go out with her, for her own sake. Because she doesn't know what will happen, but you do."

Back in the cabin, my friends are peering keenly out of the window, onto the dense green of the lower slopes of the foothills. "Look, Bill! What an opportunity for dams!"

Now we cross the lead-blue Caspian sea and are presently flying above the shore line of Baku, dotted with oil wells. Leaving Baku, we strike off northward and I am fascinated by the villages. In Persia they had been round with streets in rings and roads radiating out from the central mosque. But these Slav settlements tend to be rectangular or square like American towns. The smallest of them is a double row of houses on either side of one long dirt road— from the air they might be American crossroads towns of the 'eighties or 'nineties, except that the roofs are thatched.

Most fascinating of all is a fact which I knew but not until now could believe: that in Russia there are few connected paved highways. I see wagon trails from the villages out to the fields, and sometimes faint ones from town to town, but not one strip of clean, flowing concrete or black-top.

Also I'm trying, through this plexiglass window, to see the socialist revolution as it has affected the villages, but I can't. For all this might have been here in the middle ages. If new thatched-roof huts have been built since czarist days, from 5,000 feet I can't tell them from the ancient ones. Looking down on every village, the biggest building is still the white church, built in czarist days. In twenty-five years the Soviets have constructed nothing half as big, although here and there is what might be a school or an administrative hall.

What have the farmers got out of socialism in this quarter century of backbreaking work and bloodshed? Undoubtedly more education and better clothes, to which my friend Maurice Hindus is an eloquent and accurate witness—but nothing I can see from a mile in the air.

There are no isolated farms, but sometimes a dozen villages are in sight at once. The pattern: that single mud street with thatched houses on each side and a big white church in the center; behind each house a little strip of private garden; beyond this a vast expanse of land which is the communal farm. In one village the church, instead of being in its center, stands on top of a little hill a hundred yards away. But the path is heavily overgrown with weeds.

Now we fly over a manufacturing town. White buildings with red roofs—they tell me it is typical of southern Russia. The church still looms above all.

I read a magazine, glancing out now and then to see if the picture changes (it does not), until the co-pilot comes back to say we will swing low over Stalingrad. Diving, we follow the bends of the city itself as it follows the river—or rather, as once did the city. For Stalingrad is gone, and there remain only roofless walls like the snags of decayed molars staring up at us. Factories, with twisted machinery rusting under the tangle of roof girders. Shattered workers' apartments, like the smashed comb of a deserted beehive. It is, of course, hideous. But I have become used to ruins, starting with the blitz over London in 1940. If you coiled Stalingrad up and set it down in the ruins of London, there would still be plenty of room for Stalingrad to rattle around.

Leaving Stalingrad, we climb for altitude and I divide my time between my magazine and the window. But the picture repeats. Wagon tracks connecting the tiny villages, with their onion-spired Byzantine churches.

Finally, just out of Moscow, we see an electric power line running from horizon to horizon. It is the first thing I have seen in the past hour that I am sure was built since 1917. But soon we see the first hard-surfaced road, and that black smudge on the horizon is Moscow itself. Then its railway yards and the smoke from its factories. Tiers of workers' apartments surround each factory and are in turn surrounded by a crazy quilt of potato patches. A spacious outdoor theater is on the river banks. The roofs of the big buildings are mottled with brown and green camouflage paint.

Spiraling down we get a closer look at the railway yards. The Germans have done a neat job here, spotting craters where craters should be, and scattering few wild bombs. As we let our wheels down and begin to feel for the runway, I see, rushing past, great rows of American-built C-47's stacked on the field in orderly rows with the big star of the Red Air Force painted on each.

Two

$\mathcal{A}$ CONSIDERABLE crowd is waiting at the airdrome. First, the welcoming committee; a row of solemn Slavs in the same boiled mail-order suits we saw at Teheran. But the minute Eric Johnston emerges, a battery of lenses—movie cameras and Soviet copies of Leicas and Graflexes—close in on his profile. This over, we smilingly shake hands with the unsmiling Russians and work our way through to the American reporters on the outskirts. Practically all of Moscow's tiny foreign newspaper colony is there to cover us, and they tell us that the Russians have given us an unusually big official turnout—"better than Donald Nelson's."

A big Russian in his middle thirties wanders toward me. "Is everything all right?" he wants to know. "I am Kirilov, in charge of protocol for the People's Commissariat of Foreign Trade." Then he added a little anxiously, "I hope everything is as it should be." We did not then know that, representing this Foreign Trade Commissariat which was our official host, he was to be our constant companion or that he had been selected for the difficult task of catering to the whims of visiting American dignitaries because in the early thirties he had been sent by his government to complete his technical education at the Colorado School of Mines in the small mountain town of Golden, and so knew both the English language and the American ways.

For this task his greatest asset was to be his imperturbability. He is large, plump, pale, with dark hair and sleepy, hazel eyes. I am sure that many of the things we did irritated or shocked or embarrassed him, yet he always stared at us with the solemnity of a frog lost in reveries, unruffled as a pail of cold lard.

But we now foresee none of this and after only a casual look at

Kirilov are whisked away in American army cars to Spaso House, where Eric Johnston is scheduled to give an interview to the Anglo-American Press.

We get a quick first look at Moscow. Wide, incredibly empty streets, sidewalks full of hurrying, shabby people, walking past dingy shops in dilapidated buildings. Monotonous rows of uninteresting apartments, concrete beehives which sometimes make an effort at beauty in ornamentation. But it is half-hearted, like the architecture of an institution.

Now we come to Spaso House which, before the 1917 Revolution, was built by a beet-sugar baron, and is one of a number of such palaces in Moscow which once belonged either to the merchant princes or the Romanov nobility. The Bolsheviks have turned them over to foreign governments for embassies. Inside, all are giant forests of marble columns from the tops of which, like grapevines, trail the marble balustrades of staircases. They are as drafty as movie sets, and as cozy to live in as Grand Central Station. Out in the back yard of each is a hen house and if, at a diplomatic reception, you see Averell Harriman in the center of a Bokhara rug in this great hall earnestly talking with Sir Archibald Clark Kerr, you can be sure that they are discussing not the Curzon Line or the Future of Esthonia, but comparing notes on laying mixtures.

It was in one such august hall, its spaciousness lightly salted down with curved gilt furniture, that Eric Johnston held his first press conference, from the central master chair.

He's delighted to be here, expects to stay about a month. No, just here as a private citizen, a businessman who will discuss Soviet-American trade in the postwar period. Stalin? He has a verbal invitation to visit him from the Russian Ambassador in Washington. He won't discuss politics; he's not a politician but a production man. He believes we must have an expanding economy in the postwar world—greater exchange of goods and services between countries, which will bring a higher living standard. As a production man, he's interested in the Soviet Union's prospects for expanding production.

"Will any special organization be needed to carry on postwar Soviet-American trade?" the press asks.

"I don't know. I'm here to discuss this."

Will long-term loans be necessary?

They should be favorably considered. And on this, as on all other matters, he has come to Russia with an open mind.

Is he in Russia to lay the basis for organizing all this?

He's not here to sign contracts, hasn't discussed Russian trade with any particular American firms.

Will postwar trade be an American state monopoly?

Very firmly it won't be.

But is it possible for private business to deal with the Soviet Union?

The smaller firms can organize themselves into sizeable blocs.

"But if you're dealing with a monopoly," asks the Reuter's correspondent, "don't you need a monopoly to deal with it?"

Johnston smiles. From the English point of view, yes; from the American, no.

Aren't there forces in America against an expanding economy?

There are always forces which don't see opportunities, which think the world is already built. But in America, still greater forces see there is much to be done; that we are only beginning to develop our economy. America this year produced $80,000,000,000 worth of consumer goods—almost as much as in her peak year of 1940—on top of another $80,000,000,000 worth of war goods. Our total production is now $160,000,000,000 and we think there will be a sufficient demand in America and abroad to keep that level after the war. For it will take years to fill the accumulated shortages. There should be a period of high employment in America, England, and Russia, with higher living standards. For mankind's desires, he tells the reporters, are insatiable; the princes' luxuries of today are the paupers' demands of tomorrow.

In closing, the reporters plead for bi-weekly press conferences. For the Soviet Government has promised that he can see everything he desires, and, until he has been in Moscow for a while, he can't conceive how closely foreign reporters are held down; how seldom they are allowed to leave Moscow; how little they see or hear. And could he possibly take a press representative with him on his Urals trip?

That, Johnston says cautiously, will have to be decided later.

But now Johnston is off to call on Mikoyan, an intimate of Stalin and a top Bolshevik, who is People's Commissar for Foreign Trade, our official host. Meanwhile I prowl Spaso House. Joyce is upstairs, luxuriating in its clean bathrooms, bedbugless American sheets and the prospect of three American square meals a day. The ambassador kindly invited us to be his guests here during our stay, but I have decided to move into one of the Moscow hotels, preferably the Metropole, where all the reporters live, if it can be arranged. It may be grim, but you can't see a capital from an embassy.

Johnston returns from the Kremlin very much impressed by Mikoyan. "Highly intelligent. He'd be prominent in any country. In America he'd be a big businessman or industrialist. I told him that. He seemed pleased."

Tonight our Russian hosts, with Kirilov in charge, take us to a concert at Tschaikovsky Hall, which in New York would be Carnegie Hall. We arrive a little late and just as we edge into our box the lights go down and the performance begins. There is an excellent violinist followed by a mezzo-soprano. In between I look at the hall which seems well built but a little too ornate. Then at the crowd. It is intent on the stage and in the half-light looks shabby, except for the red epaulets on the officers' uniforms. Most of their heads are clipped, Prussian style—or perhaps the Prussians got it from the Russians?

Each act on the stage is introduced by an attractive brunette in a simply cut dress of gleaming white satin. By contrast with that shabby audience, she is a dream-princess, and so are the performers. The men on the stage are in evening dress and the women slightly spangled with sequins. But the clothes are well-cut of good materials, clean and pressed: this drab socialist audience stares at the stage as though it were some unattainable fairyland of which they get just an hour's glimpse.

A male pianist has just taken his bows and retired to the wings and they are now clearing away his grand piano for the next act.

How? Well, the slender brunette in the white satin dress is pushing it, a feat made possible because it is on castors. I find myself unconsciously leaning forward in my seat and pushing on the box rail—to help her. Joyce and Eric are doing the same. But this, it seems, is a purely Anglo-Saxon reaction, for the audience does not even rustle. Later, after watching many slender women heave pianos, trunks and crates around, we become almost as calloused as Russians. But now in the dark we look at each other wordlessly and smile.

Kirilov leans forward anxiously.

"You do not care for the pianist?"

"Oh, yes."

Kirilov looks relieved. "In this country he has large reputation," he adds, settling back comfortably into his chair, as the slender girl, pushing her grand piano, disappears behind the scenery.

Now the lights come up and we go out into the great foyer where the Russian audience is indulging in the pleasant European custom of a between-acts promenade. In the hard light of the big chandeliers I get a close look at them.

And I've never seen anything like it. Ill-fitting clothes, poorly cut, often flashy but always of tawdry materials. Yes, I know there's a war on. And the British also are shabby. But you can tell that at one time their well-worn clothes were good, while these never were.

This is the Tschaikovsky Concert Hall where seats usually go to top officials or to crack Stakhanovite workers who get high wartime wages. But their clothes can't compare with those of a meeting of the Workers Alliance in my home town of Emporia, Kansas, at the bottom of our depression. For before our WPA home relief cases would have appeared in public as shabbily dressed as this socialist soviet aristocracy, they would have gone down to the courthouse and torn the case-workers limb from limb. Yet Carnegie Hall seldom offers a better program than the one that we heard on the stage.

I note that the crowd is almost as poorly fed as it is poorly dressed. The Red Army officers are robust enough. But too many of these Russian women have bad complexions, which seem to indicate lack of vitamins. I have always thought of Russians as big people; potentially they probably are. But these people, in their twenties and thirties, were children during the hard days after the revolution; years of malnutrition show in their bad bone structure. No wonder we three average-sized Americans stand half a head higher than the Red Army officers who parade here.

A sartorial note on the Red Army. Its officers' uniforms follow the general Russian standard. But their poor material is garnished by flashy red epaulets with embroidered silver stars indicating the officers' rank. They always wear pistols in carefully polished leather holsters, suspended from Sam Browne belts, which since the last war have been abolished by the British, American, and French armies. In the armed forces of the Western countries there is little difference between the uniforms of officers and men. Indeed, the British, who are most sensitive to criticisms of former class distinctions in their army, now have a uniform battle dress for all ranks so that you cannot tell a general from a private unless you are close enough to see his inconspicuous shoulder tabs. But in Russia you are never confused on this point—the officer sparkles a quarter of a mile away.

There is also the matter of medals. In the Western countries heroes modestly keep them in their top bureau drawers, and the award is represented by a tiny bit of colored ribbon just above the upper left pocket of the tunic.

The more robust Russians do not understand such false modesty and Soviet officers' chests jingle with actual bronze and gold medals. There is, furthermore, the constant saluting. In the Western countries, both officers and men regard it as a nuisance, and officers when passing enlisted men on the streets, look the other way to avoid it if possible.

Here everybody salutes constantly and from all distances. There is more saluting in this socialist army than in any other in the world, except possibly that of Mexico, which in dress this army curiously resembles. Most of the other old czarist military caste lines between officers and men have been vigorously revived. No Soviet officer may carry a conspicuous package on the streets. Officers, of course, eat in separate messes, and on trains travel in "soft" compartments, rather than in the hard ones where the enlisted men ride.

Although Red Army officers must still spend some time in the ranks, schools like Annapolis and West Point have been established where they give promising youngsters training toward commissions. Also the Suvarov cadet schools have recently been opened, admitting sons of officers and orphans as young as eight years old.

I have already noticed a further difference. There are on the drab streets of Moscow far fewer soldiers than in either Washington or New York. The Russians have a theory that the place for a man in uniform is at the front. Few of those dangling medals ever get tangled in typewriters.

These officers in the foyer of the concert hall are apparently on leave and, except for the fact that they are undersized, are fine-looking men. They are usually blue-eyed blonds with high cheekbones, and their unsmiling Slav faces and clipped bulletheads constantly remind me of old-time Prussian officers, as they solemnly patrol the foyer with these shabby, undernourished women.

But now our hosts tear us away from this revolving crowd to a room near our box where a little between-the-acts supper is being served in our honor by the director of the theater. A table for about fifteen is set with immaculate linen. Before each napkin is the tall white wine glass, the shorter stemmed red wine glass, the tubular champagne glass, and the squat vodka glass. In the center a dazzling array of Russian hors d'oeuvres—on fifteen or twenty platters; smoked salmon and delicious Volga sturgeon, sliced, spiced ham, cold roast chicken, salami and countless kinds of sliced sausages.

But before we can begin on these, the gnarled old waiters in baggy dress suits pass around bowls of cold caviar: the fresh loose variety, its bowl resting in a bed of cracked ice, or the pressed salted kind which you slice. I take what would be a couple of dollars' worth in America. With it is served a great slab of sweet, unsalted butter, and little pastries, which remind you of mince pie tarts, if the mincemeat were unsweetened.

This initial course of caviar, sweet butter, and mincemeat pastries precedes the smoked sturgeon and sausages, and with it goes white wine. We were to find out that it preceded every meal—including breakfast—which our hosts served us during our stay in the Soviet Union.

It was, for Russians, only a light theater snack. But it was delicious and I dallied over the last forkful of rich French pastry and the last sip of champagne, talking and waiting for the curtain-call, which had not come yet.

Finally Kirilov said, "You are finished, Mr. White?"

"Oh, yes."

"Then perhaps we go back now."

As we slipped into our box, Kirilov nodded toward the stage. The house lights went down and the footlights came up. Only then did they casually explain that they had kept this underfed audience of about 5,000 waiting for ten minutes while I dallied with the second piece of chocolate layer pastry and that last sip of champagne. But no Russian thought it unusual. After all, weren't we honored guests of the Soviet Union?

This truly oriental hospitality has nothing to do with Lenin or the theory of Surplus Values. These people may be socialists, but they are also Russians. As such, they inherit an even stronger tradition from the Mongolian Emperor Genghis Khan than they do from Karl Marx.

Looking around the hall, I wonder where they keep the old people. All these faces are young: in their twenties and thirties. So were those on the streets this afternoon. What became of Russians who should now be in their fifties, sixties or seventies? Did they sicken and die during the terrible famines of the Revolution? Were they liquidated in later purges? Or have they been diluted by the terrific Russian birth rate so that they only seem to be few? Now, back in America, I still wonder.

In Russia if you decide to move, you must go through about as many formalities as you would need to get married. I want to move in with the other newspapermen at the Hotel Metropole. But in Moscow you don't just arrive in a taxi (for there are none) at the hotel of your choice. Foreigners stay at one of three hotels, but they are the best Moscow affords except for the Moskva which has been built since the Revolution and is reserved for high-ranking communists, important government officials (which is the same thing), well-known artists, and top Red Army officers.

Before going to the Metropole, I stroll through the lobbies of the Moskva. Its public rooms are in an uninteresting, classic style, which is best represented in New York by the Grand Central Station.

This barn of Guernsey cream marble has only two notes of emphasis. In the center of the lobby is a statuary group; a spike-bearded smiling Lenin has one arm, fraternally, on the shoulder of a smiling Stalin, while with the other Lenin gesticulates. At the lobby's far end, Stalin again looms more than life size, this time alone and in oils. Above the painting, electric lights burn like candles before an ikon.

There are none of these in the gloomy main lobby of the Metropole, which is understandable because it was built before the Revolution and is now maintained almost exclusively for foreigners. But just off the lobby in the offices of Intourist, which runs the hotel, there hangs the standard collection of Soviet heroes—enormous framed photographs of Lenin, Stalin, Marx, Engels, Kalinin, and Molotov.

A word here about Intourist. It is a government-owned travel agency and you can start thinking Cooks or the American Express, because in peacetime it arranges tours with hotel reservations and meals. But in Russia it has complete charge of the movements and creature-comforts of practically all foreigners, and you cannot stir without it.

For here it is impossible to drop into a restaurant for a casual meal, go to a hotel for a night, or climb on a train for a trip. A Russian belongs to his job. He and his family usually sleep in an apartment house which his factory owns. He probably eats, in his factory dining room, food raised on his factory's farm. His children attend a day-nursery which it maintains. They play games and go to movies in its culture palace and they go on vacations when it can spare them on trains which it designates to resorts and workers' rest homes which it controls.

Foreigners can function in this rigidly ordered world only if some state organization provides for their living space, transportation, food, and ration coupons, which is where Intourist comes in.

The Soviet Government realizes that it cannot force foreigners from the Western countries down to the sub-WPA standard of living, which is the lot of most Soviet citizens. Consequently, it accords foreigners privileges which in the Western world are only common decencies, but which are fantastic luxuries in the Soviet Union.

There is first of all a special diplomatic rate of exchange for foreigners. The rouble is officially presumed to be worth about 5.5 to the dollar; foreigners may buy them at about 8 cents each. At this special rate, Moscow prices become about what they are in New York; the subway is 4 cents; a hotel room is $4 or $5 a night and, when obtainable at all, butter is about 90 cents a pound and eggs are 50 cents a dozen.

The foreigner may also with his special ration book buy at a de luxe diplomatic store whose doors are closed to all Soviet citizens. Here he can get groceries, yard goods, and sometimes clothing, as well as limited but fairly adequate quantities of wines, cigarettes, and vodka.

I was accorded a large and comfortable room at the Metropole and presented with a book of ration tickets, each good for a meal in one of the Metropole's two dining rooms reserved for foreigners. It had still a third dining room for the selected Russians who were lucky enough to have permission to stay there. I never saw it, nor did they ever see ours. I am under the impression that ours was better; yet I am sure that it would have meant only trouble for the authorities had we been allowed to compare menus.

How the Japanese ate I also never learned. They too were quartered at the Metropole, but the Soviet Union, with exquisite tact, fed its Eastern guests in a dining room separate from its Western ones. However, we could pass them in the ground-floor lobby, overtake them in corridors or stare stonily over their shoulders while riding in the elevator facing them. We were icily correct with them and they with us. We would stop talking when we saw them because of course all of them knew English, but I never understood why they also stopped chattering when they saw one of us.

Being icily correct toward the Japanese was, I was told, easier now than it had been. The American Embassy has on its staff several young and spirited naval attachés and one of these was calling on an American reporter at the Metropole when a Domei correspondent stepped into the elevator facing him. It was a few weeks after Pearl Harbor and the Japanese began to grin widely. Then, by moving his eyes, but not looking the naval officer in the eye, the Japanese began to count his shining brass buttons—beginning at the bottom, slowly up to the top of his chest and then slowly down again. By the time the Japanese, still grinning broadly, stepped out at the third floor, the naval officer was rigid to the point of apoplexy, opening and closing his fists convulsively.

My hotel room with an adjoining bath was comfortable but somewhat depressing. The washbasin drain was stopped so that it took ten minutes for my shaving water to run out, leaving in the bowl a scum of soap and whisker stubble, but I soon found this is standard in Russia. There was no toilet paper but this is also standard. It is a luxury, purchasable only by foreigners at their embassy commissaries. The natives get along nicely with the newspapers, *Pravda* and *Izvestia*, or in an emergency, *Red Star*. *War and the Working Class*, the spritely weekly which is published by the organization succeeding the recently dissolved Comintern, and which attacks and criticizes foreign nations with the same vigor followed by its predecessor, is not favored because it is printed on heavier, slick-coated paper stock.

Breakfast at the Metropole, for which I surrendered a coupon, is served in your room and consists of hot tea in a glass, a lump of sugar, black bread, butter, and a choice either of caviar or one hen egg, any style. It was ample.

At lunch in the dining room are assembled the same American and English reporters you see every day, with a sprinkling of Chinese. Lunch is decent but not lavish—always a soup, then either fish or meat in modest portions, plus potatoes and a vegetable, and usually canned plums for dessert. This gives you a healthy appetite for supper, which is the slimmest meal of all—bread, a few slices of Bologna, salami, or some other smoked sausage, a couple of sweet cookies, and, of course, tea.

It was not enough and, consequently, most of the American reporters forwent it, surrendering their coupons and applying to the American Embassy for permission to buy at its commissary. They took their purchases to their rooms and each evening over hot-plates prepared messes of canned corn and stewed tomatoes and such, which they had along with American coffee and condensed milk. The meal always began with a glass of canned grapefruit juice and seemed delicious after the vitamin-starved Russian diet, which included no milk, little fresh fruit and very little meat. Most American reporters promptly lose from 10 to 20 pounds on the Russian diet. One developed a mild case of scurvy before he surrendered to the embassy commissary.

I chronicle this not to make you sorry for the press, but for the Russians, who must live on so much less.

After moving my bags to the Metropole, I stop by the embassy to change a hundred American dollars into 1,200 roubles. Once settled, I go for a walk in the town, with that comfortable feeling you have when a large roll of money is rustling in your pocket and you may buy what you like in a strange city. Slowly during my walk, I discover that there is nothing I can buy. Old clothes perhaps, but mine are infinitely better; for new ones I would need ration coupons. I see several hotels, but my ration coupons are good only for the Metropole. In London, Paris, or New York, killing an hour, I would buy a newspaper and read it over a drink— if only a Coca-Cola in a drug store. Here no one ever kills an hour. There are no cafés, bars, or hours of leisure time. The limited supplies of newspapers were sold out hours ago.

There remains the subway, which I can enter for the equivalent of four American cents. It has been proclaimed the world's best.

It is a good one, exactly like the best in New York or London, with the difference that it is cleaner and its waiting platforms and corridors are lavishly done in costly polished marbles. Yet the system is small with few stations serving only a small per cent of the people.

In the Western world no one expects effortful beauty in a subway, which is as functional as a can-opener. Nor would any transit corporation bother to provide it. Instead they would spend the cost of this polished marble on more miles of track and more stations, swelling their capitalist profits by taking in more nickels from a public eager to ride nearer to work.

Queer things can happen in a system where conventional supply and demand have been tossed out the window.

As I come out at the station opposite my hotel, I at last find something I can buy. An old lady with a cart on wheels is selling some kind of soft drink by the glass and ten people are waiting in line. I fall in at the end. From one spigot on the cart, carbonated water streams into the glass. From the second, a few drops of cherry syrup faintly stain the water a delicate shade of pink. This Soviet Coca-Cola (the glass is the same size) costs 24 cents at the cheap diplomatic rate, at which I buy my roubles. Children and adults, clutching fistfuls of roubles, wait impatiently in the line to buy this unrationed delicacy.

That evening I find still another way to spend my money. Around the corner is a movie, and the girls who run the Intourist bureau get me a ticket. The film, they explain, is the famous American picture "Jungle," now so popular in Russia—but surely, I have seen it?

I haven't. "Jungle" turns out to be a decent B picture, a screen adaptation of Kipling's *Jungle Book*. But since the scene is laid in a tiny village in India, it hardly gives a picture of life in the outside world. I had gone hoping to see how they would react to an American picture, which gave, casually, just a fair idea of American life—an American home or well-dressed average Americans getting into cars or trains.

But these girls, holding hands with Red Army youngsters, are delighted with "Jungle."

I've been out ear-biting. Henry Cassidy of the Associated Press had me over for dinner and afterwards several other correspondents drop in. Ear-biting is a technical newspaper term for a correspondent who comes to a foreign city for a short time and pumps the regular correspondents or diplomats there for the rich fund of information and background, which it has cost them years to collect, and some of which they can't write and stay where they are.

My conscience is fairly easy about biting ears here because I can answer their eager questions about America, and because, when in the past I've been stationed abroad, I've always let traveling reporters bite my ear for helpful information.

I ask about the Free German Committee and what it is up to, and the boys tell me it is still kicking around Moscow, but for the present the Kremlin is giving it the brush-off, because they feel their talks with the Americans and the British about the future of Germany are really getting somewhere. But the boys say now and then you bump into these Free German generals at the opera. They're allowed to attend, well-chaperoned, of course, and wearing Russian army overcoats over their German uniforms so they won't be too conspicuous.

Most of them are from the German Sixth Army, which fought hopelessly at Stalingrad. Why did they come over to speak on the radio for the Soviets? Some of them didn't, the boys say, in particular von Paulus * who commanded the whole army. The Soviets took American correspondents in to see him not long after his surrender. They warned them to be sure that their questions were in line with his rights under the Hague convention, to which they were rigidly adhering.

Von Paulus, they said, is a big, imposing guy with a nervous facial twitch.

"What's your name?"

* This was in June: in August von Paulus came over.

"Freiderick von Paulus!" he thundered.

"How old are you?"

"Fifty-two!" he roared again. And on all other questions he told them to go to hell, which was his right under the Hague convention.

Why did the other German generals come over? Well, most of them were either from Stalingrad or from other points on the front where German air transport had failed to get them out, and they were furious. One general had been getting mail from his wife in Berlin by parachute drop for several weeks. In her last letter, she asked him to try to send her some Russian cigarettes, which maybe she could trade on the Berlin black market for a new dress. The general, surrounded on all sides by Russians, hadn't cared much for the idea.

The boys are sure German prisoners here are being treated correctly. They say Russian civilians are sore about it. For one thing, if a German prisoner is sick he can get sulfa, which is in accord with the Hague rules because the Russians provide it for their own soldiers. Only there isn't enough for Russian civilians.

As for the Free Poles in Russia, the boys think we'll hear more of them because they insist the Poles are actually free. They say the Russians have assembled and armed several Polish divisions, which are anything but puppets. I ask about Father Orlemanski and Professor Lange, who have just left Moscow.

The Father didn't impress them as a particularly alert type. But the professor was something else again. Some of them had gone down with him when they let him talk to the Free Polish divisions, and they had come back convinced that these Poles weren't puppets.

"How about collectivization?" Lange asked them. "Do you want that for the New Poland?"

"No!" they all shouted at once. They said they wanted tractors and harvesting machinery. Maybe some big industries should be owned by the state, but not the land. The first point was to beat the Germans, and argue about the rest later.

However, toward the end, they began to clamor, "We want Lvov! We want Vilna!"—two towns which the Russians had no intention of letting them have. The Russians were embarrassed but they didn't interfere, the reporters said.

Just what, I asked, will the Russians want in Europe? That was easy, the correspondents agreed. They already had the Baltic States. They want some kind of frontier settlement with Poland, approximately the Curzon line. They want to be sure Germany is rendered harmless. Beyond this they won't want much, except to be sure that the governments in their border states—Finland, Poland, Hungary, Czechoslovakia, Rumania, and Bulgaria—will not be hostile to them. They will not be particularly interested in the economic or political systems of these states provided they are not a threat.

Of course, if through bad management, we leave a power vacuum any place in Europe and riots, disorder, and anarchy get started— they'll move in.

But what they really want is a durable peace so they can build up their own country. If we insist on decent compromises, setting up governments, not Communist but friendly to Russia, they will take it. But to carry out this policy, we may find ourselves supporting mildly socialist governments all over Europe.

Almost all the reporters now working Moscow have come here since the war. The old crowd, of which Walter Duranty was dean, is gone. Perhaps they were glad to go. The Russian friends they had made laboriously over twenty years were either shot or exiled, many for the crime of associating with foreigners, so that the few who were left were afraid to see their foreign friends except officially and at large functions.

These new boys, lacking experience of those years, carry none of its bitterness. Their estimates of what Russia wants seem shrewd and realistic. Russia wants first and last peace, but not at the price of safety.

We've been in a series of huddles about Eric's speech. It's a good one which he's been working on for weeks, and it has got to be delivered, because copies of it are already in America for release. It's a clear statement of the viewpoint with which he, representing

American business, approaches the Socialist Soviet Republic. But where should he give it? You can't just mount the first soap box.

This afternoon our host, Commissar Mikoyan of the Narkomvneshtorg (People's Commissariat of Foreign Trade), is to give a big luncheon at which he will welcome us officially to the Soviet Union. This seems the ideal time until Ambassador Harriman points out that Russians never make speeches at banquets. The speech, we point out, will take only half an hour. And another half hour, the ambassador observes, to translate into Russian, for you can't lecture your host in English, of which he understands less than he does Arabic.

But then we get a plan which satisfies everyone. At Mikoyan's luncheon Eric will deliver in English his first paragraph. Then he will sit down while the interpreter translates not only this but the entire speech into Russian. Not until its final paragraph will Eric rise again to hoist his glass in that toast which ends all Russian speeches.

The luncheon is at Spiridonovka House, another staggering czarist palace. Even Spaso would be lost in these marble canyons. On the terrace we get the usual Russian cocktail, which tastes like a Manhattan, and chat politely with our hosts. All the officials of the Narkomvneshtorg are there, and they have asked Harriman and some of his embassy staff—perhaps thirty in all.

Next me at the table is a fox-faced Russian who fills my vodka glass and then his own.

"Come, Mr. White, we drink to the second front, no? There will perhaps some day be one?"

"But that was over long ago."

"Oh, no—it is even now in the newspapers there will soon be one—perhaps, yes? So we will drink anyway."

"The landing on the Atlantic Coast? We don't call it that. In capitalist countries, the fronts are not numbered as they are here."

"How do you say, then?"

"The first front when Poland fell—with us this is number one. You remember that. The second front was in 1940 when France fell. Surely that is not forgotten in Russia, even though you were neutral. The third front is the invasion of Jugoslavia and Greece. Again you were neutral, but you remember. The next front is when Hitler attacks the Soviet Union in 1941. We were very sorry to learn it. For us it was the fourth front. The fifth front is when Japan attacks America and England and we must both fight in the Pacific. Here again you are neutral. The sixth front is when England and America land in North Africa to chase the Germans and Italians out. The seventh front is when we have landed in Italy—"

He interrupts—now he is laughing. "But anyway to drink to the new front—for you the eighth, to me the second front." So we drink. But he is not yet downed.

"Last year when I am in America, New York newspapers call it second front, and even then they demand it be started at once."

"Not all newspapers. Most of them say we should wait until our generals are ready. In America all newspapers do not say the same thing. It is because they are what is called free. It must be very confusing to foreigners."

Now comes the usual preliminary butter, caviar, and pastry, during which we are supposed also to nibble the cold smoked and jellied meats. Then the meal, course by course, wine by wine, begins building up. A soup with sherry. Sturgeon with a sauterne from the Crimea. After it, broiled grouse with a chilled white hock from the Caucasus.

Across the table, boxed in between Eric and the ambassador, sits Commissar Mikoyan. He is short, plump, dark, and immaculately tailored—like a Hollywood executive on a visit to New York. His dark suit and tie are in the best of quiet good taste.

He is an Armenian. His eyes are jet black, his face sharp, and his massive Semitic nose would come to a point except that its tip abruptly curls under, pointing down at his chin. The profile of an old Assyrian coin. Or of an extremely suave oriental rug salesman. I would guess that the Narkomvneshtorg takes few wooden nickels.

The meal pauses for grilled filet mignon and then comes the climax of all Russian state banquets, cold, shaved, boiled suckling pigs—four of them, each on its little platter.

A razor-sharp knife has separated each rib, so that the baby pork chops are as thin and white as the bread in tea party sandwiches.

The wines, two courses ago, had switched to red and with the pig we are given a rich, purplish burgundy from the Ukraine. Across the table Mikoyan is looking like an Assyrian shekel; Averell like an ambassador; Eric like a man who is about to make a speech. He is emptying his mouth uneasily and looking up and down the table to size up the audience. Joyce and I exchange looks. Now they are filling our glasses with a golden Soviet Socialist concoction known as pepper vodka and my neighbor insists that I again drink bottoms up. The boiled pig ribs are exchanged for a miniature castle of ice cream and pastry; the wine shifts to Crimean champagne.

And now Mikoyan, with the expression of an Oriental who, of course, doesn't want to sell you the rug at all, only wants, as one connoisseur to another, to let you admire the fine points of its weave and texture, rises with a smooth toast of welcome.

Eric's face is frozen into a beatific smile. Only Joyce and I know that he is wondering how those carefully sharpened cracks about the American Communist Party will sound after the satin smoothness of this welcome. But he knows what he is going to say—the speech has already been mimeographed and distributed in two languages and he can only clutch the rim of his barrel and listen to the approaching rumble of Niagara ahead.

In point of fact it goes over extremely well. When he sits down, we study the faces of the Russians to see how they are taking it. At first they are grave. Then when Eric says of the American Communists, "When you take pepper they sneeze, when you have indigestion, they belch—" one of the younger Russians hastily covers a snicker with his napkin; several others force back smiles and look down the table at Mikoyan. Finally, he smiles and now all the others smile too. At last he laughs and so do they.

Next day even *Pravda* prints a lengthy digest of it—except, of course, the reference to the American Communist Party. An American, long a resident of Moscow, had sourly predicted that the Russian papers would not carry a line.

"Anyway we are distributing mimeographed copies to the Russians at the dinner."

"Much good that will do. The NKVD will take them away as they leave."

But the NKVD didn't!

Three

A DAY or so later we are shown our first Soviet factory. Officially it's called Factory No. 38. It is in Moscow's industrial suburbs and it makes the famous Stormovik plane for the Red Air Force. Approaching it we see enormous sign boards at the entrance on which are given the most recent production figures, the names of workers who have overfulfilled their quota—only here the word is "norm"—and big pictures of Lenin and Stalin, apparently painted by the same artist who does the portraits of the tattooed man, the snake charmer, and the two-headed baby for the side-show. All this faces a square, and there is also a little raised platform in which there is also a red wooden tribune for speakers. We later discover that these are standard in all Soviet factories.

Before inspecting this one, we are taken to the office of the director, who in America might correspond to the president of the company. He is a young man of thirty-seven, Vasili Nikolayevitch Smyrnov by name, and tells us he has worked in aviation twenty-four years—eight years as director.

His office has the same standard of luxury and comfort as that of a comparable American concern with these differences: the ponderous, heavily carved furniture is stained black. At first we assume it is from some czarist attic where it has been catching dust since the nineties. Later we find it in most factory directors' offices that we visit.

Also standard are the large 2 x 2½ foot photographs of Lenin and Stalin on the wall behind the desk. From Moscow to Central Siberia we see in directors' offices exactly the same wrinkles around Stalin's eyes—precisely the same few grey hairs in Lenin's beard.

The director tells us his plant has been operating continuously here for only two years because during the siege of Moscow it was evacuated; only the walls remained. Eric immediately plunges into a series of acute questions on labor, wages, and hours, from which the following picture emerges. It proves to be true of most Soviet war factories.

The director tells Eric that 65 per cent of his employees are now women, that before the war it was about 30 per cent. Hours? The regular eight-hour day, plus three daily hours of overtime, for which they are paid time and a half, as in most American factories. But they work six days a week, which makes a working week of sixty-six hours. The director hastens to add that boys and girls under eighteen work only eight hours a day, five days a week.

Wages are paid to the plant's 10,000 workers twice a month and on a piecework basis. For a predetermined quota or "norm" of work, the worker receives 750 roubles per month. Then, if he over-fulfills this norm (and they usually do) his pay goes up on a sliding scale. So the true average would be 1,000 roubles a month, and an occasional 1,500 or 2,000.

Since the rouble has a purchasing power, in terms of rationed Soviet goods, of about 8 cents in America, the Soviet war worker gets, in terms of American purchasing power, between $20 and $40 for his sixty-six-hour week.

However, other elements brighten the picture. The worker may buy his meals in the factory's restaurant; if he chooses to eat all three there, that will be only 5 roubles a day. The factory also maintains nurseries and kindergartens. And, of course, women get the same pay as men; they are surprised that we even ask about this.

But now Eric turns to the director. What does he get, if he doesn't mind telling us? He doesn't; he receives a basic salary of 3,000 roubles a month (in rationed purchasing power, about $240) except that, if the plant wins a production banner (this one like most Soviet war plants has), he then gets 150 per cent more up to a maximum of 10,000 roubles a month (about $800). However, he tells us with a wry smile, he has no time to spend all this money.

But Eric is now back to the workers; what about their grievances? Well, they take them up with the trade union committee for their department of the plant. The director himself hears complaints twice a week. But if they don't like his decision? Then they have the right of appeal. But to whom? Even clear up to Stalin? Even to Stalin.

But now for the Stormovik factory itself, and we start trudging through. It is, first of all, poorly lit and unbelievably dirty. It has no production line in the American sense but rather a series of connected piles between bottlenecks, with women waiting idle at their machines for the line to start moving again.

It is jammed full of the best American machine tools, but seems to lack proper organization. At one point, the assembly belt is a makeshift canvas affair. The floors throughout are uneven with holes in the concrete. Piles of metal shavings are everywhere. No one bothers to clean up. Many of the girls wear gunny sacks tied around their feet. Others have crude wooden sandals with a nail sticking up between the great and second toes. In these, they scramble around in the dim light. Here they are moving (by wheelbarrow) a load of unfinished parts which spill at a bump in the floor. The girls must stop to pick them up.

Johnston falls back to whisper, "Back in the States the best rough test I know of the efficiency of any factory is its cleanliness. Any dirty shop is sure to be an inefficient one." Then he catches up with his guide and interpreters.

Maybe these people figure there are 200,000,000 Russians and that it matters little if a few are inconvenienced? But this floor could be repaired at the cost of just one of these expensive lend-lease automatic drills of which this factory has such a profusion, and then its efficiency might rise as much as 25 per cent.

Yes, I know the Russian girls are willing to endure any hardships. But a hard-boiled American production man, trying to squeeze the last thin dime of value from his workers, would start by making them comfortable with good light and tidy floors, to increase the man-hour production rate.

Now for the Stormovik plane. In front, a sheath of thick armor covers both pilot and motor, which must cut down the cruising range and make it cumbersome. I'm amazed that the heavy structural parts of the plane are made, not of aluminum, but of steel. They explain that the wings were formerly made of wood, but that now a certain amount of aluminum is used. This is true, and all of the aluminum that I see here is stamped Alcoa. Apparently Soviet aluminum production is low.

The Stormovik's rear fuselage is a long, hollow shell made of wood-plastic. The plane needs no oxygen system, as it seldom operates at high altitudes. It opens up on enemy tanks with its pair of 23-mm. cannon or sprays infantry with its twin machine guns from a range sometimes as close as 20 yards. This is possible because of its slow speed and its armor, protecting pilot and motor.

We find it also carries light bombs, and when I ask if it is a dive bomber or a level bomber, they proudly reply that it is both. Apparently they have tried to turn out a general utility ground co-operation plane hopefully designed to do everything including the laundry. However, the Stormovik's designers have done an excellent job, granted the limiting shortages of material which afflict the Soviet Union. Russia once had two of the world's biggest aluminum plants but both were overrun by the Germans.

Most of this information we pick up at the elaborate banquet in the director's dining room at the end of the inspection. There again are the red wine, white wine, champagne, and vodka glasses, the tremendous array of cold hors d'oeuvres, starting with caviar and pastry. Standing behind the table, I see a familiar face. It is the smiling steward who presided over the banquet at the Tschaikovsky Theater.

This struck me only as a coincidence. But we were just getting on to the ropes. Little did we dream that his smiling face was to haunt us like a recurring nightmare. He was, it developed, the chief caterer for Intourist, and everywhere we were entertained we were to find his beaming smile. He went ahead, of course, with trunks of pickled fishes and sausage, and hampers of wines. Whenever we entered a dining room, there he was, beaming above his crystal glasses and iced tubs of caviar, set up for business, whether the scene was a factory, a railway diner, or a picnic near abandoned German trenches on the Karelian Isthmus.

Johnston asks a number of questions about how the company designs its products, what plans they have for peacetime production, how many units they plan to turn out and at what price they will be sold.

But these the director and his assistants can't answer. They aren't holding out on us; it's clear they don't know. Such matters are decided by the Kremlin.

Between toasts Johnston whispers to me: "That director's a good man. He could hold an important job in the States. Maybe not quite the job he has here, not president of the company. But notice, he doesn't really run it here.

"He has charge only of production; in America this is handled by a plant manager, who may or may not be a vice-president. An American corporation president must think not only of production, but of new designs, new markets and uses for his products, the cost and quality of his raw materials, possibly financing, a sales organization, and what the competition may be up to.

"And you'll notice that on all such policy questions, this guy didn't know. Obviously, the Kremlin decides. Like any plant manager he does the best he can with what they give him.

"We're talking to production men. The planning brains of this thing are in the Kremlin, not in the factories."

I study the faces of the Russians around the table; they are familiar—serious, orthodox, industrious young men anxious to get on in the world—the same type you might find at a junior executives' lunch in an American factory. There they would be registered Republicans without having given it too much thought, but because the boss was a Republican and because it was the party of respectability and its hallmark would be helpful to a young man anxious to get on in the world.

Here their prototypes are Communists for the same reason. These men would average thirty-two years old. In 1917, when Communism was a revolutionary party in Russia (sometimes it still is abroad, but only when it is helpful to Russian foreign policy), these men were boys of five. When Lenin died they were twelve years old.

The Revolution was over and those young men most likely to succeed followed the Communist Party because it represented authority, power, and wealth, as has the Republican party to a lesser extent in America.

What becomes, in Russia, of the normal proportion of misfits who in America are members of the Communist Party? I am sure that on this trip I shall meet no one among these successful Soviet industrialists who would not vehemently insist that all is well in this best of all possible Socialist worlds. Still I am curious as to what they do with their misfits. I wonder that Stalin does not set up something like the United States Communist Party here in Russia, so that he can keep track of them instead of driving them underground.

Character note on Eric: he doesn't change with his environment; doesn't pretend, in Moscow, to be anything but a successful businessman from Spokane. What natives in various parts of the world may think of this is of no great concern to him. That's what he is: they can take it or leave it.

He tours Moscow plants dressed as he would to tour them in Spokane; wearing not a coat, but a heavy blue knit sweater and a wide-brimmed, pale gray hat. I too come from a Stetson country and know this for a good one.

The Russians eye it curiously as they would a theatrical costume, for they are a very formal folk. But it is an integral part of Eric Johnston.

He handles the toasts well. They formally offer one to President Roosevelt, so it would then be an insult if Eric did not toast Stalin. They drink to the success of our armies in Italy, so we offer one to the Red Army. A Russian toast is a two-minute speech—a considerable improvement on the lengthy harangues at American banquets. Eric handles his part gracefully and smoothly, but never ceases to be exactly what he is.

At the outset he explains to them that his doctor has forbidden him to drink, but that America is a country of specialization (here the Russians gravely nod) so he has brought along two assistants—Mr. O'Hara, who takes care of the women for him (the Russians solemnly appraise Joyce), and Mr. White, who does all of his drinking.

Such banter would pass unnoticed in America, but the Russians take it with earnestness. Drinking is a serious business in Russia—a test of manhood and prestige. So now they turn earnestly on me, filling my glass and proffering toasts to Russo-American relations, which it would be insulting to refuse. Down the table Eric is beaming brightly and a shade triumphantly.

I rise and say that it is true that I have entered Russia as an assistant to Mr. Eric Johnston, who is an important capitalist, and that they all know from their newspapers how American workers are exploited. But now they see it before their eyes: that American capitalists even force American workers to drink their champagne. So now, I as an American worker call upon the Russian workers for solidarity in the class struggle, and ask their help in making Mr. Johnston drink his share of the champagne.

It falls flat as I write it, but in its setting it seemed to go down reasonably well; at least, it had a temporarily calming effect on Eric.

The next morning Kirilov arrives to take us to another factory, one of the most important in Russia. For here they make the Soviet Union's automobiles. In America a dozen major companies turn out a hundred models. In this classless society one company makes one model,* and its entire output goes to its single privileged class—the top communists, factory directors, and government officials.

It has been called the Soviet Lincoln. It looks rather like a 1935 model Buick sedan with the difference that it is a sloppy engineering job. Its name, pronounced "Zees" in English, comes from three Russian words meaning "Factory in the name of Stalin."

We rode in one daily. It is too heavy for its springs; if you ride in the back seat, every time it encounters a jolt, the base of your spine thunders down through the shallow seat cushion padding with a

---

* The Gorki plant, which we did not visit, also makes only one passenger car model.

sickening bump on the rear axle. The various layers of its safety glass are prone to come unglued, so that the pane "frosts." However, its paint job, tin petticoat streamlining and instrument-panel design could compare with Detroit's nobbiest, and its tires and motor—except for occasional fits of starter trouble—seemed dependable, for it always got us there and brought us safely home.

The director of the Zees plant, Ivan Likhatchov, is a stumpy, serious little man of forty-eight who carefully cultivates a slight resemblance to Stalin. He wears a cap, grows a soup-strainer mustache, and receives us in riding trousers and high black Russian boots. At the factory's entrance, there are, of course, the usual circus-poster portraits of Stalin and Lenin, and inside are their customary photographs.

First, he gives us an over-all picture of the plant. It employs 40,000 workers, and has 12,000 more youngsters in its factory school. Formerly, it made trucks (the Soviet Union, with over 200,-000,000 people, made 300,000 motor vehicles per year at the peak compared with America's 1941 production of 4,800,000 for its 130,-000,000 people). Now it produces trucks, half-tracks and munitions for the Red Army.

This year it will make a few hundred passenger cars. The Komsomols (young communists) in the factory school started making tommy guns for the Red Army when the Germans were only 35 kilometers from Moscow, and went into production in only three weeks.

The Zees plant now has four daughter plants turning out army trucks and munitions in the Urals. Their directors were formerly shop chiefs in this plant.

Automobile production started here in 1924, the car being designed around a Soviet adaptation of the famous American Hercules Engine made in Canton, Ohio. Johnston and I exchange curious looks—I don't happen to have heard of the famous Hercules.* Likhatchov came in 1926 when it had only 670 workers. Beginning

---

* Which was my ignorance. I have since learned that the Hercules plant in Canton, Ohio, turns out a rugged tractor-type motor, justly famous in this field and doing a big job in our motorized divisions.

in 1930 the plant bought $125,000,000 worth of American machinery over a five-year period. Before the war they bought many German tools which the director says are good for precision work, although they have declined in quality in the last six years because, he says, in Germany the war came first, and also they exported inferior products.

The director tells us with quiet pride that he has visited American factories at Detroit, Flint, Buffalo, Saginaw, Pittsburgh, and Chicago, that he is a member of the Society of Automotive Engineers and a subscriber to *Iron Age*.

But now Eric starts a series of acute questions: How do they cope with the problem of absenteeism? The director is honestly puzzled by the word even after it is thoroughly explained to him.

A worker who is ill, he tells us, goes to the plant doctor to get a leave of absence. If the case is serious, in this plant his social insurance would pay 90 per cent of his wages for three months. If he is still not recovered, he gets either a temporary invalid's status or maybe lighter work. A pregnant woman gets several weeks' leave of absence before her baby, and after it. The average family, he tells us, is five children for the city worker and about eight for farmers.

But Eric persists; he's not asking about sickness—he wants to know about the problem of absenteeism. When the director finally understands, he seems amazed that such a question should even be asked, because he says, of course, they have no such cases here. Lazy or tardy workers are rebuked by the wall newspaper or denounced over the shop public address system. If it happens two or three times the matter is taken up with him by the union. We gather it is a grim proceeding.

Absenteeism seems to be as rare here as it would be in the Atlanta Penitentiary, and for many of the same reasons.

It is hard for our capitalist minds to grasp the idea that under socialism, possibly the factory belongs to the workers but certainly the worker belongs to his factory; without it he has nothing to eat and no place to sleep.

Now we tour the plant. Again it seems to have no smooth-running assembly line but a series of linked bottlenecks and connected piles. We are as great a curiosity to the workers as they to us. They look up, but they seem to have no fear of the bosses. They look him straight in the eye as an American worker would.

The Zees trucks and half-tracks look sturdy by American peace-time standards, but they can't compare with the rugged giants which Detroit pours out for our armies and those of our allies. The workers are about half women, and the rest very old men or boys in their middle teens. One of these, showing off to us, comes tearing up behind pushing a hand truck filled with half-finished parts. It weighs about ten times what the boy does (he can't be fifteen) and, what with the bad lighting, the uneven floors piled with scrap and rubbish, and his zeal to show his Komsomol patri-otism, he succeeds in pushing one of its huge iron wheels over my toe. They yell angrily at him and I try to explain by gestures with one hand—I am holding my foot with the other—that it wasn't his fault. The load was too big for him and he couldn't possibly stop it in time.

Wages here, including the director's salary, are exactly what they were at the other plant—and at most of the others we are to visit.

We go in to the usual banquet at about four in the afternoon. The usual toast, whereupon there is a pause: a worker brings in something which looks like a violin case, only inside is a beauti-fully polished tommy gun resting on a red velvet lining. Eric A. Johnston's name is engraved on it, and we later find that it is a present from the Young Communists of the Zees plant.

The next day we are herded into our Zeeses and tear across town to another dingy square, flanked by barracks-like concrete workers' apartment houses, where flapping Red banners and huge portraits of Marx, Lenin, Engels, and Stalin announce the entrance to the ball-bearing works.

It is crammed full of the newest and best American machinery, but its floors again are cluttered and the lighting bad. However, the product seems to be a good, precision-made job, although we guess that by American standards, production per worker must be low.

As we start out we are told that American troops have landed in Normandy, and the Russians seem as excited as we are—perceptibly less solemn and poker-faced. In the factory we walk under hastily erected red banners with lettering to the effect that Russian ball-bearing workers salute their American comrades in the Common Struggle against the Fascist Beast.

At one point Eric is handed a huge bouquet of lilacs with the suggestion that he present it to a beautiful twenty-two-year-old girl who is pointed out as a Komsomol and one of the most efficient workers in the plant. Smilingly, she receives it as Soviet news cameras grind.

At the regular afternoon banquet there are many toasts to Soviet-American friendship and the second front. Then Eric tries to find out something about business competition in the Soviet Union. The director of the factory insists that there is great competition—particularly to get raw materials. But who gets the most? The plant with the highest production record.

We pile back into our cars to be taken to what Kirilov describes as a rubber factory; actually it produces not rubber but tires, from rubber made (usually from alcohol) in the Soviet Union, whose scientists pioneered in this important field.

Its director, introduced as Vladimir Chesnikov, is a pleasant young man of thirty-three and under him are about 1,500 workers. In answer to our questions he explains that he gets the basic monthly salary of 3,000 roubles ($240 without the usual production bonuses because the plant isn't yet operating). They started building it only in December and began setting the machinery only six weeks ago. It should be in full operation late in 1944.

But they walk us through to see the machinery. There stands a Gordon plasticator which they say was formerly used in the River Rouge plant—set up and ready for business. On a railway siding in weather-beaten crates we see piles of 12,000 tons of American machinery—a complete Ford tire plant crated and sent to Russia last year.

Back in the director's office, Eric wants to know what percentage of their wages Soviet workers give to the war. In America it is often about 10 per cent, and Chesnikov tells us proudly that in the Soviet Union workers sometimes give as much as two or three months' salary. It occurs to us that after the Soviet worker has bought as much food as his ration tickets permit, there is almost nothing else on which he may spend his money except for an occasional movie.

When we suggest this, the director frowns and assures us that it is not quite true—that sometimes workers give money when they have ration tickets left over with which they might have bought food.

This evening I finally run into my old friend Maurice Hindus, who has been down in the Ukraine visiting one of the American air bases. In New York, Maurice lopes around town always without a hat or overcoat, showing up at parties in a black and white checkered lumberjack shirt with an orange tie. He is loping around Moscow the same way.

Maurice was born in a Russian village and most Americans who have read anything of Russia have seen the nation's progress chronicled step by step in his series of books on that village. It is now still behind the German lines, but just ahead in the path of the advancing Russian armies. The correspondents have been watching it closely for the past few weeks. In view of the fine interpretive job Maurice has done with his village in explaining Russia to Americans, will the foreign office allow him to go to the front to accompany the regiment which liberates it? In any country other than this, such a permission could be had for the asking. Although front trips here are almost nonexistent, not a correspondent would protest if Maurice were allowed to go alone. But no one thinks it can possibly happen.

Maurice, who knows more Russians than any other reporter in Moscow, tells me that the Russians liked very much *Pravda's* condensation of Eric's speech; its sparkle and its frankness. He tells me of one old Russian friend in his sixties who looked up from reading it to say, "For years we have made fools of ourselves about you, and you have made fools of yourselves about us. Let's hope that this is all over."

He also says that today all the Russians are congratulating any American friend they can find on the opening of the Normandy front—telephoning each other trying to find vodka to drink toasts. He says it was, of course, the day's big story, and all of *Pravda's* comment was on the extreme technical difficulty of making a sea landing on a hostile coast, with no attempt to underrate the dangers and the hardships. "The people here are very tense," he says. "They've gone through hell."

He wants to know about home; he's been away for months. "Tell me, Bill, is America going fascist?" he asks very intensely, and it takes some time to reassure him. It seems all the Russians want to know. The Soviet newspapers are now beginning to make the distinction between the democratic and the undemocratic capitalist countries, but they still think the line is a fine one.

And he says the Russians can't understand attacks on Russia in the American and British Press. *War and the Working Class* which would be the Comintern publication if there was still a Comintern, recently reprinted an article from the London *Picture Post* entitled, "How to Keep the Russians Out of Europe." It also reprinted Senator George's attack on Roosevelt in which he charged that the President had failed to get any commitments from Russia. "We are supposed to be fighting a war together," the Soviet bi-monthly comments, "yet these things indicate hidden hostility to Russia."

And the dozen or so Russian families into whose homes Maurice can freely go (a record for a foreigner in Moscow) share in these forebodings.

Tonight we go to a performance of Tschaikovsky's "Nut Cracker Ballet" at the Bolshoi Theater, the Grand Opera house of Moscow. It is a magnificent old czarist building decorated with a restrained lavishness rare in Russia under any regime. And the performance is beautiful beyond anything I have seen on any stage in any country—dancing, costumes, acting, and scenery are done with sweeping imagination. These people have a genius for the theater.

An explanation may be that the theater is the only thing in the

Soviet Union which can boast of an uninterrupted growth and tradition. The Bolsheviks were proud of the ballet and in both Moscow and Leningrad they kept going continuously all during the revolution. The Bolsheviks did not liquidate their actors, stage designers, directors, and artists as they did most of the upper classes in 1917 and in the ensuing Civil War.

"Destroy everything first—then build on a new foundation," was the battle cry. What I have so far seen of the structure which rises out of the ruins is often not impressive. The Bolshoi Ballet towers above everything which the Western stage has produced—unbelievably lovely.

Only the curtain seems new and even this reflects dignity. It is a great drop of gold cloth and woven into it, imperceptible at first, is an ever-repeated design made up of numerals—1871-1905-1917—the dates of the Paris commune, the abortive Russian revolt, and finally Lenin's and Trotsky's revolution.

Today, a visit to a motor factory which used to make tractor engines. Both factory and product have been re-designed and the plant now turns out dive bomber motors largely for the Stormovik —a 1700-horsepower job.

Its director is only thirty-four years old and seated next him at the table is a dark-haired woman of forty who is assistant director, and who has charge of wages, working conditions, health, and vacations.

He tells us he has 15,000 workers here and that most of them eat their meals in one building—serving goes on from eleven to five. The food is cheap and good because the factory owns and operates two farms. There are permanent operating staffs on each, but the factory workers rotate to furnish most of the labor. The factory is proud of the fact that it was heavily bombed in 1941, collecting more than 250 incendiaries and one 1000-pounder, but work continued during the alarms.

Eric mentions the fact that he also owns factories and the Russians are immediately curious. How many men does he employ?

"Two thousand," he tells them.

"And how are they paid?"

"Mostly on an hourly wage basis."

"Why not on a piecework basis?"

"Because our labor unions do not like piecework." The Russian staff is puzzled by this. They are too young ever to have known that after 1917 "piecework" was denounced as a cunning device to exploit the workers. Later, when the Soviets adopted, with much ballyhoo, the Stakhanov * system, it was presented to Russians as a socialist invention, unknown in the capitalist world. But these young men have grown up behind the veil.

"How much wages does the average worker get?"

When the sum is translated into roubles for them, they nod politely but you can see they suspect he is exaggerating.

Then Johnston goes on to explain, as they listen intently, that the head of an American factory must think not only of production, as they do, but of his sales organization, his outlets for distributing what the factory makes, new designs to compete in efficiency and price with the products of rival companies, and many other things.

They are leaning forward now, all down the long table, fascinated by it and full of questions.

How, they ask him, can an electrical company so small as his compete with a giant like General Electric? Why is he not crushed?

Eric explains that we have found out in America that after a company reaches a certain size, it becomes less efficient. Here they look at each other, exchange nods of agreement, several of them even laugh, and then they turn back to Eric.

Then they ask if the trend in America is toward large or small companies. Eric answers that there are trends in both directions. Certain operations can be done best by large concerns. But on the other hand, it's hard for an executive in New York to keep in touch with a branch 3,000 miles away in Seattle. So small, inventive

* To be more specific, when in 1931 independent trade unions were abandoned, piecework was silently introduced into Soviet factories. Later it was combined with division of labor into the much publicized "Stakhanov system."

companies, which can adapt themselves quickly to local needs, get the edge.

They are all intent on his words, and the young director has opened his mouth to ask another question, when the NKVD plain-clothes man, who is always with us, rises and firmly puts a hand on his shoulder. It seems that now we will go immediately out to inspect the plant.

This had never happened before. Maybe our time schedule was actually limited. Or maybe the NKVD, which controls what Russians are allowed to know, didn't like these spur-of-the-moment, un-censored explanations of how American business ticks, even from so honored a guest of the Soviet Union as Eric Johnston.

This motor plant seems to be a fairly well set up shop. Across one room hangs a banner in Russian: "In answer to the success of our allies the following workers have increased their norms by 350 per cent," followed by a list of names.

We glance into a workers' lunch room. The meal consists of a porridge with kasha (buckwheat), black bread and borsch—a rich meat and beet soup. It looks and smells good.

Beyond this is the foremen's dining room. They get the same dishes plus black pressed caviar. Farther on is the engineers' dining room. They eat like the foremen with the difference that they may have white bread as well as black, a generous portion of butter, and their caviar is the more expensive, loose, unsalted kind.

Now we proceed to the director's dining room, where I jot down the menu's main items: vodka, red wine, white wine, champagne, caviar, butter, smoked sturgeon, salted cucumbers (which are deli-cious), coleslaw, cold veal, salami, smoked beef tongue, and for des-sert, pastry and fine-textured chocolate layer cake.

We learn (not from our Russian hosts) that the caste system which we have seen in the dining rooms goes all through their fac-tories. They have developed enormous white-collar clerical and en-gineering staffs. But once a man becomes an engineer, he loses face and prestige if he should slip into a suit of cover-alls, as all American engineers do, and go down to a factory bench to show the workers how it should be done or to pick bugs out of the assembly line.

Until the 1917 Revolution, Russia for a thousand years was a caste-ridden feudal state. Twenty-five years can no more wipe this out than it can abolish Russian food habits or Russian verbs. So this new socialist bureaucracy, raised up out of the proletariat, instinctively stratifies itself into castes.

Although this factory's floors and lighting are better than most and its director's hospitable table far better than any American corporation president's private dining room, its production record is, by American standards, pretty sad. Fifteen thousand workers equipped with Pratt and Whitney machine tools (also some excellent German and Swiss ones) turn out only about fifteen motors a day. This is a thousand man-days per motor. A comparable American airplane motor is made with less than 200 man-days.

This morning we visit a great cooky, cracker, and cake factory, officially called the Bolshevik Chocolate Factory (named, of course, for the Party). They tell us it no longer makes chocolate—practically all of its cakes and crackers go to the Red Army. They use 50 per cent Russian beet sugar and 50 per cent American Lend-Lease sugar. In parentheses, the reporters tell me Russians complain that the American cane sugar, which they can now buy in their grocery stores, isn't as sweet as their own. They say they need two teaspoons of it to one of Russian beet sugar.

We are bundled into crumpled, slightly soiled and completely unnecessary white coats and surgeon's operating caps—unnecessary because everything is baked at high temperatures and even if we were Typhoid Marys, no bacilli could survive. But this is part of food industry frou-frou in our country as well as theirs.

The workers are also in white—so is everybody except three men who follow us through. These must be either top bureaucrats or, more likely, a new batch of NKVD guards.

The machinery is all Russian made and the operations mostly automatic. Great tubs of dough come from the mixers, are rolled into sheets, cut into shapes and these move on a belt through the furnaces like newsprint through a rotary press. The plant looks good, neither worse nor better than a big American establishment like the National Biscuit Company.

Then the banquet and, as you can guess, mountains of pastry, especially prepared for us. Only we're too stuffed to eat much. At a Chinese banquet anything you can't eat is sent around to you in pails the next day. As we leave the Bolshevik Chocolate Factory, they load three huge cartons into one of the extra Zeeses. When we get to the Metropole, we find that according to rigid Bolshevik protocol, the biggest, at least a cubic yard in size, is marked for Eric; Joyce's name is on the middle-sized one; but there is also one for the eensie-weensie bear to take to the Metropole.

When I open it in my room, it contains assorted sweet biscuits, fruit cake, chocolate-covered cherries floating in sweet brandy, and an enormous cake. I wonder what was in Eric's big box? Probably a life-size bust of Lenin done in poundcake with lemon-meringue hair. I decide to save my cake for a party which is in the offing among the correspondents and wolf the rest.

Four

*T*ONIGHT Commissar Mikoyan throws a party for us, built around a showing of a famous Soviet movie called "Volga-Volga." We also are privileged to meet Soviet movie stars, a bevy of bouncing girls in their early forties, who show the effects of their extra ration cards. Because in the Soviet Union a double chin or an extra roll of abdominal fat is a mark of caste. Like all actresses, their eyes seem too far apart when they confront you at cocktail parties. They greet us glittering with professional charm and gold teeth, and now and then the contrasting flash of a stainless steel bicuspid.

The well-known actresses were here, women whose names were headlines in current Soviet films. They were all well-dressed, except that Soviet standards in this field suggest our pink satin and seed pearl era.

I suppose I picked the Lan girl because she was quietly dressed in a simple black dress. Or maybe because she was so young she had not attained the dignity of a single gold tooth. Anyway, she was a completely charming, unaffected child who spoke rather good but unsure schoolbook English.

We talked for a while over cocktails before the cinema began. She was most intelligent, and had all the quiet charm of a well-born French *jeune fille*, or a Viennese *mädchen* of good family. I decided that if this was Bolshevik education, I was very much for it.

But there were gulfs. I made some now forgotten reference to the past, and she said in cautious English, "Oh, yes. But I have heard of that. It was just before the First Imperialist War."

This reference to 1914-1918 wasn't meant to annoy me. In her Communist histories it was the only name she had ever heard. She was most interested in American films; told me gravely how much she admired our dazzling stars, Charlie Chaplin, Mary Pickford and Douglas Fairbanks and asked for the names of their recent pictures. Yet she had also seen Sonja Henie in a recent film specially shown for Soviet artists to study. She was serious about her own work, and it appeared she was getting a few bit parts. But apparently the Soviet cinema does not push young actresses forward. Lana Turners must wait until they have more training before they can hope for leading roles.

When the movie started she offered to translate, so we went in and sat down alone except for two men who possibly were not NKVD and who took the seats immediately behind us. Eric, as guest of honor, was installed in the center of the house between two peroxide actresses, one of whom was the star of the film we were about to see.

Further down Joyce was similarly sandwiched, except that his partners were less celebrated and therefore younger with fewer gold teeth. He looked unhappy. It was clear that he was not sure what could be safely considered the age of discretion in so complicated a land as this, so he kept his hands determinedly folded in his lap, glancing warily from side to side.

Protocol was satisfied, for I was sitting still further down, with only Miss Lan, who began dutifully translating "Volga-Volga" for me. It was an extremely slow-moving comedy and on the general intellectual level of a Minsky burlesque thoroughly cleaned by the Legion of Decency. The scenes were tedious and the technique was bad. There was, for instance, a short bit in which a comedian plays a tune with a knife and fork on bottles and glasses of different sizes. Only here nobody had bothered to co-ordinate the bottle sizes with the sound track, thus shattering the illusion of reality. But the Russians never noticed it.

I began to think, watching this jerky business, what a treat it would be for this girl to see an American film—of recent vintage. Then I remembered that the ambassador showed one each week to the American colony at Spaso House. So I asked her.

But, of course, she would like to see a new American film. So very much.

Thursday, then? And would she like me to send a car to bring her to the American Embassy?

An embassy? She hesitates. Perhaps it would be possible.

She is busy on Thursday?

No, she is not busy. But she does not know if it would be possible.

But if I put in a request to the proper authorities?

Yes, she says slowly, nodding. If I did that, it would then perhaps be possible.

I know that it can be arranged that a foreigner may take a Russian girl to the movies, if the matter is taken up through proper official channels.

But before Thursday comes, I have decided against it, and not because I have forgotten Miss Lan. It occurs to me that something I write might displease them, and the matter of who told me might arise. She is a charming and attractive child, and so long as we talk sitting in front of the two men in blue serge suits, nothing could ever be brought up to mar that career for which she is working so earnestly. So good luck, Miss Lan; may fame come to you before gold teeth, and you understand now what happened to Thursday.

Slowly I am beginning to understand this place and its people. Suppose you had been born and spent all your life in a moderately well run penitentiary, which kept you working hard and provided a bunk to sleep in, three daily meals and enough clothes to keep you warm.

Suppose the walls were covered with posters explaining that freedom and justice could only be found within its bars, that outside was only disorder, strikes, uncertainty, unemployment, and exploitation of workers, while this place was being run only for your benefit.

Suppose it was explained that the warden and the guards were there largely to protect you from the malevolent outside world.

Needless to say, if anyone tried to release you or menaced you with a parole, you would fight like a tiger.

There is, however, one marked difference between inmates of the

Soviet Union and of the Kansas State penitentiary at Lansing, where I have often visited an old friend. Food and clothing in both places are about the same, maybe a little better in Lansing. But should my Kansas friend decide that his penitentiary was not well run, and express the hope that there might be a change of wardens, he would run no danger of being shot were he overheard by a stool pigeon. I concede, however, that in Russia a talented inmate can work himself up to be warden, which would be impossible in Lansing.

Public opinion here is handled with the consummate skill of an artist on a giant concert organ, whose hands run deftly over many keys to produce one marching series of harmonies.

For instance, the Russian people were deliriously happy over the news of the Teheran conference. At last Stalin, Churchill, and Roosevelt had sat down together. Finally, Soviet Russia had powerful Allies she could trust! No longer was she the pariah nation of the world.

The bureaucracy was equally pleased but not with this wave of internationalism and good feeling toward the Western world. As experts in the field of the management of public sentiment, they distrust any public emotion, which they do not instigate, or which threatens to get beyond their control. Suppose, for instance, that the Soviet Union might presently find good reason to change its attitude toward its current Allies?

They, therefore, printed in *Pravda* a little story reputedly cabled from *Pravda's* Cairo correspondent (although no such story passed Cairo's censors) to the effect that the British were negotiating with high German officials in neutral territory for a separate peace. Of course, the story was not broadcast in any of the numerous radio news programs from Moscow to the outside world (there are no personal radio sets in the Soviet Union) because it was needed purely for domestic consumption.

The story caused an indignant explosion of denials in the Western world, some of which the government complacently printed in *Pravda* when pressure was brought to bear.

But the desired effect on Russian public opinion had already been achieved. Inter-Allied good will was dampened down, to the point where public opinion could easily be switched, should this need arise.

They did not then see such a need, nor, as I write this, do they see it now. But by such stratagems they keep freedom of action to move either way with the complete backing of their people.

Russian newspapers and newsreels carry only small amounts of news about the outside world, and never anything which might arouse internal discontent with the Party's rule or the Soviet Union's standard of living. Now and then, of course, there is a slight miscalculation. For instance, Soviet newsreels, which specialize in strikes or disorders in the Western countries, ran many feet showing the Detroit race riots, including a vivid close-up of a cop beating a young Negro. The effect on the Soviet audience, according to American correspondents who were there, was electric. Some Russians even stood up. "Look"—they cried—"at that wonderful pair of shoes the Negro is wearing!"

Almost never do the authorities admit any book or movie which would give a straightforward picture of American life and the average American living standard. It is true that Soviet intellectuals have read and appreciate the artistry of *The Grapes of Wrath*. But, released for mass circulation as a movie, it is bound to bewilder the average citizen of the Soviet Union. The Joad family would not be pitied for their clothing, which except for its American cut, would be indistinguishable in a Moscow crowd.

But here is a family which, not being content with its circumstances, leaves without obtaining permission and wanders a thousand miles or so without a travel permit in search of a better job. Where is the NKVD? Why aren't they stopped? Each of these offenses is worth a five-year sentence. True, the grandmother dies on the way and obviously malnutrition contributed, but this is no rarity in the Soviet Union, nor is her funeral less ceremonious nor her grave more stark than those in most Soviet cemeteries.

Above all, where did they get the car? Since it is shabby, of course, it didn't come from the Kremlin motor pool, but the fact that it will run at all proves it must have belonged to an important factory foreman for use on official business only.

These curious, insubordinate malcontents would arouse little sympathy in the Soviet Union, and the only possible happy ending would be to have one of the younger boys join the Komsomols out in California, loyally squeal on the whole disruptive tribe, whereupon the NKVD would give chase and after exciting sequences, overtake and liquidate them at the base of a statue of Stalin.

What with all these difficulties, few American films are shown in Moscow and those are picked with the greatest care. The American films best known are Chaplin's "Gold Rush" and "The Dictator," a Sonja Henie skating picture and Deanna Durbin's "One Hundred Men and a Girl," after the Russian sub-titles were written in to bring out a heavy class-exploitation angle.

When I was in Moscow, the most popular foreign pictures were "Jungle" and "Thief of Bagdad." Both were heavily attended for they are done with the usual Hollywood skill. But since the scene of one is a Hindu village and the other is medieval Bagdad, neither portrayed normal life in the Western world and so were safe.

I did see, however, one excellent Russian picture, and did not need the language to understand and be moved by it. The story concerned a green cadet, very much on his good behavior, who arrives with his kit bag to join a veteran fighter squadron. He is at first genially hazed by the rest, gradually gets experience, shows his mettle and is slowly accepted. It depicted some highly corned-up and improbable shots of air fights, but these flights of fancy were no more distorted than the ones dreamed up in Hollywood swivel chairs.

For the most part, it was an honest, human document, telling the story of a Soviet fighter squadron. It could have been an American, British, or German story.

All nations tend to play up their own battle exploits and to neglect their Allies, and America is, in this respect, a frequent offender. But certainly Red Army advances are decently covered in stories, maps, and pictures both in American newspapers and newsreels.

The Soviet Union, by contrast, almost never shows pictures of foreign battle fronts in its popular theaters. At the time of the

Anglo-American landings in Normandy, we rushed the first films to Moscow. They were dramatic pictures of the great fleet moving into position, of American and British boys being ripped by machine-gun fire from the cliffs and on the beaches.

They were shown to the intelligentsia and to high Red Army officers, who might have a technical interest in how we handle landing operations, but they were not released to the general public.

Similarly, Russian newsreels have shown almost nothing of the Libyan desert campaign, the North African landings, the Tunisian, Sicilian, and Italian campaigns. Nor of the war at sea in either the Pacific or Atlantic. These campaigns have been dismissed with a few lines in *Pravda* or *Izvestia*.

As a result, the average Russian firmly and logically believes that his government has until recently borne, not most of the war burden, but all of it. And it is convenient for Soviet leaders that he should continue to believe this.

From time to time Stalin makes statements which are both realistic and generous to his Allies. Rather recently, he predicted that Soviet soil would soon be cleared of the invader and the armies could then proceed to follow the Fascist beast and crush him in his lair, adding that this would not be possible without the combined efforts of all the Allies.

This was, of course, printed in *Pravda* but the average reader, saturated with news of the Red Army, overburdened with personal problems, and ignorant of the extent of Anglo-American sea, air, and land effort, probably dismissed it as the kind of perfunctory gesture which all statesmen occasionally make.

Today another thundering big dinner at Spiridonovka to which Eric, Joyce, and I are asked but this time only as humble spectators, for it is given by Molotov and the guests of honor are the British and American ambassadors to celebrate the anniversary of our aid agreement with England.

Any artist could draw Molotov with a ruler—a square body on short legs, square head, jaw, nose, and eyes, and there he stands. This square face is as devoid of expression as an Indian chief's.

Litvinov is also present—a keen face, thinning, sandy hair—intelligent, alert—a benign volcano. The reporters say he is the only Kremlin resident who is accessible. He will give any of the more serious ones an hour or so, explaining Soviet policy and problems—provided, of course, they don't bother him too often.

Here is also my friend, the fox-faced Russian who sat next to me at the Mikoyan dinner, now in full-dress Foreign Office uniform. He grins, "Ah, Mr. White—and it is now the second front—come at last—yes?"

"For you the second—for us the eighth."

"That I remember well. But anyway, we drink to it—yes?"

The dinner is like Mikoyan's, even to the climactic suckling pig—or rather his cousin, similarly shaved and boiled. I am next to another Foreign Office boy (Russians apparently keep their wives and daughters away from ravening capitalist wolves) and as we sit down I exclaim in mock dismay at the array of forks and spoons, saying I hardly know which to pick up first.

My neighbor takes this with the utmost seriousness. "In the Soviet Union," he explains ponderously, "we use the English system—using first those on the outside," and gives me a demonstration.

They are tremendously formal people—not because they are Communists but because they are Russians. They may be innocent of the use of toilet paper, but when they throw an official shebang, everything must be just so, from oyster forks to medals. No wonder they were offended when Winston Churchill, visiting Moscow during the raids, turned up at Stalin's dinner in his siren suit. A czarist grand duke might have understood, but not these earnest Socialists. As Russians they must be spectacularly lavish; as Communists they must worry about the forks.

In the middle of the good-will toasts, Molotov breaks a big piece of news; tells us that today they are launching an offensive to co-ordinate with our Anglo-American landing in Normandy.

An Allied general gets briskly to his feet with another toast, expressing his gratitude for this Russian offensive, which, he says, was "specifically promised at the Teheran conference."

Check, and double check. But this to me was also news.

In the major drive which presently followed toward Warsaw and East Prussia, no one can say they did not keep faith—scraping their man-power barrel, throwing war-cripples, semi-invalids, and boys into the line. Their sacrifices from the standpoint of man power have been ghastly. Back of the front you see no young men who aren't either in uniform or limping with a wound, except the few who are in high administrative jobs. And you see absolutely no men between sixteen and forty at the factory benches.

Following the Molotov dinner, we told the correspondents of the announced attack, since it had already been launched and, of course, they filed the story. It was then stopped in censorship. Nobody questioned its truth, but the censors pointed out it had not yet appeared in *Pravda*. It is a rule of Russian censorship that nothing is officially true which has not been printed in a Russian paper, so the American reporter who decides he will scoop the Russian press is wasting his time. *Pravda* got around to printing the news of the offensive three days later.

Tonight we are taken to the Hermitage, which consists of several theaters grouped around a beautiful park. There are at least two movies and a theater for operettas. This drama form has languished in the United States, after having become the mother of our musical comedy.

It is not so elaborate or so serious as an opera, but its comedy plot is more detailed and carefully worked out. It is usually, but not always, a costume drama; the plot of this particular one was laid in the times of Peter the Great and had no direct connection with Communist propaganda except that it was a version of the Cinderella story and the whole Communist effort is an attempt to make all the Cinderella stories come true; to wave a magic wand over the pumpkin and the mice and transform them into the crystal coach and the prancing horses.

In this particular tale Czar Peter orders a young nobleman to Paris to study navigation so that he may be commissioned captain of a naval ship. But the young nobleman is too stupid to learn, so he orders one of his handsome young serfs to take his examinations and spends all his time playing around Paris.

On his return (you've guessed it) his ignorance is unmasked, and the handsome young serf is not only made captain of the ship, but is allowed to marry the nobleman's beautiful fiancée, who already loves him.

A standard character in the tradition of the American stage is the comic Englishman. As far back as colonial times, the rugged backwoodsmen laughed at his accent, his fancy clothes, and elaborate manners. His equivalent on the Russian stage is the comic Frenchman, or more often the Russian who returns from France with Parisian clothes and phrases.

As a comic character, he did not die with the Revolution, and Bolshevik Russians roar with laughter and slap their sides at him, for now he represents all Soviet citizens who have spent any time abroad.

Between acts we want to stroll in the park to mingle with the fascinating crowd. But this is impossible; for in Russia a guest must be entertained. So we are dragged across the park where the usual banquet is waiting. We can hardly nibble—we are so sick of vodka that it smells like castor oil.

Again after the last act, we are marched practically under guard to the dining room, our hosts pushing a path through the festoons of reasonably pretty girls, who watch us with friendly curiosity.

In the banquet room we find the stars of the cast are waiting to greet us. The Intourist steward, who has become to us a sinister figure, is pulling corks from champagne bottles, only what we really want is a glass of warm milk and bed.

But presently in comes a commanding figure, the actor who played Peter the Great. He bows ceremoniously, sits down at the head of the table and calls for vodka.

"My God," says Joyce. "Look!"

Peter has taken the bottle from the steward and is filling, not the tiny vodka glass, but a full-sized water tumbler.

"Look!" says Joyce. "Hey, Eric, look! He's going to *drink* it—why, he's already drunk it!"

Joyce is getting a little hysterical and Peter, noticing it, gives us a grave but friendly stare.

"Eric, he's poured another."

When Peter drank, he tilted his head but his Adam's apple did not move. It was like pouring down a drain.

"Watch out, there he goes again—some of these Russians ought to stop him— What a man! That's his third."

"How many is that?"

"Three of them!" said Joyce, "I counted. Water glasses full. Peter's not a man, he's a tank. He's a gasoline truck. Why, I bet he's got 'Esso' stenciled on his ribs!" and Joyce went off into gales.

"If we wait a few minutes until it begins to take hold, maybe we'll find out."

The gigantic actor was staring solemnly at Eric. He began talking with the interpreter. She was an Intourist girl named Eugenie —Genie for short, which Eric instantly had made into Jennie.

"He says," she translated, "that he enjoyed very much Mr. Johnston's speech in *Pravda*."

Eric nodded.

"He says," translated Jennie, "that being an artist, he has no knowledge of politics and, of course, he could not endorse any political implications the speech may have had—that would be for others to decide."

"Guess Peter likes his job," said Joyce. "Wants to stay where he is."

"He refers only to the style," continued Jennie, "and the way in which it was said. This, he wants to assure you, he enjoyed very much."

"You liked the operetta?" inquired Kirilov.

"Very much, indeed," we said, "and particularly," here we bowed to the prima donna, "the songs."

"In America you have also good songs," said Kirilov. "When I am in New York I have heard."

"We have a good song about Jennie," said Eric resourcefully. "A new song from a movie called 'Lady in the Dark.' About a girl who couldn't make up her mind. She was called Jennie like you."

"But if you would only sing it," said Jennie. "I would like so much to hear."

"Then I will," he said, and the amazing part of it was that he did. He had seen the picture only once when we were in Cairo. But he seemed as sure of the tune and words as the girl in the movie. He sang it, copying her feminine intonation and gestures.

"But," exclaimed the prima donna, "Mr. Johnston is not only a man of business—he is a true artist."

Thus spurred on, Eric launched into the other stanzas with even more vivacity. Toward the end, Joyce, for no reason that I could then see, called out loudly, "Look out, Eric!" Only when he finished I did see. Peter towered above us staring across the table at Eric. He stalked around the table, eyes glued to Eric, declaiming stentoriously in Russian.

"Look out, boy," said Joyce, "he's after you. But whatever he's going to do to you, you sure asked for it!"

"He says," Jennie translated, "that he greets Mr. Johnston, not only as an important man of business—but also a fellow artist. He salutes him."

We hardly listened, for Peter, taking Eric's face firmly between the palms of his massive hands, tilted it upward. And, then, bending over, kissed him. Although it was full on the mouth, it was brief.

Then he let Eric drop, turned solemnly, and said something to the interpreter.

"He says," Jennie translated, "that not only he salutes you, but the whole Soviet Union—"

"No—no—" said Eric, wiping his mouth on his napkin. "Tell him, never mind about anything else. Tell him he represents the whole Soviet Union." He laid the napkin down on the table and rose, very serious.

"Now, fellows—Bill, Joyce—it's late, and we have a full schedule tomorrow, and so, Kirilov, I think maybe we'd better be going now. And, Jennie, you tell these people how very nice their operetta was. Tell them we liked that very much. Tell them we don't have anything quite like it in America."

"Tomorrow," says Kirilov, "we go for ride in private steamboat down to Volga River and return." He stops. "There will"—and here his large sleepy eyes seem to be doing their best to gleam—"be girls."

Even our Russian hosts realize that after our busy schedule, we need a rest. Our idea of a program for this would be a milk toast diet. Theirs, of course, wins and differs slightly. It is a trip by boat down the famous canal connecting Moscow with the Volga River. Some correspondents are also invited.

Around noon we are driven to the landing place. Here is a huge and almost completely deserted station about the size of the Kansas City or the Cleveland Union Terminals. Its architecture is pretentious. It is over-ornamented and built with shoddy materials.

It towers dramatically above the canal, which is reached by a preposterously wide flight of steps—I would guess fifty of them—which are dominated by a titanic statue of Stalin. At the bottom is our boat, a streamlined version of a Mississippi River steamer, better than anything I have seen in America.*

To entertain us they have brought three of the plump operetta artistes. They were better by candlelight. Now we see a few double chins we had overlooked. They arrive in very formal dresses, but soon change, and in the afternoon their billowing Russian busts are encased in pastel sweaters. It's like date night at the Old Ladies' Home. Yet everybody is trying pathetically hard to show us a good time.

I go down to my cabin. Eric has a suite, which occupies most of one side of the boat. Joyce is similarly ensconced near by. I have a spacious sitting room complete with sofa, writing desk, pen, ink, stationery, and private sun deck. In my bedroom are twin beds with yellow silk spreads. It just happens that there is neither toilet nor washbasin, which, except for the bed, are the only things I really need.

* Until I saw our newest and much larger Mississippi river boats, tied up at St. Louis, after this book had gone to the printer.

The paddles are churning—through the new, white silk curtains I see the bank moving so I go on deck. On one of the long padded wicker divans, Johnston is already stretched out, shirtless for a sun bath. Two sailors, under Kirilov's supervision, come trundling out a radio-phonograph trailing a cable. This is set up in the middle of the deck.

"Now," says Kirilov, "we will have American music." Whereupon its loud-speaker is aimed at Eric and it begins to play, "Oh, Johnny! Oh, Johnny! How you can love!" An excited male voice begins to sing the words breathlessly, as though he had first been chased around the block.

I walk around to the bow. The banks sliding by might be illustrations of a fairy tale. There are tall birch forests and if it were night, I am sure a distant light would appear and walking toward it we would find the old witch and her house of stick candy.

Now and then we pass a clearing and a village of logs, with those beautifully carved doors and window frames characteristic of Old Russia. Occasionally naked girl swimmers duck down as we go by.

Here and there great piles of corded wood are stacked on the banks. They tell me this is winter fuel for Moscow but only because of the war; normally, Moscow burns coal from the Don Basin, but now the Germans have Donbas. And what coal there is goes where it's most needed.

This canal probably isn't quite as wide as the Panama but two of these great steamers can pass. About every fifteen or twenty miles there is a loading station almost as big as the one where we came aboard—but no towns are in sight. At each station a mammoth metal statue of either Lenin or Stalin commands the canal. They hold the same poses here and throughout the Soviet Union. Stalin, in his heavy overcoat and cap, strides along, swinging his arms; Lenin always gesticulates with arms outstretched.

How was the canal built, I ask. By 3,000,000 political prisoners, working with picks and shovels, and it took them only a little over two years.

I want to ask what exactly they were accused of and how many died in the building, but somehow I don't.

We float for a while through soft birch forest and sure enough, another statue looms ahead. For us they disfigure the Russian landscape but I suppose we are no more annoyed than Russians would be at the billboards which line our highways. However, the artists who paint our cigarette ads are more skillful than the monumental masons who designed these cigar-store Indians.

They are almost as hideous as our political advertisements which spring up every two years—"Vote for 'Honest Joe Doaks'—Candidate for City Treasurer—the People's Friend."

I remember a Kansas friend who was for many years a successful candidate for a county office. Tiring of nailing up posters every two years, he devised carefully framed pictures, which he hoped would stay up permanently. He would have leapt at the idea of iron statues of himself at every crossroad!

Here there are no election contests, and only one political party which constantly sells its candidate to the people. At last, as permanent political outdoor advertising, the striding statues suddenly make sense.

When Eric arises, three hours of that pale arctic sun have given him a slight rose petal pink and it is time to dress for dinner. I have already seen our Intourist steward marshaling the wine glasses.

One of the correspondents approaches.

"Bill," he says, "I want to tell you. Very curious thing happened. You know I've been intending to collect some anecdotes about Stalin over here—just the kind of little funny stories that people back home tell about Roosevelt or Dewey or Willkie—stories that bring out their characteristics and show what kind of guys they are.

"Well, I asked those artists if they could tell me any stories about Stalin. So I told them we Americans had a lot of stories about Roosevelt, and the British a lot of funny stories about Churchill, and I wanted them to tell me the funny stories the Russians told about Stalin. When they finally got the idea, they seemed shocked. Said there weren't any. Because Stalin, they said, was a great man. So, of course, there weren't any funny stories about him. Never had been. Now what do you think of that?"

I think he was only partly right. I think there once were funny stories about Stalin, and that this pick and shovel canal was dug by those who made the mistake of telling them to the wrong people.

We can only nibble dinner but the Russians eat heartily. And between courses the Sweater Girls, now changed to evening dresses, oblige us with a few vocal numbers.

When we go on deck it is dark. We are motionless in a lock while water pours in to change our level. The long arctic sunset is just dying away but I can still see the gigantic outline of a striding Stalin on the bank.

One of the British correspondents who lives up on the fifth floor of the Metropole invites me and half a dozen other correspondents up for a party, and I take as a contribution my Bolshevik factory cake.

The party starts about 10 o'clock with sandwiches and black coffee, brewed over an electric stove—and my cake. The host has persuaded the Metropole maid, an old lady of seventy named Nina, who has looked after him for several years, to serve and wash dishes afterwards in his bathroom. At about ten-thirty a couple of Russian girls arrive. One is touching thirty, with the usual sallow, pimply Moscow skin and shabby clothing. The other is about twenty-four and the prettiest Russian girl I have seen. She has a black dress with white collar and cuffs, and white bobby socks. But the amazing thing is not where she got the silk dress, but how in Moscow she has found enough vitamins to clear her skin.

Someone puts a record on the portable, we roll back the rug, and our host calls for Nina to bring cake plates and coffee cups for the girls. Nina eyes them with intense disapproval, shoves the plates into their hands and goes out banging the door. It shakes the room.

Our host laughs.

"She's adopted me. Any Russian girl who comes in here, Nina is sure is a tart. When, now and then, one of them does spend the night, Nina puts the picture of my wife and kids where it's the first thing I'll see when I wake up."

And now for a note on sex in Russia. In the outside world Russians have an awe-inspiring reputation for promiscuity. It is unfounded. It grew up in the days when the Bolshevik Party denounced fidelity as a bourgeois fetish and proclaimed the new freedom in these matters, along with legalized abortion and post-card divorce. But even in those days the reputation was unfounded, for although divorce could be had for the asking (and some individuals got dozens), the rate for Russia as a whole was less than the American divorce rate. The average Russian seemed reasonably content with one wife.

Now divorce is difficult and abortion illegal in Russia and promiscuity politically unfashionable. Yet life seems to go on at about the same cadence that it always did. One gathers that these matters are governed by deep instinct and are little affected by the official preachings of church or state, and that this is true not only of Russia, but for the rest of the world as well.

Having said this, I must add that the Moscow foreign colony is definitely underprivileged in this field. In part this is due to matters of taste, for the legendary Russian beauty turns out to be mythical in Moscow; at least she does not exist in the absence of adequate amounts of fresh fruit and tomatoes. The women are drab, sallow, and tired, and on the street dismally unattractive.

There is among the Moscow foreign colony the story of the young consular secretary who one day comes to work and remarks, "By the way, you should have seen the girl in the subway this morning. Lovely looking kid. I don't think she was just looking at my clothes. Tomorrow morning I'm going to take the same train."

At this point his chief rises, puts a hand on his shoulder and says in a fatherly way, "My boy, you've been here too long. We'll have to get you out for a vacation."

"This morning," says Kirilov, as we climb into the waiting Zeeses, "we visit fur factory." In his bright lexicon, a factory is any place where something is produced. This one turns out to be a collective mink farm, a few kilometers out of Moscow. It was once a village. The houses still stand along the mud street. The biggest, which probably belonged to a thrifty kulak who was liquidated in the thirties, is now the administration building. The communal kitchen and dining room is in the second biggest house. A nursery school is in a third.

In the director's room is the usual picture of Stalin, the usual carved furniture. The director, however, is a lean, gentle farmer. His face and neck are weather-beaten. So are his hands. So are the faces and hands of his assistants. These are rugged, intelligent farmers such as you might find in the Farm Bureau Office of Lyon County, Kansas.

This director tells us he is thirty-six; like all farmers, he looks ten years older. Then he gives us some statistics. His collective has 1,200 hectares (hectare = 2½ acres), of which animal cages occupy about forty. It raises not only minks, but silver foxes, sables and martins. Mink pelts, he tells us, bring almost $12 each, and at a wholesale price of about $800, you can buy the seventy necessary for a coat, which will retail at about $2,500. It takes about sixty-five sable skins to make a coat, and these pelts are sold at prices ranging from $50 to $600 each. He tells us that only one or two sables are born in a litter and it sometimes takes a hunter two weeks to find and kill a single animal. Wild sable pelts sometimes bring $500 each. The darkest and silkiest made up into a coat bring as high as $45,000.

And where are the skins from this farm sold? Practically all of them in New York. In normal times, also London and Paris. Only a very few in the Soviet Union.

I get a brief attack of social conscience. Here this half-starved nation is forced to put skilled farmers to raising useless animals for the cream of the foreign luxury market so that Russia may buy useful machines.

We now are taken for a walk among the cages. I know nothing about mink farms, but this one is orderly and clean, and the sturdy farmers seem to know their business thoroughly. The supervisors, both men and women, are "agronomes." That is, they have degrees from agricultural schools in veterinary science.

A girl wearing heavy canvas gloves steps into a cage, picks up one of the squirrel-like minks. It squeals, hisses, and bites viciously— its eyes red with hatred of us and of its destiny.

We pass the nursery school, and I peek into its curtained windows. It is nearly three o'clock, which is rest-time for five-year-olds the world over and these clean, well-fed children are sleeping soundly in their tiny beds. On the rack near the basin is a peg for wash cloths, and over each the child's name. It looks very like the nursery school our daughter goes to in New York. But on the wall there is a huge picture of Stalin, for once smiling and holding a child in his arms. Political education begins early here.

The white-coated Intourist steward has by magic arrived in the dining room and is opening his wine bottles on the long farm table. I wonder what happens to all this opened wine. We drink so little, and it will spoil quickly.

The meal is different for he has apparently supplied only wine, caviar, and dessert. The other courses come from the farm itself and are delicious—good country soup, cabbage, roast duckling, roast pork, and salted cucumbers, all washed down with beer. Honest, decently cooked food. As refreshing as a long drink of well-water on a hot day. Above all, we are with farmers and I feel as though I am back home.

The director's wife, a serious, weather-beaten farm woman who has a college degree, is telling us through the interpreter about the problems of raising the animals.

Eric, in high spirits, asks if they have any skunks.

The answer, when it comes, is no.

"Tell them that when we don't like someone in America, we call them a skunk!"

This is translated and the farmers nod gravely.

"Da-da," says the director, which in Russian means, "Yes, yes." Only sometimes the phrase strikes the American ear as comic.

Eric looks around the table with his contagious smile. "Da-da!" he says, mimicking a baby. And then, pointing his finger around the table, he says "da-da-da-da-da-da-da-da" as though it were a tommy gun mowing them down. This American sense of humor somewhat breaks down their Russian gravity.

At this point one of the waitresses—they are all healthy, big-bosomed, barefooted farm girls—brings a bouquet of field flowers from the collective's garden, which is presented to Eric.

He rises superbly to the occasion. Getting up from his seat, he presents it to the director's wife with a bow. She also rises.

"And tell her," says Eric, with his contagious smile around the table, "that in America it is the custom to kiss the wife of the director."

But she draws away.

"She says," translates Jennie, "that this is not a Russian custom."

"Tell her that it is an American custom."

The weather-beaten woman said something slowly and firmly in Russian.

"She says," Jennie translated, "that we are not now in America."

In the end, however, Eric Johnston won. For when we went outside to have our pictures taken, he seized an opportunity, in front of the Russian movie camera, to kiss the director's wife lightly and playfully on the brow. This is a mutually educational tour.

Coming hard on the heels of this experience is a visit to what Kirilov calls a meat factory, which is, however, not a stock farm but a packing house. Since it is food, we are again garbed in rumpled, slightly soiled white. It differs little from an American packing house, but they show us something which they say is a Soviet invention. The cow, instead of being slugged with a hammer, is struck just at the base of the skull with a javelin, tipped by an electrically charged needle. This stuns but does not kill. Her heart continues to pump out blood after her throat is cut and while, suspended by the horns, she moves down the dis-assembly line to be skinned.

I say "she" advisedly for Soviet beef consists almost entirely of worn-out old milk cows, calves, or an occasional bull whose romantic fires have burned to embers. Almost no cattle are raised to ma-

turity purely as beef. Here it is the end product of the dairy business, as in fact it is over most of Europe.

In the Soviet Union tenderness makes little difference since, due
to the lack of refrigeration, almost all red meat is prepared as
smoked sausage. During our entire stay in the country, only twice
were we offered steak.

But at the banquet which ends the packing house visit, the table
is piled high with countless kinds of sausage. I am stuffed like a
Christmas goose with Soviet food. It would be delicious if I were
even vaguely hungry.

As we leave, three enormous cartons are hoisted into the car
and I have visions of sausage feasts at the Metropole. Each box must
contain the equivalent of a year's meat ration for a Russian. If I
distribute them among the correspondents, beautiful Russian girls
will come flocking to their parties from as far as Leningrad, thus
contributing to the peace and dignity of the resident Foreign Press.
However, this is not to be, for Eric and Joyce, remembering the
faithful servants who wait on them, distribute all three boxes among
the Russian servants who work at the embassy.

My traveling companions have in them the seeds of true great-
ness—they are ever mindful of the humble.

We were surprised at this plant to find that the basic wage was
only 500 roubles a month—instead of the customary 750. However,
the fact presently comes out that workers who overfulfill their
norms (almost all of them do) get an extra dividend, not in money
but in meat, which is infinitely more important.

I see now it was a mistake for me to take a day off, staying at
the Metropole to talk to the correspondents, for Joyce and Eric
return wide-eyed from today's trip. They visited what I suppose
Kirilov must have called a penis factory. In point of fact, it was a
large Russian military hospital, a section of which is devoted to the
repair of genital wounds. They have here developed a surgical
technique to supply penises for men who have had theirs blown
away in battle.

The operation * starts with a fold of skin from the abdomen, one end of which is detached and transplanted below. When circulation is re-established, it is moved and the other end is transplanted. All of this being repeated until it is in a position where it can be sewed into place for the exterior of a penis. There follow a series of delicate operations to re-establish the functions of the organ.

When this is healed, the soldier is released, with orders to report back in six weeks. Sometimes he is not satisfied, and they then make adjustments.

Usually, however, he returns smiling and is taken into a ward full of genital cases just arrived from the front—depressed youngsters often on the verge of suicide. He gives an account of his holiday, and they sit up wide-eyed with new hope.

Genital wounds are relatively rare in war, as a man instinctively protects this area, even more carefully than he does his eyes. There could be no better measurement of the astounding casualties the Soviet Union has suffered than the large number of cases which have gone through this treatment. Surgery can be learned only from practice, and the senseless slaughter of war has given these Soviet doctors so many thousands of these rare cases that in this operation they surpass the world.

Such injuries are rare in the tank corps and uncommon in the air force. They are most frequently found in the infantry, where masses of men must leave protection to rush enemy positions. The backbone of any army is its infantry but this is especially true of the Red Army.

Although visiting Soviet doctors have free access to Allied hospitals on the Western fronts, it is most difficult for Allied medical observers to visit Soviet field hospitals. This is not entirely because of the traditional Russian suspicion of foreigners. They are a proud people, and conceal their weaknesses. Their general standard of

* This operation is brilliantly described for American doctors by the famous Soviet surgeon A. P. Frumkin in his article "Reconstruction of the Male Genitalia," in the October, 1944, issue of the *American Review of Soviet Medicine.*

medical care cannot compare with that of the Western countries. They spend freely on the more spectacular branches of medical research,* but under this top crust, the average Russian doctor has less training than a good American nurse. So when permission to visit a Russian hospital is refused by the Soviet method of delay and postponement, the real reason often is that the Russians know the foreigner would learn nothing new except the meagerness of their equipment. For the general poverty of the country extends to medicine. Yet even though Soviet doctors have less training than American doctors, their people probably get better medical care than do many Americans in the lower income groups, who cannot afford good doctors and yet are too proud to go to charity clinics. And Soviet medical training has made great strides in recent years.

Jennie and I (she is Johnston's interpreter and therefore constantly with us) are beginning to have a number of quiet jokes together. She is a discerning girl with a good sense of humor. I early confessed to her my liking for the Finns and ever after, when they came up in the conversation, she would remark disdainfully, "*Your* friends." So I now humbly refer to them only as "those four-headed Fascist beasts."

She is pushing thirty and was born in Leningrad, which is Russia's center of culture much as Boston was America's in the nineteenth century. She came from a comfortable middle-class family,

---

* Before going to Russia I had read in popular American magazines accounts of the experiments of the Soviet scientist Burdenko in removing and preserving live nerves to be used in replacing nerves destroyed in paralyzed limbs.

After arriving in Moscow I was told that when additional information on this process was asked, the Russians had replied that it was a military secret. This I chronicled in my book, and it appeared in the condensation published in the *Reader's Digest*.

Since then I find that the Soviet government has given to American medical journals and schools what seems to me ample information on the nerve grafting and preservation process. I think my previous statement, as published in good faith by the *Reader's Digest*, was unjust to Russian scientists. They seem to be giving us everything, including the blood bank technique which they originally developed, and which has saved thousands of American lives.

probably learned French and German at home as a child, and also studied for the ballet, but apparently failed to make the grade. After the Revolution she passed a normal Soviet girlhood. She joined the Komsomols, which in American terms is a combination of the Girl Scouts and the Young Republican Club. She also belonged to the Society for the Godless, their Epworth League.

Her present job as interpreter for Intourist by Soviet standards is an excellent one. Since she deals exclusively with foreigners, she is supplied with good clothes as a soldier is issued a uniform. She is probably paid little enough and undoubtedly sleeps in a room in some rabbit warren with other Intourist damosels. But in no other job could she earn enough to supply herself with silk stockings, decent shoes, a presentable wool suit, a supply of fresh blouses, and an occasional shampoo. Nor could she eat as well as she does when on duty with us, where she averages at least three lush gorges a day. Although we are by now so surfeited that unfolding a napkin is almost as painful as having our tonsils out, it is still infinitely better than the dreary Soviet rations. I hasten to say, both for truth's sake and for Jennie's, that these are my unsupported deductions: as a loyal Soviet lass she gave me no hint. But I had only to look at the rest of them.

Her job also gets her around the country. She has in the past escorted the Germans and Japanese about the country on tours not unlike ours. She has shepherded trainloads of German Jews who had bought their tickets in Berlin, clear across European Russia and Siberia to Vladivostok. She has interpreted for British and American sailors at Murmansk.

She has followed all her country's shifts of policy and each has meant that she must deal with new breeds of foreigners. We Americans are the last, or to put it more cautiously, the most recent. Sometimes she mixes her English with German, because to a Russian, the two languages are very alike. For instance, there was that toast at the rubber factory. It had been a long day and Jennie was tired.

"The director says," she translated, "that he wishes to drink with Meestair Jawn-stone to the long endurance of German-American-Russian friendship."

"Watch out, Jennie," I whispered across the table, "you've got the wrong year."

Five

TODAY I go to visit Eric and Joyce at the embassy and am invited to lunch. Never have simple, vitamin-stuffed dishes like canned pineapple, and tomato soup made with condensed milk tasted so good.

Afterwards Joyce and I follow Eric up to his room.

He brings out a list. "This is the itinerary Kirilov gave me that they've worked out for the Urals trip. And boys, it's too long. Lot of places I'd like to see, of course, but my chamber meeting starts the twelfth and I absolutely must be back for that. Kirilov will understand.

"I've crossed out some towns on it. But if we visit Magnitogorsk, Omsk, Sverdlovsk, Novosibirsk, Alma-Ata, Tashkent, and Ashkhabad, that'll get us to Teheran on the eighth in time to get home by the twelfth. Joyce, you give this revised list to Kirilov—he'll understand.

"Now to get all those towns in, we should leave here not later than Wednesday—yes, that's right—Wednesday we should go."

Just before Johnston left America, the Soviet Ambassador promised his Russian trip would include both an interview with Stalin and a trip to the front. The latter is now going to be delivered, only we are to visit not the German front but the Finnish. Perhaps this is a graceful Soviet tribute to my special interest in the Finns.

It is necessary first to go to Leningrad. The reporters are excited because Eric has agreed to take half a dozen of them along. So far none of them have been able to get near enough to the battle lines to hear a gun. A Soviet "front trip" usually consists of a trip in a de luxe Pullman in the general direction of the lines, a perfunctory interview with the sector's commanding general, inspection of some abandoned German trenches, and at the end, champagne and vodka at the officer's mess.

This time they hope it will be different, so they wear whatever odd bits of uniforms they picked up at other Allied fronts—khaki fatigue caps with "U.S." pins on them and bits of British battle dress—with one exception, a motley crew. The party included Dick Lauterbach of *Time* and *Life*, Bill Lawrence of the New York *Times* and Robert Magidov of NBC, but certainly its most conspicuous member was a pushing, plump, semi-bald correspondent, who had recently arrived in Moscow representing an American newspaper syndicate. He had elbowed his way into the party and turned up at the train resplendent in a brand-new American officer's summer uniform gleaming with brass buttons, campaign ribbons, and correspondent's insignia—as fresh as though he had just stepped out of the Pentagon.

He was promptly dubbed "The Field Marshal" and it was clear that he didn't think this joke quite as funny as the rest of us did. Although he went with us everywhere, he saw very little of either Leningrad or the front, being constantly preoccupied with the problem of whether any given group of Red Army soldiers approaching would or would not salute him.

Eric, Joyce, and I traveled in what, when we left Moscow, was a private car at the end of the train. It was clean and comfortable. Its rear half contained a long table and there, of course, was the Intourist steward, laying out the sliced sturgeon, uncorking the champagne, and opening the cans of caviar.

But just before dusk, the train was halted at a junction and a ramshackle boxcar was hooked on behind. Two anti-aircraft machine guns were bolted to its roof. Some straw was also piled there and on this sprawled the gun's crew—half a dozen Red Army boys. The Soviet Union was taking no chances with the safety of the titular leader of American business.

Thirty or 40 miles farther on we are halted again at a siding to let a troop train pass us on its way to the Finnish front. It contains perhaps a regiment, and is mostly flat cars. Artillery, trucks and tanks are mounted on these, straw is piled around them. Some of the blond soldiers are sleeping on the straw; others astride the guns or tanks watch the green countryside go by.

I remind myself that this is a regiment which has probably been pulled out of the line farther south, to be thrown without rest against the Finns. Even so, by Western standards, they look shabby. They have been haphazardly piled aboard this rickety train. Everything seems improvised. The equipment is battered, a little rusty and considerably lighter in construction than ours. Were it not for the Slavic faces, this might be a Mexican regiment on the move.

In many ways Russia is like Mexico. Both peoples have been basically agricultural, with no great aptitude for industry and still less experience. The general poverty of Russia, as far as I could see, is no less than that of Mexico except that it is a cleaner poverty. Also the standard of health is better in Russia and this has cut the infant mortality rate. Russian doctors do not have the problem of persuading the peasants to accept what medical care they are equipped to give. In Russian villages the people aren't asked; they are told.

It is now bedtime, and I undress in the compartment, which I share with Joyce. It is a little larger than an American Pullman compartment but it lacks all the ingenious contraptions with which Western nations make limited space useful. There is no washbasin. There is no toilet. The only mechanical device is the bolt on the door.

I climb into my upper berth and Joyce, below, switches out the light and is soon snoring. After half an hour, I discover that another missing gadget is a ventilating system. In this confined space, the temperature is rising, and with it an odor. It is like being locked in the vault of a small and none too solvent state bank, unprotected by the Federal Deposit Guarantee.

There is, however, a remedy, and I reach out for the door which leads into the corridor. Then I remember that among the perils which constantly threaten Joyce in his travels, is the menace of fresh air. During the day his system can tolerate moderate amounts of it, but at night he takes every precaution, particularly here where they have the further complication of Socialist fresh air.

Gingerly, I reach out to the door and push so that it opens noise-

lessly. About three inches. Joyce's snores subside, and then omi-
nously cease. There is a sudden bang as the door slams shut. I call
out, "Joyce?"

"Yeauh," he mutters. "Those damn Russians. Opened our door.
Give us all pneumonia."

In the morning the long table is again set for breakfast with the
wine and vodka glasses. What we want is orange juice, toast, and
coffee. What we'll get is that standardized Intourist orgy.

This section of the railway line was bitterly fought over, and the
people have begun to come back, living in the abandoned dugouts
in the sides of the deeper grade cuts. They are women, barefooted
and in rags, and an occasional child. Their miserable laundry, which
they have washed in ditch puddles, is drying on the barbed wire.
German trenches look exactly as they did in the last war—well
braced with timber expertly sawed to size, well made duckboard in
the trenches' bottom, and neatly piled sandbags on the parapet.
In such things a most orderly and thorough people.

With us on this trip is a chunky young colonel, assigned from
the Red Army staff in Moscow to explain military matters.

"Yes," he agrees through the interpreter, "they make excellent
trenches, always." Then he adds, "It is a people which must have
its comfort." The train comes out onto level ground and we see
that these ragged women, who plow barefoot through this mud,
have planted little potato patches in clearings of the debris of concrete pillboxes, barbed wire, and the rusting ruins of wrecked tanks.
The women stare blankly with beaten down, blue eyes at the train
windows, while sitting at our breakfast table, we stare at them over
the row of wine glasses.

"Now somebody," said Eric, "ought to do a magazine piece about
these Russian women. Look at them out there—back working already—clearing things up. The women of Russia! Probably the
engineer and fireman on this train are women. Look at all the
women we've seen in the factories. Those women out there don't
shrink from hard work! They're practically keeping Russia going!
The magnificent women of Russia! No, thank you, Kirilov, don't

think I'd care for any more of that wine. Almost never take it. You haven't got any just plain water, have you?"

We glide through a wood as heavily blasted by artillery fire as those of the Somme in 1916. Only a few shattered, branchless trunks protrude above the shell holes. At this point the Red Army's excellent artillery had to blast the Germans out of every inch of ground.

The colonel tells us that these German fortifications were built at the time they cut the railway line, completing the encirclement of Leningrad—in late 1941 and early 1942. This encirclement was only broken by the Russians late in 1943.

We now pass a railway siding where the heavy machinery of a factory stands loaded on flat cars. It is a former Leningrad plant, returning from its wartime exile in the Urals.

As we drive from the Leningrad station to our hotel, we get a good look at the city. It is a beautiful, spacious, well-planned town, built over two hundred years ago on the shores of the Baltic by order of Peter the Great. Its site was an uninhabited salt marsh and it was completed in about two decades.

As part of a drive toward Westernization and modernization Peter built his new capital on the shores of the Baltic, giving Russia a window on the civilized outside world. There is in its beautiful, clean architecture little suggestion of Russia, for the good reason that the architects were all French or Italian. The city might be part of Paris except for its churches and except for the fact that its public buildings and palaces are painted lemon yellow, which was the color of the czars.

It is, of course, now run-down and dilapidated. Yet, somehow, we all felt we were back in Europe, in a gently cultured, comfortable world.

Russians, who are proud of the war-sufferings of Leningrad, are always annoyed if you mention the fact that the town is less damaged than London. Actually the beautiful old central part is almost intact, except for broken window glass and nicked cornices. Shell or bomb craters are rare.

During our Leningrad stay we are put up at the Hotel Astoria, one of the relics of czarist grandeur. Eric has what could be no less than the former Romanov bridal suite and we inspect this with awe. There is a large dining room, a spacious sitting room and a thundering big bedroom with matching double beds covered in silk brocade. The rooms are done in the lavish style of czarist days, and there are several pieces of porcelain bric-a-brac, thick with china cupids tickling each other or else pinching the gilded bottoms of angels.

Best of all, the light switches seem to work, and the bathroom's beautiful plumbing is clean. There is no smell, nor is there any scum around the lower part of the hand bowl, so its drain must be unclogged—truly a novelty in Russia.

What the china cupids in Joyce's room are doing to his angels, I do not know, for I have a slightly less luxurious suite (twin beds, sitting room, and bath) farther down the hall, which I invite Dick Lauterbach of *Time* to share with me.

The correspondents are excited, for a few days here are like a vacation. In Leningrad book stores you can still pick up occasional second-hand copies of French, German, or English books, relics of pre-Revolution middle-class libraries. Looking out of our tall French windows, over the housetops, we might be in Paris or Vienna. Even the venerable maid who looks after our room remembers a few words of French, the language of the czarist educated classes.

Outside the tiny island of our hotel, there is only the monotonous Soviet poverty, in the shop windows and in pinched faces of the people. Yet something still lingers in the beautiful wide streets and in the simple, well-proportioned lines of the houses, as orderly as a Bach minuet. The new order has not quite laid the graceful old ghost of European St. Petersburg, which lingers in a delicately proportioned window, in a beautifully bound but now forgotten volume on a shelf.

Opposite our hotel is St. Isaac's Cathedral, but there is no hint of Europe in its architecture. It squirms with Byzantine ornament over which float onion-shaped spires. It is Russia, and back of Russia, the Eastern Empire of Constantinople, and back of that Bagdad and the temples of Asia.

Above St. Isaac's door is an inscription in Old Slavonic (the ancestor of modern Russian): "God, with your help, we uphold our Czar." The Bolsheviks have not bothered to change it. The doors are closed; maybe because of bomb damage to its roof, or possibly it has been locked for years.

Leningrad's sidewalks are empty of people; sometimes in a huge square there will be no one in sight—a sharp contrast with teeming Moscow. Before the war Leningrad had 3,500,000 people. The government gives no figures on the number who starved during the siege, but estimates vary between 500,000 and 1,500,000. The rest were evacuated except for a skeleton force which remains. It is like strolling through Pompeii.

Before the war most of Russia's highly skilled precision workers lived here (again the European influence) and it was the center of Russia's precision industries—cameras, optical equipment, telephone instruments, radios, electric light bulbs, dynamos, and fine machine tools, which, however, were only about 10 per cent of the whole, for Leningrad also made many tractors and comparable machines. Most of this factory equipment and the people who worked at it were loaded into freight cars and hauled halfway across Russia to the Urals, Siberia, or the Chinese border, where they are now operating.

But now our program begins. We are taken to Leningrad's city hall and there we meet the official architect of the city—Alexai Baranov. On the wall is a huge map of future Leningrad. Some of this grandiose plan had been built before the war; most of it is still only on paper.

When it is done, old St. Petersburg will be a back-eddy of moldering history. In the new Soviet megalopolis of the blue prints, boulevards will slash through it, housing developments will rise stretching far down the shores of the Finnish Gulf. They will carve a great park of Culture and Rest out of the present city near the old Fortress of Peter and Paul. A new square in honor of the 1917 Revolution will be opened up in front of Smolny Institute where Lenin organized the overthrow of Kerensky and brought the Bolshevik Party to power.

They tell us Leningrad's intellectuals continued with this planning during the blockade, as both architects and people were sure their town would never fall. Like everything in Russia, it is very impressive in its blue print stage. Eric is presented with a beautifully printed monograph on old and new Leningrad, issued while Leningrad was still under siege.

Back into our Zeeses and on to the new Palace of the Soviets, the hub of the future city. We move toward the suburbs but the buildings don't trail off in size, as they do toward the edge of an American town, where the yards gradually get bigger, garden plots appear with now and then a cluster of crossroads filling stations, grocery stores, and billboards.

Instead we drive down a wide street between rows of six-story concrete barracks-like workers' apartments. Suddenly the city stops as abruptly as the noise of a pistol shot. Beyond the last apartment are the open fields of a collective farm, whose buildings we can see in the distance.

But near us is not a shack, a shed, a bungalow, or an old fence. We have emerged into open fields of grain and potatoes.

An American or European city grows like a plant—naturally, freely, sending out roots and shoots in search of water or sunlight, twisting, bending, groping tentatively this way or that. Broadway was once an old cow path; the Paris boulevards trace the sites of the medieval city's walls.

Now and then our cities need (and get, although this is often too long delayed) a major face-lifting operation—slums are scooped out to be replaced by parks, or a boulevard cut through to drain off traffic, when the city's natural growth has proved its needs.

Here a city follows, not the contours of the land nor the desires of the people, but a blue print on a drawing board. Suppose those people in that six-story concrete workers' barracks had been able to choose; would not some of them have preferred modest bungalows here in the outskirts, if the collective farm were permitted to sell them a building lot and a small garden?

If allowed this much freedom, one might want the right to quit his factory job and start a crossroad store, exploiting his neighbors by selling them merchandise from a temptingly convenient location, thus disrupting the plans of the Soviet Food Commissariat.

They would point out that under capitalism such little men often make mistakes, locating crossroad stores where there is no need for them, and then go broke.

A spokesman for capitalism would answer that so would most Soviet enterprises if they had any free competition. But here competition with the state is outlawed, so inefficiency is protected and the people accept it because they know nothing better. Occasionally some Russian expert returns from abroad with the news that keen capitalist competition has developed a cheaper, quicker way of doing something. Then, if he can get in to see the important commissars and beat down the natural inertia of a bureaucracy, the new system is installed throughout the Soviet Union. But more often than not capitalism pioneers, while socialism only copies.

Somehow those six-story concrete barracks, dropping off sharply into empty fields, tell us more vividly the story of rigid socialist planning than anything we have seen.

Our hosts are proud of the straight new concrete highway on which we are riding. This section of the New Leningrad is being built on "The American Plan," they explain.

Someone gathers courage to ask them what, exactly, is this American Plan.

But surely, we must know! Anyway, the American plan of city building is to build the concrete roads first, even before you are ready to put up the apartment houses.

But now we are approaching the Palace of the Soviets, a tall, impressive building which towers over the empty fields just off the highway. Its architecture is pleasantly simple; along the façade facing us is a row of tall, thin white columns, which might be mistaken for marble. Getting closer, we see their stucco surface is already peeling. Beneath is a hollow, shell-like tube of bricks.

Like most new Soviet buildings, it reminds us of the structures that rise suddenly from the exposition grounds of American world's fairs—always grandiose and impressive—designed to amaze or amuse but not intended to last after the gates are closed.

As we walk back toward our cars, the reporters tell me that the Kremlin's new plans for rebuilding the devastated regions show a sharp trend away from these concrete workers' barracks, which they have been building since the Revolution. Instead they are planning cottages, each with a yard or garden-plot.

This reflects the whole change in Bolshevik thinking—a move back to the family as a unit—away from easy abortions, community kitchens, and free divorce.

It has taken a bureaucracy almost a generation fiddling with blue prints and human happiness to arrive at this simple conclusion.

But maybe this has always been a nation of blue prints. After all, old St. Petersburg was just as abruptly and rigidly planned on the salt marshes. And again that enigma which we meet almost every time we see something fantastic: is this a manifestation of Communism or is it because these particular Communists are Russians—a race grandiose in its plans but sloppy in its execution of them?

Leaving the Palace of the Soviets, we continue on out the paved road. When it ends, we bump over ruts to the German fortifications. They are neat and orderly like German entrenchments everywhere. At this point the German line ran through a little cluster of houses, which was a co-operative farm and had been heavily shelled by Russian artillery because near it the Germans located one of the big siege guns which pounded Leningrad. The Germans got their gun out but its great emplacement remains, a careful job of concrete work and camouflage, which the Russians show us with respect.

But the little co-operative farm buildings took a pounding—doors were blown from their hinges, all the glass is gone and also the roofs, although some of the beams remain.

Already the people are returning. We see three ragged women picking about the ruins, trying to put on one end of a room a temporary roof which will shelter a stove from the rain. A shy, chunky, nineteen-year-old girl, dragging from another ruined house a heavy rafter, passes us on the path. She is in rags, but they are clean rags. We stand aside to let her pass. She avoids our eyes. Her hands have calluses as thick as those of a stonemason. We watch the prints which her bare feet leave in the mud path as she goes on up toward the other house, dragging the beam. So Russia is built.

Now at last we turn back toward Leningrad. The reporters tell me its people are tremendously proud of their city, and regard themselves as culturally superior to the rest of Russia. They are also proud that they were able to hold the Germans for weary, starving months at the city's gates, and finally hurl them back. They are contemptuous of Moscow which they have always regarded as an overgrown peasant village, but particularly now because of the panic which swept Moscow when the Germans were at its gates.

To make conversation we ask our Leningrad hosts, riding with us in the car, when Leningrad evacuees will be returned to their proud city.

They tell us calmly that most of them probably will never return. For Leningrad was evacuated, not by districts or by classes, but by factories. These were scattered beyond the Urals, all over Siberia and Russian Turkestan. Most of these factories will probably stay and, of course, their people with them.

New and even more modern factories will be built in Leningrad. New people will be brought from other parts of the country to run them. These things seem to be no problem in Russia. But we wonder about the people. Will the mellow old buildings of Czar Peter give the new people the pride which the old ones had in their city? Will the former Leningraders back of the Urals remember with pride that they were citizens of a city which was Russia's window on Europe? Or will the proud tradition, which survived even Bolshevism, melt to nothing? Clearly, it matters little to these brisk young Russians who are now rebuilding Leningrad.

Few of them, it develops, were born in the city. Like American city managers, they are specialists in government. They do a job in one town, are promoted to another, and thus climb the ladder of bureaucracy.

We were halfway across Leningrad, going to our hotel, when Eric had a happy impulse.

"Kirilov!" he suddenly called, "stop the car, let's get out here for a minute—right by this church. I'd like to go in and look around. We've never seen one, you know."

"I do not know," said Kirilov, "if the church is open."

However, it was and we streamed inside. It was as over-decorated as a lace valentine but gloomy. Presently, an old man appeared and began switching on dim little chandeliers. Kirilov said he was the warden who would show us around. And then the warden apologized that today the priest was not here to meet us. The old man said we were in the Church of St. Nicholas.

"It has," translated Kirilov without cracking a smile, "a miracle-working ikon."

The church was built in two elevations and as we climbed the stairs, we heard singing and discovered that we had blundered in on choir practice. At one side of the main altar were lights and here the choir was sitting around on folding chairs. They were all women in early middle age, very well dressed by Soviet standards and decently dressed by ours. There were perhaps a dozen. They went on with their singing, paying no particular attention to us. It could have been choir practice any weekday afternoon in any Episcopal church in America.

The music was an old Greek choral chant, and very beautiful. Presently, there appeared a tall, plump, blond man in his early fifties, who wore a white shirt and clean, stiff collar, a dark tie and a blue serge suit, which fitted him rather well. Had it been in America, I would have guessed him the owner of a comfortable small business, and head vestryman in the church. That seemed to be his position in this one.

Kirilov told him who we were. He had read of Mr. Johnston and was much flattered that we should pay his church this unexpected visit, smiling us a hearty welcome. He apologized because the Father himself was not here, but volunteered to show us the various altars and the miracle-working ikon, switching lights off and on and being frugal of electricity, since, as we knew, a church must pay staggeringly high rates for its current.

We asked how the money was raised for keeping the church in repair, and were told that the state took care of this, so we looked more closely. At least it came up to the standard of other Soviet public buildings.

I go into detail about this simple incident because all of it surprised me. I had expected to find the church deserted, except for a few ragged, superstitious old women.

But these people, on our surprise visit, were not old, and were decently dressed. Clearly, they or their husbands held positions of some consequence—engineers, maybe, professional men or minor administrators—yet they had no fear of jeopardizing this by attending church.

Kirilov and the other Russians with us represented a party and a government which has bitterly opposed their church. But they stood in no fear, nor did they make an obsequious fuss over him. They went about their business. The head layman treated us exactly as would his opposite number in America if a member of the city council showed up at an American church with distinguished foreigners in tow. If there were any sinister undertones, I was too stupid to catch them.

So much for what I myself saw of the Russian church; now for what more skilled observers told me. First, bear in mind that Communist Party members continue their private contempt for religion. They regard such doctrines as the forgiveness of sin and the immortality of the soul as childish superstitions on a level with palmistry. It is highly improbable that anyone holding to any of these beliefs would be regarded as fit for membership in the Party, which in Russia is the only road to power.

However, the Orthodox Church is now, for all practical purposes, the officially established church of the Soviet Union, with a representative on the Council of People's Commissars, corresponding to a cabinet post in the Western countries. For this change, Hitler is largely responsible.

After the 1917 Revolution, most of the Orthodox Church leaders emigrated to the Balkans, and Hitler, as part of his invasion plans for the Soviet Union, seized on this historical background. He established a number of Orthodox churches in Berlin, including a cathedral, and earmarked millions of reichsmarks for their support. After he invaded France, he commandeered silk to make religious vestments. When he entered Russia, he proclaimed himself the Protector of the Russian Church; every German army quartermaster was equipped with a supply of these vestments as well as sacred church vessels, and churches were everywhere re-opened in the Ukraine.

When the Communists dropped their anti-religious propaganda, in the schools and on the stage, and suspended the official publication for the Society of the Godless because of a "paper shortage," their critics in the outside world insisted that these moves were only to impress foreigners.

These critics were wrong; the Party had sounder domestic reasons for changing their policy. For the Germans were making headway in the Ukraine with their religious propaganda, and whispers were going all over Russia. Not only was it popular with the older people, but many of the young were joining the Germans. During the final stages of the Ukrainian mop-up, the Red Army came on entire regiments of Ukrainians in German uniform. The numerous "Russians" whom the Americans captured during the Normandy landing were undoubtedly some of the same.

As a further answer to this German propaganda in the Ukraine, three dignitaries of the Russian Orthodox Church were invited to see Stalin and on September 4, 1943, a formal reconciliation was effected and the Church got its place on the Council of People's Commissars. This is a complete reversal of the action of January 23, 1918, which separated Church and State in Russia. The Metropolitan of Leningrad also was given a high Soviet decoration for his part in encouraging the morale of the people during the blockade.

A further explanation of the change is that the Bolshevik Party now feels strong enough to tolerate, even to recognize, the Church. The clergy have loyally supported the war. And the principal reason for the Party's original opposition lay in the fact that the

Church had in previous generations preached unquestioning obedience to the czars. The Party has not overlooked the fact that a patriotic, nationalistic Church can be as useful to their regime as it was to the Romanov dynasty. So many of the churches reopened by the Germans in the Ukraine remain open, particularly in Zhitomir and Odessa. Even some of the clergy who came in with the Germans are permitted to officiate. The State printing presses in Moscow are now turning out beautifully printed religious books for the use of the Church, and it has consented to the establishment of a seminary for training priests, so that the faith will not die out.

But although the Church is now recognized and tolerated, it is not officially encouraged. The Party realizes that the new policy is popular abroad, and strengthens in America and England both its own position and that of its friends in those countries. Consequently, it encourages all news stories and picture layouts coming out of Russia portraying the new state of affairs.

The Party was delighted when the Metropolitan Benjamin, canonical representative of the Russian Orthodox Church for the Americas, in 1942 told Canadians that separation of Church and State in Russia was not more severe than in all other truly democratic countries. Of course, such statements never appeared in the Russian press. Marx called religion "Opium for the people." The private attitude of the Party would be, "If the people still want opium, why not give them a little? We are strong now, and today the Church is patriotic."

Something of the basic attitude toward the Church, however, may be seen in a little thing like electric light rates. A state-owned store pays only 1.16 kopeks per kilowatt-hour for its current, a home user is charged 5.5, while a church must pay 41.

While the Bolshevik regime has finally arrived at a comfortable and probably permanent living arrangement with the Orthodox Church, the case is far different with the Church of Rome. This has become important only since the war, when the Soviet Union absorbed the Baltic States and parts of Poland, all of which contain many millions of Roman Catholics.

Some concessions have been made. After Hitler's attack on Rus-

sia, the Soviet's Polish prisoners of war were released from intern-
ment camps and presently organized into several divisions originally headed by General Anders. While these troops and their
families were on Russian soil, the Soviet government permitted the
teaching of the Catholic religion to their children in special Polish-
language schools, organized for them by the Soviet Department of
Education. Anders was also permitted to have thirty-seven Catholic chaplains for his seven divisions.

Regardless of the basic contempt of all Communists for religion,
the Orthodox Church is a purely Russian institution, and its clergy
are now as completely obedient to the Kremlin as they were
once subservient to the Czar. But the Pope, an Italian living in
Rome, is another matter. Like the Nazis, who in these matters are
only paler copies of the Communist political system, the Soviet
Government permits outsiders to have little contact with, and certainly no authority over, the people within its borders. So as long
as the Soviet Union contains within its frontiers a considerable
Roman Catholic population, any agreement between the two could
only be an armed truce.

It is late when we leave the church, but our hosts insist we must
visit the Leningrad Defense Museum, which turns out to be an
enormous world's fair type of exhibit telling the story of the city's
recent siege. At such things Russians, who have a native sense of
drama, are at their best.

In the central lobby there is a bronze statue of Lenin, addressing
the people during the Revolution while standing in an armored car.
There are dozens of groupings. We are shown how Leningrad's
luxury and precision industries mobilized for war; a perfume factory makes disinfectant, a radio assembly line turns out shell-timing
devices.

Here is the telegraph apparatus connected with the line laid under
Lake Ladoga, Leningrad's only communication with the rest of
Russia during the siege. There are pictures of the transportation
system across Ladoga's ice; the top layer had melted, but cars were
traveling hub-deep over the lower one.

A scale model of Leningrad's bread factory shows how it operated without electricity or running water. A collection of lamps was made from bottles after the electricity gave out. There were also exhibits of the daily bread ration as it had to be successively reduced because of dwindling supplies. The smallest was 125 grams (about 4 ounces) on December 25, 1941.

We are shown pictures of people pulling the bodies of their dead on sleds through the streets toward cemeteries. But the reporters tell me that bodies frequently were kept in the house or buried after dark, so the survivors could continue using the food card.

A most interesting series of montages is devoted to the partisans; explaining how organizers are parachuted into occupied areas, how the bands camp in the forests. There are photographs taken from German prisoners showing the execution of Russian girl partisans.

Why did not France use the partisan technique in 1940? Largely because, once the Maginot line had been broken, every realistic Frenchman knew the Germans could reach the Pyrenees at will. But it was always clear that the Russians—no matter how badly beaten—would never run out of land into which they could retreat, since the Pacific was 7,000 miles away.

Occupied France in 1940 thought (and not unreasonably) that the war was over. Not until Russia and America had entered did the French people change their minds, and only then was it possible for the British and Free French to organize the Maquis and establish airplane contact with them.

The case of Russia was never hopeless, so from the outset it was as easy to organize civilian resistance in the occupied area as it later became in France.

Many romantic things have been written about morale, but it is usually a by-product of facts. When a situation is favorable, morale is high; when it becomes hopeless, morale vanishes. We Americans and the English can criticize the French for thinking that the war had ended in 1940 with a German victory. However, the Russians can't, for they also believed it, and their propaganda machines abroad were doing everything possible to weaken England and stabilize that victory.

Late that night, very tired, as we trudge back up our hotel stairway, we see, passing Johnston's suite, our customary breakfast banquet table already set with its vodka and champagne glasses. But next morning the prospect is too grim to face. Dick Lauterbach and I arouse everybody's jealousy by ducking the breakfast banquet for a simple breakfast in our room.

A little furtively we emerge from our dog house to join the rest of the party as it rises from its breakfast of chocolate cake and champagne to visit the famous Leningrad electrical plant, now named for Kirov, Stalin's close friend, whose assassination in 1934 started the big political purge of the Communist Party.

The plant's director is Gregory Mukhin, a gray-haired man of fifty-three who tells us he was an assistant for nine years and director after 1941, when he succeeded his former boss, who took most of the plant's machinery with him behind the Urals. The present plant, he explains, employs only 3,000 people. Before the war 6,000 worked here. It is now producing no consumption goods —only generators, hydro-electric turbines, and electrical equipment for the Red Army. Their generator sizes range between 1,500 and 100,000 kilowatts.

But before we start our inspection, the director tells us the story of his plant during the siege. The German lines were only 5½ kilometers away, and more than 1,500 eight-inch shells fell in the area. Early in 1943 they started restoring the plant and even at the hardest time more than a thousand workers were turning out small motors for the front which could be used for charging batteries. These were sent out of Leningrad by plane. Recalling those bitter days, the director's eyes fill with tears. The spirit of the workers helped them go on, he tells us. They were convinced Leningrad would never surrender. Most of the workers lived, ate and worked in the plant. In 1943 they sent out to war plants in the Urals, where machinery was desperately needed, a 100-ton engine and also a 50-ton generator. Both were hauled on sledges over Lake Ladoga's ice.

In this factory they maintain an industrial school, where 500 high-school-age boys are taking a two-year course.

At one point girls working at a row of benches are winding and assembling a small electric motor. Eric says it is a standard type which sells for $55 in America. He knows, for he makes and deals with electrical equipment at his Spokane factory.

They tell us that 250 people work in this division. They turn out 400 motors a month. So we do a little figuring. At American prices, these motors would bring a monthly total of $22,000. If this sum were divided equally among the 250 assemblers here, each would get $88 a month, which is almost exactly the wages they do get, in terms of the actual purchasing power of the rouble.

But this leaves nothing whatever for general factory overhead or the wages of the management, nor does it allow for the cost of the wire and metal parts, since these people only assemble.

Obviously, if their factory is to make a profit, that little motor must be sold for at least double what it would cost in America, and this because of the inefficiency of Soviet production methods. One worker turns out only $1\%_{10}$ motors per month. Is it unskilled management or unskilled labor? Whatever the answer, the picture is the same in almost every plant we visit.

This factory is also badly lit and dirty. Going from building to building we thread our way among scattered piles of twisted, rusting metal rubbish. But since it was long under bombardment, it is only fair to assume that this time the Germans, not the Russians, are responsible for the disorder.

Strolling through the plant, they stop to show proudly a device which was made to the order of the great Russian physicist, Joffe, who has been engaged in splitting the atom. The central part of it appeared to be a large, solid steel kettle-drum, but was probably a magnet.

One of the reporters tells the story of a famous Russian chemist, who after the Revolution found an honored position on the Oxford teaching staff. However, the Bolsheviks, who have a deep respect for science, kept after him to come back, offering him not only honors and salary, but unlimited research facilities, and finally they succeeded in persuading him.

A few years ago they were entertaining a group of British and American scientists, and the old Russian chemist, now a highly honored professor, was brought out to greet them at a big dinner. He was, of course, delighted to see his old friends again and was warm in his praises of Western universities, of Oxford, and in particular of Massachusetts Institute of Technology which he had often visited. There, he said, one found the true scientific spirit, a fine atmosphere for the search after pure truth—a great assemblage of minds.

"But, professor," piped up an eager young Komsomol, "what about our Soviet universities? You say nothing of them."

"Young man," said the old chemist, "in our Soviet universities we teach the students many important facts. But at M.I.T. they teach them to think."

The authorities, of course, didn't care for the remark but the old man was an honored world figure and could get away with it.

Now we enter the main Kirov plant and have our initial session with Nicholas Puzyrev, a stocky man of forty-one, its director.

He starts out by telling us that this factory is rich in tradition—during the Revolution it furnished many soldiers to Lenin's army. Trotsky was the military commander at that time, but, of course, his name cannot be mentioned.

Before the war, the director says, his factory employed 32,000 workers. How many now? He dodges—almost the only time anyone has refused to give us a frank answer. Anyway, several thousand, he says after hesitating. It was probably a legitimate military secret. The plant functioned all through the blockade, producing mostly ammunition for Leningrad's defenders. And the number of workers has "slightly increased" since the blockade's high point. Now its principal work is the production of tank motors.

The workers had their greatest casualties in the early days of the bombardment, the director explains. Later, they learned to take cover when the German artillery opened up. But we should hear the story from the workers themselves in the plant.

He conducts us down a long assembly line and stops at a particular grinding machine presided over by a beautiful girl—the only attractive one in the room. She is tall, blonde, and blue-eyed but her Slav face is unusually grim. She is a Stakhanovite * Komsomol † and can't be more than twenty-two. We ask about her production record, and she explains that she works not for the extra pay but from hatred—her father and mother starved during the siege. At the factory, she says, the workers ate grease from the guns and oil from the machines. From nowhere, a bouquet of flowers appears, is slipped to Eric, who presents it to her. She receives it with a faint smile and goes on with her work.

The correspondents remember her—she talked to them when they toured Leningrad five months ago.

Leaving the plant, we pass through rows of workers' apartments and are surprised to see how little damage a single shell does to the great concrete beehives. It will open out only one or two cells in the honeycomb.

We also see a string of rusting streetcars backed up on a siding. Once they took workers into Leningrad. During the siege they were placed here and filled with gravel and dirt to serve as fortifications in case the Germans broke through the line a few kilometers away. The Germans didn't, and now green grass is growing out of the dirt-filled windows. But the lines stayed in this position, they tell us, for 900 days. You could hear German machine guns plainly in Leningrad—cannon twenty-four hours a day. Now all is quiet.

They drive us from Leningrad to Peterhof, the great palace built by Peter the Great just outside his capital.

The Germans occupied Peterhof and all Leningrad's other suburbs. For instance, Ligova was a suburban town of 35,000. When the Russians reoccupied it, they found not a living soul. The same with Pushkina, which had 50,000, and Peterhof, which had 45,000.

At last we are in sight of Peterhof—a beautiful palace rather faith-

* A worker with a high production record.
† A member of the Young Communist League.

fully copied from Versailles, but painted the Imperial lemon yellow. It stands in its beautiful gardens, a stately roofless ruin—burned by the Germans.

Before the fire it was looted. They found gold chairs in the mud of German trenches and dugouts. We ask if the looting was organized. The Russians say, unfortunately not—otherwise there would be some chance of getting it back after the war. Individual German officers—sometimes soldiers as well—would go into the palace, cut down huge pieces of the great gold embroidered draperies, and send them home to their thrifty wives—"But look—Hans sent me this from the Palace of the Russian Czars!"—treasures carefully preserved during all the turbulence of the Revolution.

A few villagers who remained saw the Germans take the 30,000 catalogued pieces of furniture, bric-a-brac, and draperies out of Peterhof—an enormous Gobelin tapestry was the prize of a general —before they lit the fire.

After the Revolution the Bolsheviks made Peterhof a museum and public park where the workers came to spend their days off. The Russians are sure that only in the Soviet Union could such a miracle be; they wouldn't believe that French workers picnicked by the thousands at Versailles every Sunday.

Directly in front of Peterhof, a canal has been cut through the forest leading to the near-by Gulf of Finland. And now, from nowhere, appear hampers of sturgeon sandwiches and vodka bottles and the grinning Intourist steward. We picnic on the banks of the canal near an enormous stone lion. Just before she leaves, Jennie runs over and pats him on the nose. She explains, a little embarrassed, that when she was a very small child her mother used to bring her to Peterhof on Sundays to play, even though the civil war was still going on. She was always allowed to pat the lion. Her mother is dead now, and her family is scattered she doesn't know where, as so often happens in the Soviet Union, but still she didn't want to leave Peterhof without patting the lion good-by.

This evening our Leningrad trip comes to a climax with a big dinner given in Eric's honor by Popkov, whose title I suppose

would be Mayor of Leningrad. Anyway, he is head of the local
Soviet and more important still, he is for this region Stalin's right
bower in the organization of the Communist Party, second only to
Zdanov. Like an American city boss, he runs the town, regardless of
what title he holds.

We are brought to an elaborately furnished old czarist palace
in a park on the Neva's banks, and sit around in a stiff gold and
brocade room on uncomfortable gold and brocade chairs, drinking
Russian cocktails—those syrupy Manhattans—and sizing up Popkov.
He is young, small, swarthy, bullet-headed. He has a habit of
peering suddenly at you and then maybe grinning and maybe not.
He talks directly with no wasted words. We like him.

He apologizes because his wife and family were evacuated and
cannot meet us. It is the first time this has happened in Russia. So
far, these important Bolsheviks have entertained us like Moslem
princes—without mentioning their hidden families.

It is not quite time to sit down so Popkov (he is, of course, surrounded by his own experts and assistants) invites us for a brief
stroll through the graveled walks of the park along the Neva.

We look back at the palace. I ask its name.

It has no name, he tells me; it is simply his office.

"I thought it was probably the Winter Palace."

Popkov gives a little self-satisfied laugh at this. He has come a
long way, but he hasn't quite moved into the czar's quarters yet.

"No," he says, "only an old palace I use for my office."

Then at Eric's request he tells of the siege. He was in command
the whole time. They kept in Leningrad, he tells us, only that part
of the population needed to defend the town. Then they organized
air-raid defenses and started improving Leningrad's communications.

After many weary months, the blockade was finally broken. To
get the railway working, the Russians rebuilt two bridges in twenty
days. When this was done, the problem was to free the city, so the
people were put to work supplying the army with tanks, machine
guns, and ammunition from the restored factories.

He had not finished the narrative when we went in to dinner.

The palace dining hall and table were what you would expect, something out of an eighteenth century set in the movies.

We were impressed and showed it, and this pleased Popkov, who had settled into his great throne at the head of the table.

They started passing the caviar.

"Next we will have soup," said Popkov expansively, "and this evening there are two kinds. Of course, we have plain cabbage soup" —here he paused—"but then we also have a special broth—" and this he described in considerable detail, stressing all the rare and special things that went into his super soup, and ending, "Which will you have?"

"The cabbage soup," I said, maybe a little too promptly.

"Not the special broth?"

"Just the cabbage soup."

In the end I got the special broth. So, in fact, did everybody else. I was about to protest, when it occurred to me that just possibly Popkov had been showing off, and that his kitchen, being sensibly run, had only made one kind of soup.

The dinner now began to jog along. Popkov turned loose with a couple of Soviet funny stories, one of which was mildly dirty and the other mildly anti-Semitic. I begin with the latter.

"It seems," said Popkov, or rather the interpreter for him, "that the First Imperialist War of 1914-1917 created such a rumpus that it penetrated Heaven, so the Lord God sent Saint Peter down to find out what was the matter. Next day he got a telegram: URGENT. NOT HAVING PROPERLY COUNTERSIGNED TRAVEL PERMIT HAVE BEEN THROWN IN JAIL BY THE CHEKA. PLEASE OBTAIN RELEASE EARLIEST. PETER.

"The Lord God sent Saint Paul, and next day got this telegram: WHILE MAKING INQUIRIES FOR PETER ENCOUNTERED CHEKA POLICE AND NOT HAVING PROPER IDENTITY PAPERS AM HELD IN JAIL FOR INVESTIGATION. IMPORTANT SEND HELP AT ONCE. PAUL.

"So the Lord God sent Saint Jacob, this also being a common Jewish name in Russia, and the following day opened this telegram: PETER AND PAUL RELEASED WITH APOLOGIES SITUATION COMPLETELY IN HAND AWAIT YOUR FURTHER ORDERS. JACOB, CHIEF OF THE CHEKA."

The mildly dirty story concerned the wives who were evacuated from Leningrad during the siege and the girls who remained and took their places. It was all couched in terms of fighting Communist war slogans, and is funny if you have become a little bored by them, as most Russians are.

The evacuated wives, for instance, learning of what was going on in Leningrad, took as their slogan, DEATH TO THE FOREIGN INVADERS!

But when the wives returned, the girls who had taken their places adopted as their slogan, NOW WE GO UNDERGROUND TO BECOME PARTISANS AND CONTINUE THE STRUGGLE SECRETLY!

Eric now came back with a couple of safe ones which the Russians seemed to enjoy, but then it was time to get to work, toasting our old friends, Marshal Stalin and Gospodin Roosevelt. After that we relaxed again.

Popkov, by now, was reasonably mellow, leaning back in his chair. He said he was delighted to have us with him. He hoped we were learning about Russia, which maybe we hadn't understood. Now, for instance, he said, there were some things he certainly didn't understand about our country.

And the principal thing, he said, squinting at us, was this: Here we were, fighting a war together, or anyway Russia was fighting, and maybe we would be soon. But in spite of that, we let a Fascist Press exist in America, clearly fascist because it frequently criticized Russia. That, he said, he certainly could *not* understand; why we would let Russia and her leader be criticized in America.

Now, of course, this was Eric's show and I was only hooking a ride. But I wanted to handle this one and signaled as much to Eric. He gave me a nod to go ahead.

So I got up and said that I could well understand his confusion. And that perhaps I could clear it up because I was not a businessman but that I ran a newspaper, and so could speak for them. America was a free country, and therefore had a free press. And while most Americans supported both President Roosevelt and Russia, all of us would fight anyone who tried to stop criticism of them. Because a country where criticism is dead, is not free. This right to criticize, I said, is the most important freedom for which we are now fighting.

Then a curious thing happened. Some of Popkov's henchmen at the table were old-timers—men in their fifties and sixties. They were smiling and nodding approval. One thin old man, who might have been an architect, even had his hands poised to clap, but then he looked at Popkov and he didn't clap.

At this point Joyce got up and said that in a free country we always criticized our friends. We had been supporting and criticizing the British ever since this war began in 1939, and we saw no reason why we shouldn't do the same with Russia.

Then Eric got up and smoothly settled everything, freedom of the press, Russia, England, and even Popkov, who had been a little bit taken aback by it all, and who now said that this freedom to criticize was a most interesting thing, and he hoped we didn't mind that he had himself used some of this American freedom to criticize America.

Leaning across the table, I told him that we didn't mind at all, that we had plenty of this freedom in America, and if one day he came to visit us he would find he was free to criticize our leader, our government, or anything else he cared to.

So then he filled up his glass and mine, and grinning, said he suspected me of being a *khitre moujik*, a back-handed Russian slang compliment, which means "sly farmer"—one who knows more than he appears to.

So I said I was sure he was a *khitre* proletarian, and after that we got along very well. We all liked Popkov. He meets you head-on. He is tough but this is a tough country and only tough men can ride this broncho. Talkers don't last. Kerensky and Trotsky weren't quick enough on the draw. These combination city-manager-Little-Caesar types are the only ones who can handle it.

Six

THIS MORNING we start for the Finnish front and the reporters, against all experience, are hoping. All previous front trips have gone no further than the headquarters of a general. But Eric Johnston, even in America, was promised a look at the fighting. So this time— Just maybe—

We drive over one of Russia's few paved highways—from Leningrad to Viipuri. Until 1940 it was Finland's second largest city. Russia took it by the treaty of that year.

In 1941 the Finns again reoccupied it, continued to their old frontier and then dug in a few kilometers beyond. In these trenches they stayed during 1942, 1943, and half of 1944, making no attempt to advance in spite of German pressure on them.

They were there until a few weeks ago, when the Russian drive easily crashed through their first carefully prepared defense line, and then their second. We are told that they have now been pushed back to their third, which is just outside Viipuri.

In 1939 Russia sent almost identical notes to Finland, Lithuania, Latvia, and Estonia, demanding the right to send the Red Army in to occupy military bases in these countries. They all protested vigorously. In the end, all but Finland gave in to Russian pressure.

Finland argued that although the Russians insisted they only wanted occupation of these bases for the duration of the war, once the Red Army was in their country, it would be impossible to get it out. The Finns decided that under these circumstances they would rather go down fighting.

Their belief proved to be correct. The three Baltic States were presently swallowed by the Soviet Union. Because the Finns fought they got a respite, although in the treaty of 1940, they lost Viipuri, their second largest city.

The Russians profited greatly in experience by that little war. They were badly mauled in the first months of fighting because, being overly impressed by the success of German tank tactics in flat, treeless Poland, they had tried to copy them in Finland, a rolling, heavily forested country studded with lakes and swamps.

After early setbacks they corrected their errors; they reorganized their general staff, changed their tactics, and in the opening months of 1940 they did the simple and obvious thing, which they should have done at the outset; namely, they abandoned all open tactics in the north, brought up their big guns (which are excellent and which they possess in great numbers), banked them hub to hub in front of the Mannerheim line and blew it to bits, after which the Finnish infantry could offer only token opposition to the Red Army masses.

In the peace which followed in February of 1940, the Russians got permanent possession of Viipuri, and the right to garrison, for the war's duration, a tiny peninsula called Hango, hardly larger than Gibraltar, which from a naval standpoint dominates that end of the Baltic.

World attention was then diverted from Finland by the invasions of Denmark, Norway, and France but much went on in the Baltic area. Russia was holding those "plebiscites" which ended the independence of Latvia, Lithuania, and Estonia, and although she had signed a peace with Finland, she brought forth new demands, insisting on the right to bring troops overland across Finnish soil, to garrison Hango. Finland protested violently, pointing out that the Hague Tribunal's definition of an independent nation was one which had no foreign troops on its soil. But the Western powers were occupied, the Red Army threatened to march again, and Finland could only give in.

Immediately she yielded, the Germans came forward with demands. They had captured Narvik in northern Norway and were having trouble garrisoning it by sea. They insisted on the right to move German troops through Finland to reach Narvik by the back door. Finland protested, but the Germans pointed to the precedent set by the Russians in the matter of Hango, so Finland yielded—as Sweden later yielded to similar demands. World conscience was now of no effect in the Baltic Basin, which had become a totalitarian sea, and knew no law but force.

Skip now to June 22, 1941, when Hitler attacked Russia. As his armies crossed the border he spoke to the world over the radio. Several paragraphs were devoted to praise of Finland's 1940 resistance to Russia. Germany was now ready to defend the integrity of little Finland, he said. And even now German troops were on Finnish soil.

Technically this was true. It had been explained to the Finns, who had no foreknowledge of the attack on Russia, that these German divisions were only en route to Narvik.

But the Russians jumped to the conclusion (as Hitler intended they should) that Finland was already in the war. The Finnish version of events is that the Russians immediately began bombing Finnish cities, that the Finns sent unanswered notes of protest. Historians will settle this point. At present we only know that the Finnish declaration of war on the Soviets came four days after Hitler's attack, indicating the obvious reluctance of many Finns.

Of course all Finns bitterly resented the loss of Viipuri, as we would resent it if the British took Chicago, explaining that they needed it for strategic reasons. Undoubtedly many of them welcomed war for they wanted Viipuri and would embrace any ally who gave them hope of getting it back.

The Russians, of course, were quick to claim that Finland's entry into the second war completely justified all their suspicions of that country which had led them to attack her in 1939. Russia, they had argued, needed Viipuri only to protect near-by Leningrad, to guard against the likelihood that in the event of a Russo-German war the Finns would permit the Germans to use their country as a base. And now, Moscow proclaimed, the expected had happened.

There is in history some justification for this belief, for Finland is the Ireland of Russia. European culture originally came to Finland through the near-by Swedes, who owned the country for many centuries. In many Finnish towns a majority of the people are of

Swedish descent and until very recently Swedish was the language of business and culture.

But Sweden got on the wrong side in the Napoleonic wars and consequently lost Finland to Russia. However, the early rule of the czars was not oppressive. The Duchy of Finland was not incorporated in the Empire but given an autonomy, which would today be called dominion status. While the czar nominally ruled as its grand duke, Finland's free parliament governed the country, and the Finns enjoyed civil liberties unknown in the rest of Russia.

This continued until about 1907, when the czars decided to Russify Finland, began appointing Russian officials to Finnish posts and imposing Russian as the official language. The Finns, consequently, seized the first opportunity to break away, which came with the Bolshevik Revolution, just as the Irish seized the opportunity of World War I to try to break away from England with the Easter Rebellion of 1916.

There followed a bloody civil war. The Russian Bolshevik Party in Helsinki failed to seize control of the government. But their leadership was liquidated certainly with no more thoroughness than their opposite numbers under Lenin and Trotsky across the border. And in this civil war the Finnish anti-Bolsheviks were helped by Germans, whose principal motive was to weaken Bolshevism, just as Germany had tried to weaken England by landing Sir Roger Casement in Ireland by submarine.

The average Finn has the same deep dislike for Russians that most Irish have for the British, with, however, one difference. In comparison with England, Ireland is a somewhat backward underdeveloped agricultural country. But Finland is a much more highly developed nation than Russia. It has a neat, orderly Scandinavian culture, a high standard of literacy, well-cultivated farms, tidy modern cities, and well-managed little industries. And this has been true for several centuries.

They regard themselves as in the plight of Massachusetts, were it unfortunately situated in Yucatan and in constant danger of being overrun by Mexico. This poor view which Finns take of Russians dates from earliest times, although the fact that the Russians have since exchanged the dictatorship of the Romanov dynasty for that of the Communist Party has done little to improve it, just as it would not help Ireland's relations with the British if the latter set up a Bolshevik dictatorship in London.

Consequently, like Ireland, Finland frequently looks for help to the foes of its oppressor, and in both cases this foe is Germany. There is, however, some difference in the oppressors. Just as Russia wanted bases in Finland, so England wanted anti-submarine bases in Ireland. But when Ireland refused, England (mindful of her own conscience and of world opinion) did not press the point. She did not persuade herself that she had been brutally attacked by those fascist demons, the Irish, and try to overrun the small island by force of arms.

Finland, like Ireland, would undoubtedly have preferred to remain neutral in this war although, again like Ireland, the sympathies of her people are strongly anti-Nazi, for her people are even more staunchly democratic than the Irish.

And even with German troops on her soil, she has refused to persecute Jews. An American Jewish organization recently made a survey of their treatment in various European countries. It reported that, of all the German "satellite" nations, only Finland had stood firm in refusing to pass legislation discriminating against the Jews.

Indeed, until after the final Russian drive against Finland started in June of 1944, Finland had refused all offers of alliance with Hitler, and had refused to permit German troops to take part in her offensive against the Russians in the region of Viipuri. When this drive had regained Viipuri and the other territory taken from Finland in 1940, Finland then advanced her troops a few kilometers, occupying several hills, which she said were necessary for strategic reasons, and then dug in to await the end of the war, making no attempt to further threaten near-by Leningrad. A few Finns were not content with this, and volunteered to serve in a Finnish battalion organized by the Germans which fought against the Russians on the central front in German uniform, along with similar Spanish and Vichy-French battalions. But these Finns lacked the official sanction of their government.

Finland also gave the Germans air bases in the far north from which their planes attacked Allied convoys bringing military supplies to Russia at Murmansk, making this the most dangerous of all Allied ports for our Merchant Marine.

In general, the attitude of the democratic and patriotic Finnish people toward the war was mixed, because they wanted the impossible: a victory for the democracies combined with the return of Viipuri.*

They were not much less mixed than my own feelings as we started out on the old Viipuri highway toward the Finnish lines, about two hours from Leningrad.

It was a beautiful June day, and the countryside was vividly green. The land is rolling, with patches of woodland and not many houses. We share the road with truckloads of Red Army boys rolling toward the front. Curiously enough, none of them seemed to have steel helmets, which are also rare in Moscow. Perhaps steel is scarce, and they are issued only when men are within range of enemy artillery.

Then we pass still a more curious sight—to our Western eyes—the wounded coming back from the front—heads in bloody bandages, arms in slings, but jolting along in horse-drawn carts. They are the kind we often whisk back across the Atlantic by plane.

Maybe it was not typical. From three creaking wooden cartloads it is not safe to assume that human suffering is so cheap in Russia that you take a man to battle by truck but, once his fighting usefulness is gone his time is not valuable, and a horse cart is fast enough. Only there were the trucks and the carts on the only front I saw.

Conclusions drawn too quickly are dangerous; for instance, all of the motor transport I saw at this front was Russian Zeeses except for three American trucks and two jeeps. However, the correspondents say that on the other fronts, this proportion is

---

* For the record I should like to add that the final indemnity was set at a figure which it will be possible for the Finns to pay and the Soviet Armistice Control Commission to date has shown no disposition to interfere in the internal affairs of the country.

reversed, and that American transport is an enormous part of the whole.

Our macadam road now mounts the crest of a hill, and below us in the valley and on the hill opposite we see the outworks of the Finnish defense line, behind which they camped from the fall of 1941 until June 12, 1944—about a week ago. The valley is thick with barbed-wire spun like spider web on a stubbly forest of waist-high posts. The green hill beyond is scarred with zigzag trenches. The wire, of course, crossed this road but now has been cut, and we see the tank traps—stout, triangular wooden boxes which the Finns filled with stones, having little concrete. The Russians say they were ingenious. Now they lay piled at the roadside, along with the severed ends of barbed-wire. Here and there a red flag waves, with the Russian inscription, "Attention! Mine field!"

We pick up at this point a gaunt old Red Army lieutenant—a man in his middle sixties, who has been detailed to explain the defenses to us. He says that the offensive opened at half-past four in the morning when the Red Air Force plastered Finnish airdromes. At six o'clock an artillery barrage was laid down on the Finnish barbed-wire and pill boxes. They kept it up for twenty-four hours and at dawn of the next day the Russian tanks went in, followed by the infantry picking its way through the mine fields. By evening it was all over, and what was left of the Finns was in full retreat toward their second defense line, some twenty miles back. This lasted no time at all. He says the Finns are now fighting just outside of Viipuri, at a third system of strong points which occupies the site of the old Mannerheim line of the 1940 war. And back of this there is only one other—something the Finns have called the Line of State Defense.

In between these lines the old man says the Finns make no real attempt at defense, but fall back very rapidly. While we are stopped, a number of Russian tanks pass, big ones and good-looking, on their way up to the front. Continuing, we presently pass the only evidence of German help to the Finns we are to recognize on this trip—the overturned wreckage of a tiny tank with a swastika painted on one side. It is so small it could not possibly hold more than a crew of two, and looks very like the British scout tanks, which I saw around Dover in the fall of 1940, and which were all the armor Britain had salvaged from Dunkerque. This one is camouflaged, not brown-green but a tawny, desert yellow, and might have been some of Germany's salvage from her African campaign.

Behind us comes a dull roar and we look up to see a formation of Stormoviks on their way toward the Viipuri front—flying unusually high for Russian bombers, the reporters remark.

Finally at about noon we arrive at the little village of Terijoki, which I had visited almost five years before when it was a front-line town on the other side of the Russo-Finnish lines. But that was in winter and the houses were buried deep in at least a yard of snow, which also blanketed the spruce trees. A carload of us, with a Finnish military conducting officer, had driven out toward the Russian lines and had stopped in Terijoki for lunch and to warm ourselves by a porcelain stove against the bitter cold.

But now all is changed. It is another season of another year, and I come to Terijoki the guest of another army. It could almost be another town for the hub-deep snow is gone, revealing the neatly painted Finnish houses with white picket fences around their ample yards. It might be a Vermont village.

Only the grass of the lawns is untidy, the flower beds ragged, and the houses deserted. For the Russians tell us that when Finland abandoned this region under the treaty of 1940, the people preferred to withdraw to Finland. When the Finns reconquered this region in 1941, they did not bring the people back with their armies—suspecting that they probably would not be able to keep it.

So for four summers the flower beds have seeded themselves and the grass has grown high. The village is still deserted except for a couple of Red Army soldiers who have built a little fire on one lawn, and are warming their chow over a kettle.

Now we stop, and Kirilov leaves us to visit the local commander who will decide how much farther and by what road we may go to the front.

A quarter of an hour later, he comes back and imperturbably motions us to follow. We drive to the outskirts of Terijoki where there is a huge grove of trees on the shore. Kirilov's car stops and so does ours. He gets out and so do we. Just ahead through the trees shine the blue waters of the Gulf of Finland.

An American jeep, manned by two Red Army soldiers, stops behind us. They get out, and bring up hampers covered with napkins, from some of which protrude the necks of bottles. Kirilov strolls over. But the front, we ask.

"The commander has said today we can go no farther. There would be danger."

We argue, plead, expostulate.

"The commander has said he cannot be responsible for the safety of Mr. Johnston. There would be danger."

We express dismay, chagrin, consternation. We point out that we have been nowhere near the front.

"The commander has said no further. Now we picnic." Already they are handing the sandwiches out of the hampers, opening the vodka and champagne bottles. With a glass of vodka aboard him, the old lieutenant smacks his lips approvingly and becomes very spritely. We ask him if he had service in the First Imperialist War and he says even before—in that of 1905 against the Japanese, and proudly tells us much of the now forgotten czarist general under whom he served. We look out over the Gulf of Finland, which when I was last here was frozen solid, and the Finns were fearful of tank attacks by sea. There is a blue shadow low on the water which they tell us is the great Russian naval base of Kronstadt. Further along another shadow they say is Peterhof, which we have visited. Just out of sight around the point they say is the smoke of Leningrad.

When I was last at Terijoki, we went on up to the lines and crawled through a long communication trench in the bitter cold, crouching as Russian machine-gun bullets whipped snow on its sandbags. Now we watch two Red Army boys who have left their clothes on the beach and are splashing each other waist deep in the water. The Field Marshal, resplendent in his correspondent's uniform, strolls toward the beach in the hope that they will stop splashing to salute him.

Cupping my hand to my ear, I hear a faint, muffled roar, which could either be Russian artillery, pounding the Finns as they battle desperately to hold Viipuri—or it could be only the wind.

Kirilov hands me a smoked sturgeon sandwich.

I have had a Soviet front trip.

We now turn back toward Leningrad but presently stop, for our Russian hosts have a Finnish atrocity to show us. Our cars pull up before the blackened walls of a once pleasant, not too pretentious country house with huge elms and nice flower gardens. They explain that it once belonged to a famous Russian artist called Ilya Repin, long dead. When the Revolution came in 1917, he left Russia to build this house—not too far from Russia but still on Finnish soil. A few years before his death, he was induced to return to Russia.

When the Red Army took this territory after the 1940 war, they made this house into a museum, for Repin is an honored figure in Russian culture. The Finns then recaptured the region in 1941 but when they retreated last week, our hosts explain, they fired this Russian museum and it burned to the ground. Undeniably true; the ashes still smoke as we walk listlessly around.

The plump, blue-eyed Red Army colonel, who is with us poking in the rubbish, picks up a newspaper. The interpreter reads for him part of its feature article which is in fulsome praise of a British general who, the Finnish writer predicts, will play a dashing role in the eagerly expected Anglo-American invasion of Europe.

The colonel, a handsome and efficient product of Soviet education, brings this in perplexity to me, as an authority on Finns. Because why would these fascist hirelings, the Finns, be in possession of a newspaper which praises a British general who is fighting their brother fascists, the Germans?

It is no use. He could not understand. And if he did, it would only get him into trouble. I see now why the Soviet government goes to such pains to keep foreign newspapers away from them.

So I only shake my head in pretended perplexity.

✦

He is a very nice young colonel—certainly not over thirty-five—handsome but with a flat nose and a thick neck, and ordinarily imperturbable. But that evening on the way back to Leningrad in the lounge of Johnston's private car—after the usual banquet and while the waiters are clearing away the champagne glasses and coffee cups—I get into a three-cornered argument with him.

He and Jennie, the interpreter, say that the Germans are sure to yield soon, because they cannot endure the hardships to which Russian soldiers are accustomed. But I say that nevertheless, Germans are good soldiers.

They grudgingly agree, and then add that Americans and British are also too soft and too fond of comfort to make the best of soldiers. Jennie says she has traveled with Americans and she knows. They are always complaining loudly of their comfort.

I agree that our soldiers complain, but maintain that when discomfort is unavoidable, Americans will endure it as well as any other nation. But when it comes through stupidity or inefficiency, when through bad organization our troops are improperly fed or clothed, then they yell their heads off. And I say we think this makes for a better army.

At this point the young colonel, gleaming in the new red and silver epaulets which recently have been awarded Red Army officers, says any such discussions make for bad discipline. That the soldier's only duty is to obey, and this is why the Red Army is superior to any in the world. I argue that while in the American army we also have discipline, we feel it is also the duty of a soldier to use his head; that we encourage initiative in the field. This is a little mixed in translation and the colonel begins to flush angrily. He says there is, of course, also initiative in the Red Army.

So I smooth it all out with a speech to the effect that I'm sure our armies are very much alike—that of course the American Army has discipline and I am equally sure the Red Army has initiative. Then everybody is happy—at least on the surface.

There is no doubt that Jennie's stories of Americans are accurate, for the Soviet standard of living is a shock to anyone from the Western countries. During the world depression, a number of young

English and American workers, intellectually inclined, took passage to the Soviet Union because in this land there is always work for everyone.

Swept away by the enthusiasm of the first few weeks, they surrendered their British or American passports and took out Soviet citizenship. Within a year practically all of them were back, clamoring at the doors of their former embassies, pleading for help to get out of Russia.

It was, of course, impossible. They had freely given up their passports and with them their rights, and under any interpretation of international law they were indistinguishable from any other Soviet citizen, bound to their assigned jobs and with no hope of leaving.

And when they exercised their former Anglo-Saxon rights to protest about living conditions, they got the treatment meted out to any other Soviet citizen who stirs up discontent: they were arrested and thrown into labor battalions. All trace of them was lost and no longer could they plead with their embassies in Moscow.

But one man's family made persistent inquiries for news of him, and his legation brought pressure to bear on the Russians for at least some information. So after some months, it was announced that the man had died in his labor camp, that according to law his effects had been sold, and the legation was given a check for 15 roubles to be turned over to his next-of-kin abroad. These relatives, however, would not believe that he was dead, and darkly suspected that it was worth those 15 roubles to the Soviet government to be rid of the tedious inquiries.

A note now on the Red Army: Americans frequently express amazement that it should have been able to resist the German attack, and feel that its exploits are a miracle.

The Red Army is good. Russians make good soldiers. They are well disciplined, competently led, and equipped with good rifles and plenty of heavy artillery which they handle with skill. But this is not all. Soldiers must be young, and the military strength of any nation is determined not only by its total population, but by the number of boys in their late teens and early twenties. Because of the enormous Russian population and the swelling Slav birth rate, in the Soviet Union 2,000,000 boys each year attain the age of eighteen, as opposed to only 500,000 Germans—a four to one superiority.

Considering only military effectives, the miracle is that any German soldier was able to set foot on Russian soil. They were able to penetrate to the suburbs of Moscow and Leningrad and range as far as the Caucasus (1,500 miles from Berlin) not only because of Russia's technical poverty and the disorganized state of her industrial development, but also because at the time the Red Army lacked experienced officers. Her initial air force, for instance, could not compare in quality with that of the Germans. Much of it was smashed in the first few weeks of fighting.

If the Russian air force is primitive, this is no reflection on the skill of Russian pilots, who rank among the world's best. But Russia lacks the skill to turn out good planes. Of all branches of any air force, long-range bombers such as the British Lancaster and the American Fortress and Liberator require the highest degree of industrial skill for production and operation in large numbers. They are almost totally absent in the Red Air Force.

The men who plan the Red Air Force have skillfully designed it around the country's many shortages; they have concentrated on production of the Stormovik, a slow, low altitude strafing plane. Since this efficient little tank buster usually operates at treetop level, the Soviet fighters which protect it have no need for high altitude equipment.

Of the 10,000 planes which America has delivered to the Soviet Union the Russians like best the Bell Aircobra, which is a light, low altitude, ground co-operation plane, similar in function to the Stormovik. It is standard Red Air Force procedure immediately to remove all high altitude flying equipment from most American planes, replacing the weight with extra ammunition.

Lacking night fighters and radar, Soviet targets within range of the Luftwaffe are particularly vulnerable to night bombing, and the standard Russian method of defense is ground fire from anti-aircraft batteries, such as was used to protect Moscow. However, lacking radar to guide their fire, the gunners can shoot only at the sound, which is a rough indication not of where the bomber is, but where it was several seconds ago. Therefore, to be effective, batteries must be massed about the target, vomiting continuous fountains of fire during a raid, an expensive procedure.

One day we inspected the Moscow exhibit of captured enemy war equipment. It was a beautifully arranged display open to the public, and included everything from Italian uniforms to the newest and biggest in German Tiger tanks. New, it should be said, only to the Soviet Union for they had been introduced in Africa to match comparable British and American equipment, and after the fall of Tunis they were brought to Russia. Still wearing their desert camouflage they were captured in the Crimea.

After inspecting all this, I asked Jennie, an unusually intelligent and well-educated Soviet girl, if they had any captured German radar. She had never heard the word. Thinking the Russians used another, I described it as an electric device which detected airplanes at night or through fog without the use of sound. But she had heard nothing of this and went off to consult the general in charge.

Returning, she said he knew what I was talking about; that such devices existed, were used by the Germans and had even been captured but they were kept in another place for study and were not on view. In the Western world, every bright fifteen-year-old knows the general principles of radar. But two hundred million people in the Soviet Union will probably never hear of it until it can be manufactured there.

America's most vital contribution to Russia was not planes but trucks. Of course Russian factories have provided most of the Red Army's motor transport. But this huge agricultural nation is incapable of producing enough to fit the size of its army or its sprawling geography. It was for want of modern transport that, when fast-moving German columns punched their 1941 lines in a dozen places, the Russians had to fall back in disorder, leaving thousands of precious heavy artillery pieces and hundreds of thousands of prisoners in German hands.

But by 1942 American trucks began flowing into Russia in volume. Without these it would have been impossible for the Russians to have followed up their major victory at Stalingrad in 1943. Stopping an enemy advance and removing his armies from your soil are two different problems. It does no good to get the enemy on the run unless you can pursue him. Without these trucks, the Red Army would still be stuck in its own bottomless Ukrainian mud. With them it was able to pursue, and when the Germans made a stand at a river or a provincial city, to deal the next sledge hammer artillery-infantry smash which knocked loose the Wehrmacht and kept it continually off balance and retreating.

The top Russians do not underestimate the value of American aid. If the lesser ones seem unappreciative, it is only because, in spite of vigorous protests such as that of Admiral Standley, they have not been told the extent of it.

For instance, the correspondents tell of a front trip on which they were being escorted through reconquered territory by a Red Army lieutenant. Far down the road, they saw a jeep in a ditch. Russia makes no comparable car, but quantities of jeeps have arrived through Lend-Lease, with instructions in Russian stenciled in Detroit, and are familiar now all over the Soviet Union.

"Is that a German jeep or an American jeep?" the correspondent asked.

"Neither one," said the lieutenant, "it's a Russian jeep. Your American jeeps are too flimsy to use on these roads at the front. Five thousand kilometers and they fall to pieces. Here we use only Russian jeeps."

The war's climax came in 1943 with the successful defense of Stalingrad. The Germans had by this time been dealt a crippling blow to their air force in the great battles with the British in Africa. Russians point out scornfully that this African campaign involved few men; however, it required masses of highly complicated transport and machines.

Furthermore, the RAF and the Eighth Air Force in England were by then pounding German industry, and the Germans had to strip the Russian front of Messerschmitts to defend their home factories, so that for the first time the Russians had superiority in the air. Lend-Lease, including thousands of trucks, was now pouring in, the German lines of communication were perilously extended, and for the first time it was possible for a Russian army to move quickly out to envelop and cut off a German army, as theirs had been enveloped so many times before.

After that, Germany's superiority in weapons was slowly reduced by Allied air poundings, while Russia's supply increased. Her own factories behind the Urals were working; new ones were equipped with American machine tools. By the summer of 1944 at least half of the Red Army's road transportation was being supplied by 210,000 American military trucks, 40,000 jeeps and 30,000 other military motor vehicles. She also had 5,600 American tanks and tank destroyers, and was using $225,000,000 worth of machine tools —a total of $5,750,000,000 worth of Lend-Lease aid. At last Russia's crushing superiority in man power could become effective.

But as the Anglo-American offensive opened in France, the Soviet government loyally kept her agreement, made at Teheran, to start a drive from the east. In order to do this, she was drafting for front-line duty men who had already been discharged with wounds and others previously rejected for serious physical defects—the dregs of any nation's power. But the Soviet government kept faith.

One reason for the success of the Red Army is that the breach between its old-line, experienced officers and the Communist Party is now completely healed. Originally the Red Army was burdened with a system of political commissars whose duty it was to watch the officers, keep the army politically sound and under the Kremlin's thumb, and whose authority could under certain circumstances exceed that of the unit's regular commander.

This division has now gone. The political commissars have been absorbed in the army, with regular military rank and duties. Political education continues, but not to the neglect of military training. The political commissar is now the official pepper-upper—the morale officer of his unit. Membership in the Communist Party always carries heavy responsibility, and this continues in the army. Party members are supposed to set an example to the others—not only in efficiency but in bravery under fire, and as consequence the Party had had more than its share of casualties. Its membership, formerly 2,500,000, was increased to 4,000,000, but many of them have been killed.

But the Party is strong in the army, and a man who wished to advance must usually join. A Russian general will not be removed because he has neglected this, but the Party must be sure his views are sound. It is much more solidly welded to the army than before, although you still get occasional old-line officers who scoff at political commissars.

The army's achievements have given it a great pride in itself and some little contempt for the outside world. Reporters say that when it invaded Rumania, the officers laughed at the uniformed doormen, and had only scorn for the beggars and bootblacks who solicited them.

The Moscow correspondents have a deep respect for the competence of its leadership and often, when irritated by the stupidity of a Russian civilian official, they would remind each other that some of this was temporary, as all the country's really intelligent and efficient men were in the Red Army.

Seven

RETURNING to Moscow, I have my first experience with Soviet censorship. I submit a news story on the Leningrad trip, which includes the sentence that "The Finns were fighting hard for Viipuri, *which prior to 1939 was Finland's second largest city.*" The censor passed the story except for the italicized words. They contain no military information—nothing which is not in every child's geography.

But Russia has the most rigid political censorship in the civilized world. The reporters explain why this cut in my copy was made. When the Soviet Union claims territory, no Moscow story may mention the fact that it once belonged to another nation. And this goes not only for the Karelian Isthmus but also for the Baltic States. They are now parts of the Soviet Union and no hint can be cabled from Moscow that they were ever independent republics.

In other fields the censorship goes much further and makes no attempt at consistency, except on a day-to-day basis. Early in the war the Soviets were proud of their scorched earth policy, and *Red Star* severely criticized American generals for not burning Manila before we evacuated.

Now, however, they are preparing a bill for property damage to be presented to the Germans and since this began, no mention or hint of "scorched Russian earth" has been permitted to leave the Moscow censorship. Presumably, the great Dnieper Dam suffered only from German vandalism.

Moscow correspondents say the most severe political censorship was imposed on their stories of the Katyn Forest Massacre, which is not surprising because this subject is one of the most delicate of the war, strung around a plot as exciting as any detective "who-done-it."

Katyn Forest is near Smolensk and it is the grave of some 10,000 Poles, mostly officers, who were shot in the back of the head. On these facts everyone agrees. But on whether this slaughter of help-less war prisoners was done by Russians or Germans, there is vio-lent disagreement and some evidence both ways.

To understand the complexity of the case, a little history is neces-sary. When, in 1939, the Germans and Russians divided Poland, the Russian share of the loot included more than 180,000 prisoners of war, of whom 10,000 were officers. A few were generals. The most distinguished of these, including General Anders, were con-fined to Moscow's Lubianka prison. The rest of the 10,000 officers were sent to three prison camps in the Russian towns of Starobielsk, Kozielsk, and Ostaszkov. These camps housed twelve Polish gen-erals, sixty-nine colonels, seventy-two lieutenant colonels and in all 5,131 regular army officers and 4,096 reserve officers. Few of the last had been captured in combat. Most of them had not yet been called up for duty, but, when Russia occupied her half of Poland, obeyed the Soviet summons to assemble.

The Polish officers were reasonably well treated at the three camps until April, 1940, when the Soviets began evacuating them, telling the men they might be sent back to their homes. They left in groups of from twenty to sixty every few days during April and early May, first being loaded into prison cars. As to what be-came of them after that, the Poles have a few clues. Most of the 10,000 vanished from the earth except for 400 who were finally taken to a camp at Gryazovets. There they were allowed to write letters to their families. But from the answers they received, inquir-ing as to the fate of their comrades, it soon became clear of the thousands of officers who had been at the three camps, they alone were writing letters home.

More than a year passed and on June 22, 1941, Hitler attacked Russia. The Polish government in London immediately offered the hand of friendship to the Soviets, suggesting the formation from prisoners of war in Russian hands, of a Polish army. The Soviet government quickly accepted. General Anders was released from his prison cell, installed in a comfortable hotel room with apologies, and with Soviet co-operation began forming his army.

Poles, released from prison camps all over the Soviet Union, began flocking to his headquarters, but there were almost no officers.

General Anders was at first not alarmed, believing that they probably had been transferred to some far-away Arctic labor camp and presently would turn up, as thousands of others were doing. But as months went by and not one additional officer reported he became concerned.

In November of 1941, Polish Ambassador Kot got an interview with Stalin to discuss this perplexing problem. The Marshal appeared genuinely astonished.

"Have they not been released yet!" he said, and in Kot's presence, rang up the NKVD and said the prisoners who had been in those three camps should be released at once, because "the amnesty applies to all Poles. They, too, should be released."

A month passed, during which the Poles were collecting, from the 400 survivors of the three camps, a list of the names of their missing brother officers. On December 4, when Stalin received Generals Sikorski and Anders, they took with them an incomplete list of 4,500 names. This time Stalin expressed no surprise or indignation. The Poles felt he answered evasively, suggesting that the 10,000 officers might have returned to German occupied Poland or fled over the Manchurian border. Knowing how closely the NKVD supervises all travel in Russia, it was difficult for the two Polish generals to believe that such a large number of officers could have accomplished this journey undetected, and Anders told Stalin as much, venturing the counter-suggestion that perhaps the NKVD, short of labor, was still holding them in some far-away Siberian camp. "If they haven't released any such prisoners," said Stalin, "we will compel them to do so." And picking up his telephone, he called General Pamfilov at NKVD headquarters, again issuing orders to release all Poles who had ever been in the three camps.

More time passed but not an officer turned up. However, disturbing rumors circulated among the Poles. Among the 400 survivors there was a belief that the other officers had been sent in the direction of Smolensk. In one of the cars in which the 400 were evacuated, they had seen, scrawled on the wall, a hasty message in Polish. They guessed it had been left behind by a certain Polish Colonel Kubya, who had been evacuated ahead of the 400, and who had promised, before he left, to try to leave a clue as to where they were being taken. This message read, "The second stop after Smolensk, we are being taken from the cars and loaded into trucks." This, however, meant little. Katyn Forest is seventeen kilometers beyond Smolensk, but the 400 had then never heard of Katyn Forest.

But a really disturbing rumor began to circulate. It seemed that, a few months *before* the German attack on Russia, the NKVD had assembled several Polish staff officers, including a Colonel Berling, and suggested to them that possibly a Polish army might be organized to fight the Germans. At a conference with Russian NKVD officials, Beria and Merkulov, Colonel Berling agreed, provided it was organized "irrespective of political creeds," and then added that, at the three officers' prison camps, "we have excellent army cadres." Whereupon, Merkulov answered quickly, with some embarrassment, "No, not these men. We have made a great blunder in connection with them." Only rumors, perhaps, but they disturbed the Poles.

But the Poles kept their misgivings out of print, anxious to preserve friendly relations with their new Soviet ally. Considerable time passed, and then on April 13, 1943, the German radio announced that in Katyn Forest, near Smolensk, which they then held, they had discovered mass graves of about 10,000 Polish officers, each killed with a bullet through the back of the head. They said that Russian peasants in the vicinity had told them that these prisoners of war had been murdered by the NKVD in the spring of 1940, giving dates which would correspond closely to the time the prison camps had been evacuated. The Germans also claimed that letters and papers found in the clothing, as well as the condition of the bodies, indicated that the men had been murdered in the spring of 1940. According to the German story, the peasants had delayed showing them the graves because of their great fear of the NKVD. Names announced over the German radio corresponded with those of Polish officers missing from the three camps. This German announcement created much confusion among the Poles.

Two days later, Radio Moscow took cognizance of the German charges in a bitter broadcast in which it said that "these German lies reveal the fate of Polish officers whom the Germans employed in construction work in that region." The next day, April 16, the Russian news agency, Tass, issued a communiqué explaining that these Polish prisoners, who had been employed by the Russians on construction work west of Smolensk, had been captured by the Germans during the Soviet retreat from that region in the summer of 1941.

But this explanation did not satisfy all Poles. Their officers had been evacuated from the three prison camps in April, 1940. Ever since the Russo-German break in June of 1941, the Polish government had been trying to get from the Russians some hint as to where they had been taken. Only after this German broadcast do they learn from the Soviet government that the officers had been taken to the Katyn Forest region, with the additional statement that in 1941 they were captured and murdered by the Germans.

Why had the Soviet government let them hunt and hope for nearly two years?

However, the Polish government in London was cautious. On April 17, the day after the Tass explanation, the Polish Cabinet issued a statement denouncing the "profoundly hypocritical" indignation of the Germans, who had been guilty of even greater crimes against Poles than this which they charged against the Russians. At the same time, they announced they were going to ask the International Red Cross at Geneva to investigate.

But on April 21, Radio Moscow blasted the Polish government saying that such a proposal would be "collaborating with Hitler," and attacked General Sikorski, its Premier, saying that his appeal to Geneva "proved how influential are the pro-Hitler elements in the Polish government."

The next day Berlin announced the discovery of a third mass grave at Katyn. On the day following, the Red Cross in Geneva said it "acceded in principle" to the request for an investigation, but could only act if Russia, also a party to the dispute, would join in the request.

On April 26, the Soviet government broke off relations with the Polish government in London, and set up in Moscow her own "Union of Polish Patriots" which, according to the London Polish government, was made up of Polish Communists unknown to the people of Poland.

However, anxious to conciliate Moscow, the London Polish government on May 1, withdrew its request for a Red Cross investigation. Berlin, which had agreed to the investigation, went ahead with a propaganda field-day of its own. The Germans invited a committe of twelve distinguished European experts to examine the bodies at Katyn. It should be noted, however, that of the twelve, only one, Dr. Naville, Professor of Forensic Medicine at Geneva, was from a neutral country. The others were from universities in Belgium, Bulgaria, Denmark, Finland, Italy, Holland, Rumania, Slovakia, The Protectorate, and Hungary—countries either allied to, or occupied by, the Germans.

These professors were either deceived or convinced. They issued a unanimous report to the effect that the Polish officers had been dead for three years (which would date the massacre in 1940 when the Russians held Katyn) as proved by the condition of the bodies as well as by papers found on them and from the testimony of natives.

However, the German triumph was short-lived, for the Red Army presently reoccupied Katyn, and on January 22, 1944, issued a communiqué saying that a Soviet investigating commission had been called to settle, once and for all, the Katyn Forest dispute.

It should be remarked that if the German Commission was a 90 per cent Axis party, the Russian Commission was a 100 per cent Soviet picnic. Their experts—distinguished Russian academicians—determined that the Germans, following their occupation of Smolensk, had carried out the mass shootings in the autumn of 1941, and in 1943, "calculating to set Russians and Poles at loggerheads, tried to ascribe this crime to the Soviet government." The Russians charged that in the spring of 1943 the Germans had even brought to Katyn Forest, Polish bodies from other districts, and had used 500 Russian prisoners of war in the work of removing from the Polish bodies all documents which would incriminate the Nazis and substituting documents which would tend to incriminate the Russians, after which the Germans had shot the Soviet war prisoners.

The Russians also cross-questioned those local peasants who had previously testified that they had held back information from the Germans in fear of the Russian NKVD. These peasants now testified that they had signed statements for the Germans only because they feared the Gestapo.

The evidence of German guilt gathered by the Soviet Commission is detailed, complete, damning, and it answers all questions but this one: if the Polish officers were still alive in the summer of 1941 and could be captured by the Germans, why were the Poles not told this at once? Why were important Polish government officials allowed to go wild-goose-chasing all over the Soviet Union for nearly two years in search of their army's officers, when the Russians knew the men were already in German hands?

When the Russians retook Katyn Forest, they invited the Moscow correspondents to inspect the graves of these Poles, murdered, they insisted, by the Nazis. Most of the Anglo-American correspondents—trained observers—believed even before they went that the Germans had done the killing.

It was difficult to say with certainty when they had been shot but an observant reporter noticed that one Polish body was clad in long, heavy underwear, and mentioned it to the Soviet doctor in charge. The doctor remarked that most of the bodies wore either heavy underwear, or overcoats, or both.

That seemed to point to the theory that these Poles must have been shot during April, 1940, as the Germans claimed, rather than in August and September, 1941, after the Germans moved in, as the Soviet government was contending.

When this point was raised with the Soviet conducting officers, there was considerable confusion and the Russians finally argued that the climate of Poland is uncertain, so that fur overcoats and long underwear might be worn in September.

The reporters preferred to believe the stories of their Allies in which most evidence pointed toward German guilt. Even so, Moscow censorship struck out all the qualifying phrases.

If a reporter would write *"I am not a medical expert but doctors say* the condition of these bodies proves they were murdered by the Germans," the censorship would strike out the qualifying phrase (which I have italicized), leaving only the bare charge.

Also stricken out were all phrases indicating any doubt in the correspondents' minds—such words as "in my opinion," "probably," or "evidence we were shown would tend to prove," with the result that the stories as received in America were as firmly damning of the Germans as *Pravda's* editorials.

The truth is that no one but the Russians and the Germans—and some Poles—know what went on in Poland and the Baltic States between September, 1939, and June, 1941—the period of the Russo-German pact, because reporters from all neutral countries were rigorously excluded and foreign consuls expelled. The censorship vacuum can only be filled by rumors, reports from the Polish underground to its London government and an occasional whisper which reaches Moscow.

This is equally true of the Baltic States, Estonia, Latvia, and Lithuania. Although this territory had been a part of the Czarist Empire for 200 years, the three small nations preserved their identities as did the Finns and the Poles. They seized the opportunity to break away from Russia in 1917, becoming part of the *cordon sanitaire* of buffer states which French diplomats set up to insulate Europe against Bolshevism.

The people of the three Baltic countries are thrifty and orderly, and they soon established a standard of living comparable to Scandinavia with whom they had many ties. They were also inordinately fearful of Russia—a feeling they shared with most small countries having a common border with the Soviet Union.

In the summer of 1939, when the Anglo-French Military Mission was in Moscow trying to negotiate an alliance with the Soviet Union one of the Soviet demands was the right, under certain circumstances, to occupy the three Baltic States.

The British demurred. When I was in London in February of 1940, an intelligent young man in their foreign office gave me their position.

"Here we are," he said, "supposedly defending the rights of small European nations. We could hardly start by delivering three of them to the Russians as a price for their alliance. We have to consider opinion in the States. What would your people have said to that?"

"They would have been in favor of almost anything you had to do to win the war without their having to get in," I said, and I still think I was right.

Hitler, however, had no such qualms, or need to consider American sympathy for small nations, so he signed with the Kremlin. In a matter of weeks, Russia's demands were dispatched to the Baltic States. The Red Armies moved in to garrison all strategic points and all foreigners were moved out. Once they were there, events moved rapidly. The three governments resigned, to be replaced by Communist cabinets which immediately ordered plebiscites on the question of whether they would petition for union with the U.S.S.R. It was then announced that the people had voted yes by majorities of about ten to one. But no neutral observers were present, and the Red Army was the only witness.

The immediate effect, according to Moscow observers, was a flash of prosperity in Moscow. The Baltic States had been prosperous, and in Moscow stores there appeared well-made, smart-looking shoes, print dresses, men's suits, countless shiny items of consumption goods and minor luxuries, which indicated that the living standard of those prosperous little countries was being equalized with the drab Soviet average.

There was no other direct news, but many rumors.

To understand why the Baltic States and later Poland's eastern provinces voted by such staggering majorities for union with the Soviet government, it is necessary to know the meaning of the term "social engineering," as first coined and later practiced by the Communist Party.

Communists recognize that in newly occupied areas many individuals cannot adapt themselves to the Soviet system. They learned this during their own civil war. So each such province constitutes a problem in "social engineering."

Least likely to adapt themselves are those individuals who have functioned successfully under the preceding regime, particularly the people beyond school age. The Soviet blacklist includes all who have held positions of trust in the former state—governors, members of parliament, state or municipal clerks and employees, local police or frontier guards, and, of course, large landowners as well as conspicuously successful manufacturers, merchants, and farmers. Prominent on the list are officials in trade unions or political parties other than the Communist Party, Socialist leaders being held in even lower esteem than the landed gentry as traitors to the working class.

The Soviets wisely conclude that the very fact that these people have been leaders under the old order will make them, at the least, undependable citizens of the new. Consequently, the leaders are arrested for deportation immediately, the smaller fry being rounded up at a more leisurely rate during the ensuing months.

Rarely are they shot, for social engineering is a science with no place for the emotion of hate. Shooting can be wasteful, therefore the members of the classes to be removed are customarily sentenced to ten years in a Soviet labor camp.

Meanwhile plans for elections proceed. With all such "enemies of the people" disposed of, the Soviet propaganda apparatus moves in, the Red Army taking a prominent part. The Communist Party organizes local workers' and peasants' committees, which nominate candidates for delegates to the regional Popular Assembly.

Shortly after the Soviet occupation of Eastern Poland, such elections were held in Polish Ruthenia and in the Polish Ukraine. *Pravda* boasted of the Red Army's work, saying that "thousands of its men and officers carried on an immense political work among the population. The soldier-political-worker was everywhere."

Only one candidate runs for each office and he is Communist-approved. A tremendous effort is made to get out the vote, with Party workers from Moscow and Red Army soldiers touring the countryside in trucks. Banners, parades, and speeches imply that anyone who fails to go to the polls thereby declares himself an enemy of the new state.

Most curious of all, from our Western standpoint, is the fact that soldiers of the occupying Red Army are permitted to vote in these elections. Once at the polls, the voter's identification card is checked by the Communist election officials, and the voter is handed a ballot. He is told that he may either drop this in the ballot box or he may retire behind a screen and make changes in it. He does not need to be told that if he does step behind the screen, this fact will be remembered. Few changes are made.

The assembly made up of delegates so elected, meets a few days later. In occupied Poland such assemblies passed standardized resolutions taking over the authority of the old government, requesting admission to the Soviet Union, confiscating large estates, and praising "our great leader, Stalin."

In relation to the economy, social engineering makes rapid changes. In Poland's eastern provinces the old Polish zloty was pegged to the Soviet rouble at a figure most advantageous to the hundreds of thousands of Soviet visitors with the result that the shops were quickly stripped both of luxury items and of staples. After a short period, the zloty was declared worthless.

State-owned stores were substituted for private shops which were taxed out of existence, and although the land was not immediately collectivized, each farmer was notified what share of his produce must be sold to the state at the low official price. In place of the old Polish system of free labor unions, a new system was installed under which a worker who is constantly late or who quits his job faced several years in a prison labor camp.

In addition to the 180,000 war prisoners, an estimated 1,500,000 civilians were removed from Poland in the early part of 1940, as a part of the social engineering program.

These people were moved in transports similar to ones I saw in the Leningrad freight yard and which had been used to move Russian factory workers back of the Urals. A Soviet transport is an ordinary boxcar with two small, high, barred windows, a stove with its pipe protruding through the pipe roof, and a hole chopped in the floor for a toilet. Between thirty and forty deportees are locked in each car, which is almost the size of the famous French "40 and 8" troop transports of the last war.

Most deportation round-ups were conducted by the NKVD late at night when the population is most docile. The people are told whatever story will make them most amenable to the order. For example, the wife of a Polish officer who had been killed at Katyn Forest (although she did not then know it) was wakened, told that special arrangements had been made for her to join her husband if she would pack and be ready to leave in an hour. After dressing herself, her small son and packing her bag, she arrived on her front step—where she found all the other women on her street also waiting with packed bags and realized that the journey ahead was not a special dispensation to her.

It is also an axiom of social engineering to separate families, not as an act of needless cruelty, but because men are suited for stronger, more rugged work than are their wives and daughters, so heads of families are sent to special camps. But if they are told this at the outset, the emotional scenes which follow cause needless delay. Consequently, the only instruction given by the NKVD in the home is that the head of the family is to pack his toilet articles separately since men will go to another place for sanitary inspection. Therefore, not until the family is on the station platform do they discover that the head of the family is locked with other men in a car separate from those into which they are locked with women and children. It may be several days before they learn that the men are now en route to an unknown labor camp. It was the practice to send men to lumber and mining camps in northern Siberia, while women and children did better in the brick yards and co-operative farms in southern Kazakstan.

There was much unavoidable confusion. Although the cars were supposed to be opened daily, sometimes through neglect, they stood for days on sidings, and when they finally were opened it was nearly always necessary to remove a number of bodies of those who had died from general weakness induced by thirst or cold. But none of this was deliberate, and in such large mass population movements, oversights are inevitable.

If the new colonists were often not welcome on the co-operatives to which they were assigned, this is not because the Russians are heartless; but in Kazakstan, for example, the co-operatives were too often only a group of mud huts on an arid plain, where there were already too many mouths to feed. Newcomers were a burden on these struggling communities, as they would be in our dust bowl settlements, and they were further resented because the remnants of their belongings were finer than anything the natives had seen. Yet many of these tragedies had eventual happy endings, for following Hitler's attack on Russia and Russia's temporary reconciliation with the Polish government in London, the captive Poles were released and allowed to leave Russia with General Anders' army.

Russia's postwar plan for Poland is not necessarily a fair sample of the governmental set-up she will demand in her other border states. Poland is a special case. The Poles have undergone so much social engineering that a truly free and democratic Poland might not be as friendly to Russia as the Soviet Union feels it has a right to expect on its frontiers after winning a war.

It is unlikely that Russian armies, occupying other neighboring states, will practice social engineering to anything like the degree that it was applied to Poland and the Baltic States. These things were done in the honeymoon period of the Stalin-Hitler pact, when Molotov was proudly proclaiming that Poland had forever vanished from the map, and a Russian alliance with the "war-mongering capitalist democracies" was unthinkable. It is trite to say that today the Kremlin's thinking has greatly changed.

The science of social engineering cannot be deflected by personal tragedies, since its objectives are the building of a strong, loyal state. And it should be said in defense of the Soviet government that under similar circumstances it has treated its own people exactly as it did the Poles.

Soviet social engineering as applied to Poland and the Baltic States has a purpose which we can understand even though we do not approve; and it should not be mentioned in the same breath with the savage and senseless butcheries which the Germans were perpetrating at Lublin on their side of the partition line.

It is easy to see why Soviet censorship is severe in matters that involve social engineering. A less harmful manifestation is its sensitiveness to any hint that Russia might be radical. A reporter, describing an abrupt alteration in certain Soviet methods, referred to "*revolutionary* changes," but the timid censor struck out "revolutionary." They also don't like references to the Communist Party, feeling it is unpopular in the outside world.

This type of censorship was imposed on a cable sent from Moscow by a correspondent concerning Maurice Thorez, leader of the French Communists, who spoke over Radio Moscow to occupied France. I give below a paragraph from this cable, and the italicized phrases are those which the Soviet censor struck out:

"Maurice Thorez was giving the French underground its instructions by radio from Moscow, but he spoke as an individual *and not in the name of the Communist Party*. He urged them not to indulge in *revolutionary* uprisings but to submit to the Allied High Command. He also discussed the postwar role of *the Communist Party in* France."

The censor refused to let reporters say that Thorez never attended the large diplomatic receptions in Moscow, that he was the father of a child born there, or that his exclusion from Algiers by the French Committee of Liberation had been a blow to his health. The censors admitted it was true, "but it can't come from here."

If, in the course of a news story, a prominent Russian is identified as "a member of the Communist Party" this fact is almost always stricken out by the censor.

"Listen!" a correspondent once shouted through the wicket window, "are you proud that a man is a member of the Party, or are you ashamed of it? What the hell is this anyway, the Dies Committee?" In this instance he got the phrase reinstated.

Ordinarily, however, the Soviet blue pencil is not a "consultative censorship"—you cannot argue with the censors or give them your reason, nor will they give you theirs, when they hand back a mutilated cable.

Their reply is always, "We can't discuss this with you. It's been decided."

If the correspondents persist and become importunate, or show a resentment to which Russians are not accustomed in dealing with their own subservient press, the censor will say sternly, "Mr. Smith, I must remind you that you are in the Soviet Union!" The reminder is usually unnecessary.

The censorship, of course, excludes everything which might give the outside world an unfavorable impression of conditions within Russia. A correspondent may not give the size of the monthly bread or meat ration allotted to each citizen, nor may he say that favored classes get special rations. He may not say that outside the meager scope of rationing, prices for the necessities of life bought on the free market have become wildly inflationary, surpassing anything dreamed of in the American black market. Nor for months could he say that the government last spring re-opened its commercial stores where people may buy—without ration cards—these same free market commodities at the same fantastic prices.

One explanation is that Russians are a proud people, ashamed to have such facts proclaimed to the world. But the result is that the world has only a meager idea of the sacrifices the Russian people are making. Likewise, they conceal exactly how many hundreds of thousands of Leningraders starved during the siege.

The foregoing illustrate definitely established policies of the Soviet censorship. There are in addition its occasional whimsies. A minor bureaucrat in that office will occasionally strike out a whole paragraph from the story of an experienced correspondent with the remark that he found it "uninteresting," or considered it "unimportant."

A story was recently submitted for censorship in two parts. The second half was assigned to a competent girl who passed it without alteration. But the first half fell into the hands of a dull youth who struck out the last three paragraphs. Usually no explanation is given; in this case, he deigned to remark that he thought the story ended better without them.

Correspondents who resent the censorship most say that fully half their troubles come not from the rules but from the censors' stupidity, or their limited knowledge of languages, and complain that all the intelligent men in the Soviet Union are now in the Red Army. One censor, handling a story which described Ilya Ehrenburg, Russia's famous war writer, as a "Francophile," struck out this word and reproved the correspondent: "How could you say such a thing? During the Spanish War Ehrenburg was with the Loyalists!"

When he finally understood that the English word "Francophile" means one who loves not the Spanish dictator but the French Republic, he let it pass.

Censorship in the Soviet Union is handled by a minor bureau of the Foreign Office and in charge of a functionary called Apollon Petrov, a former professor of Chinese history at the University of Leningrad and also a former Soviet Consul at Chungking.

Most modern countries maintain bureaus like the British and French Ministries of Information, the American Office of War Information or the German Propaganda Ministry, which make an effort to supply foreign correspondents with any standard information about their countries the reporter may need.

The Soviet Union possesses no such facilities, and Moscow correspondents say that the avowed function of the Petrov Bureau is not to help them but to prevent them from getting news, although occasionally it telephones them at three o'clock in the morning promising an important announcement, and they hurry over to receive a mimeographed statement that in the Socialist Soviet Republic of Uzbekistan, infant mortality has, in spite of the world struggle against the fascist aggressors, dropped this month by $1\frac{3}{10}$ per cent in comparison with the same month of 1943.

Petrov, in particular, and his assistant censors in general (excepting one girl, who, reporters say, is pleasant mannered and intelligent) are despised by the Anglo-American Press with an intensity which goes far beyond the bounds of reason.

One correspondent in a fit of exasperation, ripped in half a large map hanging on Petrov's wall. Another, when handed back a story badly mutilated, tore it into bits, and accounts then differ as to whether he laid the pieces on Petrov's desk or tossed them in his face. The Russian Foreign Office can truthfully say that no other nation would tolerate such behavior by correspondents.

The correspondents can truthfully say that nowhere else in the world does such provocation for it exist. They would not mind the vitamin-starved diet or the bleak living conditions of wartime Russia if they were not treated as tolerated spies—cut off from any real human contact with a people they admire and herded into the institutionalized life of the Hotel Metropole, talking only with each other or with the small diplomatic colony, reading only the controlled Russian press, and then having their daily work messed about by what under any circumstances would be the world's most rigid political censorship, and which is in addition in the hands of men who are often mediocre.

Consequently, Petrov has become the focus of their frustrations. Since many of them are fervent admirers of the Russian people and have a keen interest in their social experiment, they have come to believe that if only he were removed, all would be well.

I came for only a brief stay; not long enough to get caught up in this whirl of misunderstanding. My career did not depend on trying to force the truth through Soviet censorship. I filed only one story and could consider the cuts with some detachment.

I met Petrov and found him businesslike and courteous. Perhaps because he readily granted my routine request I judged him intelligent. I felt that he was only carrying out long-established policies of the Kremlin.

And if his underlings often make stupid mistakes, one of the basic reasons is the language barrier. For Russians, owing to their enforced isolation, are almost as bad linguists as Americans. Only a few have more than a smattering of any European language other than their own. I doubt that the Foreign Office could assemble a more competent staff in wartime.

Russians, who sincerely believe that their *Daily Worker* is the only free paper in America, and probably think that their Moscow censorship brings order into an otherwise chaotic scramble of capitalist distortions, certainly must regard the foreign correspondents, and in particular the Americans, as a problem. They already enjoy food and housing privileges equal with those of Russia's most privileged classes; for this they show no gratitude, but demand permissions to travel and a license to criticize, undreamed of by the Russian press.

While correspondents may never visit the front, they are occasionally taken en masse to recently liberated cities or to rear area military headquarters. On these they are always escorted by an assistant censor, one of whose duties is to verify everything that happens. Because if the censor fails to see or hear something on the trip, the reporters, when they return to Moscow, are not allowed to report it. It didn't happen. Even in routine stories from Moscow, the censors usually blue-pencil anything which has not appeared in the Russian press, so there is no such thing as a news beat or an exclusive story. A reporter can work for weeks gathering material for an article, only to have the whole thing killed because it has not appeared in *Pravda*. They view his independent activity as bordering on espionage.

"What's a front trip really like?" I asked a group of correspondents.

"Well," said the oldest, "the first thing is a tour of a liberated city, where they feed you a lot of food and vodka and show you a lot of damage—"

"—With particular emphasis on the churches destroyed," said the second correspondent.

"Next, they take you to see the mayor," continued the oldest correspondent. "He's usually forty-one years old. They tell you that he's been a Party member since he was twenty-two and had lived in this town three years."

"And during the invasion he was always transferred to be the mayor of some Siberian town, and has just come back with the liberating troops," said the third correspondent.

"All these Communist mayors look like brisk American city managers," said the second.

"Anyway," continued the oldest, "he always gives you how many square meters of living space they had before the invasion and how many they have now."

"Then they always get out their map, showing how Humpty-grod will be a bigger and better city after the war, and you look at that," said the third.

"And then," said the second correspondent, "they bring out the Secretary of the Soviet Atrocities Commission."

"That guy," said the third correspondent, "is one of our oldest and dearest friends."

"Now take it easy," interrupted the oldest, "don't give White the wrong angle."

"But in every town the story is more or less the same," said the third correspondent.

"Why shouldn't it be?" said the oldest. "After all, the Germans didn't change their methods."

"I know it," said the third. "What I object to is that the Soviet people sometimes stretch the figures. The solid provable truth is always so shocking that it's almost incredible. I guess the Soviets are so shocked themselves that they think the outside world won't be as shocked as they are unless they stretch it."

"Sure," said the second, "like the kid who comes home from the circus and tells you the elephant was bigger than the tent."

"Well, to go on," said the oldest, "he always tells us how many Jews the Germans killed here—say 80,000. We privately estimate it couldn't have been less than 40,000. Then he tells us how they did it."

"Gave them notice to appear in their best clothes and all their valuables because they were going to be moved. Then marched them all out to a ravine and shot them."

"Always made them undress first," said the third correspondent. "Of course, they take us to the ravine."

"And it's always full of bodies," said the second.

"Only in Kiev where the Germans shot 80,000, they dug them up again just before they left (or rather they made Soviet war prisoners do it) and burned the bodies so there would be no trace. Then they shot the Soviet war prisoners."

"All but three who got away," said the second correspondent. "We talked to them."

"By the time the Germans left Kiev, they knew they were licked," said the oldest.

"And they didn't want to be criticized," said the third.

"No," said the second. "They didn't want that."

"And they're proud that they're an orderly people," said the third.

"Next the Russians take us in cars out to see some German fortifications," said the oldest.

"And after that always the general."

"What does he tell you?"

"All any general ever can in any army," said the second. "Which is never much."

"Hell," said the third, "generals were never there themselves. All they know is what someone tells them. You can have the generals. Even these Soviet generals."

"But don't forget," said the oldest, "when you get up with the army, everything gets better fast. Because they're smart, and strictly business, and they do it well."

"They do it very, very well," said the third.

"With what they have," said the second.

"Which is the best the country has," said the third.

"What else happens?"

"That's all," said the second.

"Except they give you a lot of vodka and pour you back on the train," said the oldest.

"And you've had a front trip," said the third.

Eight

I HAVE just been pricing food in the Moscow government-run stores and in the uncontrolled free public markets and at last I understand how and what these people eat.

A war-plant worker who exceeds her quota makes about 1,000 roubles a month, which at the cheap diplomatic rate of exchange is $80 and will buy about that much in terms of the state-controlled prices for rationed goods.

But the quantities which she can buy on the ration are so meager that she can't spend more than about $6.50 a month for rationed food.

In America, any worker who lost his food coupons could still live magnificently on unrationed goods. He could fill up on milk, eggs, fish, poultry, bread, and unlimited amounts of fresh fruit and vegetables.

In the Soviet Union everything which has any possible food value is either rigidly rationed or else is unobtainable except at fantastic prices.

The Soviet food ration, which she must buy at her assigned grocery store, gives the worker about nine-tenths of what she must have to keep alive and working. For the other tenth, and for any food delicacies she wants, she must look elsewhere.

The first place to look is in the free market or Rynok, where farmers bring produce for sale.

A note here on the farmer. He lives on a collective or state farm, where he does his share of the common work. When the crop is sold, certain overhead expenses must be met, just as in capitalist countries. There are the state taxes, which take a substantial share. His collective probably owes money for farm implements it has bought from the Machinery Trust, and these installments must be paid. The Collective has probably pledged itself to buy a tank for the Red Army, so taking these items together, nine-tenths of what it raises must be sold to the State at the low-pegged official price.

But not all. A small surplus of produce usually remains, and this is distributed among the farmers, who are free either to eat it or bring it to town for sale in the free market, at any price they care to ask. This is also true of what each farmer raises in the small kitchen garden tract which is allotted him. It is supposedly only large enough for his family's needs, but usually something is left over.

In America commission men make the rounds of farm houses in trucks, buying surplus vegetables for resale in town. In the Soviet Union both the farmer and the commission man would get a five-year sentence, because that is exploitation. For the commission man hopes to sell what he buys at a profit, and is thus guilty of exploiting both farmer and the worker. To avoid this crime, the Soviet farmer must take time to hitch up and go to market where he sells personally what he raises, and the hungry housewife may go by subway clear across Moscow to find him.

The Moscow Central Rynok is a large, crowded, fairly clean pavilion, which resembles a farmer's market in any fair-sized American town. The rouble-per-kilo prices I translate into American dollars and cents per pound. But remember that on this same basis, our Russian warworker gets a total of $20 a week.

With this, at the Rynok, she may buy all the eggs she wants (but with no guarantee of their freshness) at $13.10 a dozen. And bread, too. She probably can't afford a whole loaf but may buy as big a chunk as she wants at the rate of $5.67 per pound. Here is some mutton (or perhaps goat)—a bargain at $11.34 per pound —more than half her week's wages.

Has my lady a sweet tooth? Well, an old peasant woman is selling chunks of sugar beet at 80 cents a pound. But if she wants much of that honey at the next booth, she must save her money for he is asking $15 a pound. It's much sweeter than the watery beet.

Then there are assorted items. Across the way an old lady is selling a calf's head and its four knuckles. She wants $18 for the collection, with the hair on and glassy eyes open, attracting a few flies.

Another wrinkled old lady is selling a bunch of peonies. Obviously, they were planted at the corner of her house, and she is selling them just before the petals get too limp. But no one is going to buy the entire bunch since she is asking (and getting) $1.60 per flower.

Across the way a man is selling a crudely made wooden coat-hanger for which he wants $1.02. It is a fair copy of the kind which in peacetime an American cleaner sends back with your suit for free. This sale is legal in Russia because the seller whittled it himself.

Potatoes are $1.05 cents a pound. No wonder our lady-shopper has a little garden plot, and tries to raise all she can herself. Here are ripe currants in a jelly glass. The man wants a dollar for them, but, of course, he keeps the glass.

The currants made into jam would be good on cottage cheese—cheese you can buy here for $6 a pound.

Now for milk. An old lady has a huge pitcher of it and a queue is waiting to buy. The price is $2.65 a quart. But, of course, you must bring your own bottle, except that these people can't afford more than a glassful. Is it inspected? Who knows? Maybe the old lady scalded her big pitcher and maybe not. But look closely—the customers are inspecting. The old lady pours a few drops into a customer's palm. The customer tastes it. Yes, it's fresh—so she buys. Most of the people of the milk line are holding freshly scoured American-made tin cans to carry the milk home in.

In the yard outside are other things. This girl would like to sell some stockings—they're only slightly used and carefully mended. When she sells them, she will undoubtedly go in and buy some food with the money. She wants $6.25 for the cotton ones and $25 for the rayon pair.

Shoes? Yes, you can buy them. A man is selling his extra pair, somewhat worn but they look fairly stout, for 1,000 roubles—

$80 in our money or exactly a month's salary for our warworker. But if she should want a pair of new evening shoes, she would have to save for several months, as they would cost her $333.33 per pair.

But here are a couple of big, strapping girls who are obviously selling something else. They are all fixed up with lipstick, red shoes, red pocketbooks, and red ribbons in their hats, their eyelashes smeared with stove blacking, and they are giving the farmers the eye.

Now, of course, prostitution has been abolished in the Soviet Union; woman's most precious gift is no longer to be had for money. But, friend, do you happen to have an extra quart of milk, a bottle of vodka, a pound of pork, or a pack of cigarettes?

Here a girl is selling a sweater—probably to buy food, since it is warm now—and this is a real prize of soft, English camel's hair or cashmere. Probably, it originally came from one of the embassies or maybe a soldier occupying the Baltic States in 1940 brought it home. And any Russian would call it a bargain at $56. Still, this is June. She could get much more next October—but she's hungry now.

However, remember that these food prices listed above are exceptional; our $80 a month Soviet warworker has already bought with her ration book at the government-controlled store about nine-tenths of the food she uses and has paid only $6.50 per month for it, at low-pegged, state prices.

On the way home from the market we stop at a government-run commission clothing shop. If you have any old clothes to spare, they will buy it, sort, wash, mend, and iron it, and put it on sale here. This specializes in children's clothing and they ask $12.80 for a five-year-old size white dress with a dab of embroidery. Cheap for wartime Russia, but you can't buy many on a salary of $20 a week.

The Soviet government's problem was basically that of our own: its people were getting high war wages, but there was nothing to spend them on. We solved it partly by taxation and partly by selling our people bonds, so that after the war, when industry was retooled, they might sell the bonds and buy merchandise at normal prices.

Of course, war bonds are sold in Russia, many of them even bearing interest. But a large proportion of Soviet war financing consists of outright gifts solicited from individuals, factories, and co-operatives, either in cash or in kind. Also, as we shall see, the government gets money by charging fantastic prices for luxuries in state-owned stores, thus putting part of the war on a solid pay-as-you-go basis which would delight a Vermont Republican.

But the Russians are skeptical about bonds, because a man who owns one has purchasing power which the state can't control. His whims constitute a danger to the state economy. Maybe he will take a notion to start buying before the government is ready to sell. Maybe he will prefer a radio instead of a wooden table, and create a sudden shortage in radios!

So long as he is dependent on state wages, he is on a hand-to-mouth basis and his purchasing power can be controlled. He will get a radio only when they are ready to make radios, and the first sets will go to those whom the government thinks most deserve them.

But if he owns a bond, or if he has hoarded his high wartime wages under the mattress, the whole carefully planned economy is threatened.

The Soviet government has met this peril most ingeniously. In April of 1944, it began re-opening what it called "Commercial Stores." In them the government will sell you almost any luxury item in food or clothing you want, at prices about equal with those in the free market from which I have just come, and without asking you for ration coupons.

In American terms, the Soviet government is running its own black market as a state enterprise in order to skim from its workers the bulk of their war wages.

When peace comes, they hope to have most of the worker's savings in the hands of the government (which will have no obligation to repay him, as our government must redeem its war bonds) and he will be back on a hand-to-mouth basis, dependent on his government-controlled salary.

It is a different system. In America a man who saves money is regarded as a sound and valuable citizen. In Russia he is viewed with suspicion as a hoarder, a potential capitalist to be watched for the criminal tendency of exploiting his fellow workers by giving them jobs.

Now let us step into one of these government-owned "Commercial Stores" and look at the goods and the prices—along with our $20 a week Soviet warworker. She has left her ration book at home but this black market is perfectly legal—the government makes the profit—not some racketeer. The government will sell her their cheapest grade of baloney for $13.20 per pound or boiled ham at $26.46 per pound or bacon at $24.57 per pound. A dressed chicken is cheaper—only $13.20 per pound.

Beef—about the grade America uses for soup meat—is $13.62 per pound, mutton $13.20, and pickled herring dripping from the barrel $13.20 per pound.

And not only staples, but luxuries. If she plans to have a few friends in for a snack, there is sliced, cooked sturgeon at $13.20 per pound, black caviar at $19.73 per pound; almond meats the same, and also hazel nuts.

She can toss up a little omelette out of these really fresh eggs (you can never be sure in the free market) for only $1.25 per egg, and take home a pint of this nice, fresh, thick cream for $8. Or Swiss cheese at $20 per pound. All these items are clean, nicely packaged (at the free market she must bring her own bottles or wrapping paper) and she can be sure she is not getting short weight. So she would probably rather go here than to the free market—if she can spare the time.

For outside this store a long line stretches around the block; shabby warworkers eager to pay these prices. Inside there is another long line to the cashier's desk. It takes the better part of a day to get in, buy a few items and get out again. For this is one of only twenty "Commercial Stores" in Moscow.

Their purpose was not only to drain off the warworker's surplus buying power, but also to keep this surplus out of the hands of the farmers, where it would be equally menacing to the government's postwar plans.

The government, of course, had already tried patriotic appeal; there are countless drives urging factories and collective farms to buy tanks and planes for the Red Army but this was not enough.

There remains considerable money now in the hands of the farmers who have been selling food at the fantastic free market prices for some time. With the money they have been paying fantastic prices for second-hand clothing.

Last summer the government opened a chain of clothing stores exactly like its commercial food stores, where new, stout, warm clothes, including many luxury items, are on sale at black market prices. Thus, it will take from the farmer all he has saved from selling food in the free market to city workers.

Any foreigner, looking at all this, is amazed that the people do not protest when the government takes over the functions of the illegal black market. On the contrary, they seem glad to buy these things, and count the new shops among the other blessings of this society.

"This government is afraid of money," said the American who was showing me around the market. "Their real rewards aren't in terms of roubles. If you belong to a privileged class, they let you trade at certain luxury stores from which others are barred. Their rewards are medals and decorations, some of which entitle you to ride free on the trains, or admit your children to universities without tuition. Factories which exceed their production norms are rewarded with tickets to the opera, or given the privilege of buying luxury items at a greatly reduced rate.

"Money is always kept secondary. The authorities are suspicious of it. They are afraid that it will accumulate into great fortunes which will destroy their system.

"Because of the way they have been educated, they can't understand our system. If you try to tell them that we control great fortunes by breaking them up with inheritance taxes, they don't believe you. Because such a thing could not happen under capitalism as they have learned about it in their textbooks."

As we walked home I was struck again by the drabness of the stores and apartments.

What is missing is competition. Nobody bothers to put up a striking store front or a beautifully arranged window display. The grocery stores are all run by the food trust, the clothing stores by the textile trust. It is a matter of considerable indifference to the government even in peacetime whether the public chooses to buy its socks or sausages at one particular drab government bureau, or at a similar branch several blocks down the street.

Some effort is made to present the merchandise attractively, just as our post office would prefer to put out pretty stamps. But it doesn't greatly matter, any more than Kansas particularly cares whether its auto license tags are prettier or easier to screw on than those of neighboring Oklahoma.

The architect who drew the plans for that dreary workers' apartment had to please, not the people who live in it, nor the promoter-owners who hoped to keep it rented, but the government officials who approved his drawings. The tenants live there not because they like its façade or its plumbing, but because it belongs to the factory where they work or because they lack the necessary prestige or political connections to wangle more square meters of living space in a better one.

This does not mean that either the Russian people or the Soviet government do not want beauty; there are many sporadic and bungling efforts in that direction: it means that they have a poor system for getting it. For competition has gone from Moscow's shops and buildings; over everything rests the dull, unimaginative hand of a bureaucracy which, in the absence of competition, produces only a dreary mediocrity.

The way to understand capitalism is not to memorize the long words economists use. It is to go some place where they don't have any, and see what they do instead.

Under our way of doing things, a man who saves money instead of spending it to have a good time, performs a useful act. For out of such savings our factories are built and our farms improved.

These Socialists can argue that when saving and spending are left up to the individual, they can get out of control and wreck a nation's business structure. Panicky saving can stop all business activity and throw millions out of work. They can argue that the greatest waste of capitalism is not the money we spend feeding the unemployed, but the valuable man-hours of work which our nation loses when these millions are either idle, or when they are employed by the state in ways which do not compete with private business, which means that they are producing little of practical value.

But are capitalist depressions any more wasteful of human energy than this bureaucratic society with its inefficient method; where almost every activity is a state monopoly, and where there is no competition to force inefficient businesses to reform or go broke? True, these people don't stand in line at employment agencies. They work terribly hard and stand in line to pay $1.25 for a really fresh egg. In peacetime they stood in line for other things. They work terribly hard but produce so little that the living standard is less than was that of our jobless on work relief. During our depression as many as 15,000,000 people of our 130,000,000 were for a few years down to this low WPA living standard.

But in the Soviet Union about 180,000,000 people have been on an even lower living standard for twenty-five years, and only a few privileged million know anything better. During this quarter-century the Soviets have controlled one-seventh of the world's land surface, rich in natural resources.

They explain this low living standard by pointing out that the Russian people lack technical experience and that Russia's resources are largely undeveloped. But to correct these things they have had almost a quarter of a century of peace—which is a long time.

Temporarily, money has little value. Everyone has far more than he needs to buy his ration limit. The unofficial currency in Russia is vodka. The average citizen may buy a pint a month for about $5 but if he does not care to drink, it has a very high trading value. If he slips a bottle to a shoemaker, he can get his shoes mended. It will also procure a cheap abortion although one performed under fairly sanitary conditions would cost much more.

There are, in Russia, several categories of rationing corresponding to different strata of the Soviet caste system. The Red Army, for instance, is extremely well fed, particularly in the front lines. And Soviet officers are given a 50 per cent discount when they buy at the newly opened commercial stores.

The Kremlin is luxuriously fed through its own commissary. Whenever one of the foreign embassies is giving a big, formal dinner, the Kremlin obligingly provides them with delicacies which otherwise would be unobtainable in the Soviet Union at any price.

Foreigners are about as well fed as the top Bolsheviks (except, of course, for the very top, who live in the Kremlin). They get ample meat and bread rations, may buy four pints of vodka a month, and so on down the line.

For ordinary Soviet civilians, there is a sliding scale, which may be pretty well judged by the bread ration. A first-class warworker gets 600 grams a day—which is more than a pound. A second-class worker gets 500, an office employee (not an executive) gets 400 and a dependent (old people, children, cripples) gets 300 grams.

Writers, actors, singers, musicians, and other artists are in a special luxury category, not only for food, but for clothing and living quarters.

But the whole picture was nicely summed up by William Henry Chamberlin, a veteran Moscow correspondent, who has written several scholarly books on the Soviet Union. Chamberlin was caught in Bordeaux the week that France fell, and watched the city seethe. The streets were thronged with homeless people, they were sleeping five and six in a room, grocery stores were sold out, there were long lines waiting to get into restaurants.

Chamberlin surveyed all this and finally in his slow drawl, remarked to a fellow correspondent (who quoted it to me in Moscow), "You know, it takes a great upheaval, a catastrophic defeat in war and a national convulsion to reduce a nation to that state of affairs which is normal, everyday life in the Soviet Union."

"Today," says Kirilov, "we visit vegetable factory." This, it develops, is an enormous state-run greenhouse a few kilometers beyond Moscow, which was started a number of years ago by our host, Commissar Mikoyan, when he was head of the Commissariat of Supply. Its purpose was to provide Moscow with a year-round supply of fresh vegetables.

In an open air garden, fresh cucumbers are not ready to pick until the middle of July. This hothouse begins to deliver them in late February.

First, the director. He is small, wiry, and sunburned, a farmer type in any country. Eric starts in with some questions about financing.

Last year they produced 10,000,000 roubles' worth of vegetables, the director tells us, on which they made a profit of 3,000,000, and this was used to enlarge the farm.

These figures are based on the low fixed price at which this farm must sell its vegetables to the state grocery stores. If they were sold in the free market, the profit would be in terms of billions.

The farm, they tell us, has a production norm, and its workers get a third of everything produced in excess of this, given to them in a vegetable dividend toward the end of the year. This they may either eat or sell in the open market, and is, of course, in addition to their wages of 500 roubles a month for which they work ten hours a day, six days a week. These wages are low by war-plant standards, but remember they may eat or sell vegetables at free market prices—or trade them for clothing. Money is always secondary in the Soviet Union.

Now we begin the tour. First a huge hothouse for tomatoes, where the workers (90 per cent are girls) pick them green at an even size to ripen on frames.

The size of the place is staggering. They tell us there are more than 30,000 square yards under glass. In addition they have 22,000 cold frames, each more than a yard and a half square. We see long vistas of tomato plants. Peak production here is 100,000 pounds of tomatoes a month.

In the next building are long alleys of pumpkins. This I can hardly believe. For with us pumpkins are so cheap that no one would dream of raising them under glass.

This plant is the largest of several other vegetable factories which supply Moscow, they explain, but its production equals that of the others combined. That would allow one pound of tomatoes a month in winter for about 200,000 privileged people out of Moscow's millions.

And the price? The director tells us they get in winter ten times the price of tomatoes raised in summer in the open air. No wonder 30 cents of every dollar is profit, in spite of the fact that they must heat the greenhouses from September to May in this sub-arctic climate.

In America such a spread would bring quick competition: somebody would invest money in railroad cars to bring them up from the south in winter. Certainly in America no one could afford to produce hothouse pumpkins, since they are cheap to raise, keep so well, and are so easy to ship.

But here a state monopoly has no competition to uncover its mistakes; instead they can point with pride to their 30 per cent profit.

The plant is clean and seems efficiently run, following the most modern methods. They also show us their live stock which they explain is not for sale, but for the use of members of this co-operative. They have flocks of fine-looking chickens, geese, turkeys, and ducks, all of carefully selected breeds; the pens are immaculate.

No dinner in Russia was better than the honest meal we sat down to in the big dining room. True, the Intourist steward hovered around, uncorking champagne and spooning out caviar. But we could ignore him, for they had good, simple dishes cooked on the farm—cabbage soup, roast pork, roast duck, and homemade dumplings.

These Russians are fine farmers. It is the fault of the system if what they are doing may in part be silly. They are doing it efficiently and well.

On the way back to Moscow we turn into the driveway of what was the estate of a czarist nobleman, and is now a museum. When Peter the Great was forcing Russia to turn toward Europe, this nobleman sent several hundred of his young serfs to Italy to learn the arts. When they returned they were architects, portrait and landscape painters, sculptors, opera singers, and actors.

He put them to work renovating his palace in the Italian style. It became a forest of slave-produced statuary and paintings and included a theater for the ballet.

The slaves had learned a smooth technique and certainly no one could criticize their volume. We pass down lanes of Venuses, Neptunes and swans tampering with the honor of Ledas. But as art it is as dead as the autocracy which inspired it.

A group of clean, bright-eyed Soviet school children are being taken through by their teacher.

The old, courtly caretaker and his wife bow us out after we have signed the guest book. Jennie whispers, "They are of the old regime, those two."

"You have seen them before?"

"Never. But I know by the way they speak Russian, and their manners. One can always tell the former people. They are of the old times."

Probably an old lawyer, or an old teacher and his wife, who found for themselves this little haven against the social storm which destroyed their class. To find such a haven was not easy, for an estimated 20,000,000 people died during the civil wars—most often from starvation. And of these, few were rich aristocrats, for before the first world war only 30,000 people had taxable incomes of more than $5,000.

There is in Moscow a society called Voks, organized by the government to maintain cultural relations with the outside world. And this afternoon Voks honors American business, which means Eric, accompanied by Joyce and me, with a party at the comparatively modest mansion which is their headquarters. Not more than twenty-five Russians are there, but the list includes every well-known Russian name in the arts. There is, of course, the composer Shostakovitch, the sculptress who did the gigantic statuary group for the Paris exposition of 1937, and the immensely popular writer

Ilya Ehrenburg, of whom I have also heard much from the correspondents.

For many years he served as Tass correspondent in Paris, which is the only Western country he knows well, and is at ease in the French language.

He is a short, stocky little man who in Moscow dresses in the kind of unmatched English tweeds affected by French intellectuals. His political line in relation to the Germans is indistinguishable from that of the late Georges Clemenceau. This has not always been the line of his government. Until the Teheran conference, where it became clear that the Anglo-American powers would raise no serious obstacle to their annexation of the Baltic States, the Soviets maintained, in Moscow, a Free German Committee of captured generals. Stalin had emphatically said that the war was not against the German people but only against Hitler's clique. A separate Soviet peace, signed with any German faction other than Hitler's, keeping intact the German army, was possible.

Since Teheran, however, when Stalin, in exchange for various assurances, accepted the Anglo-American "unconditional surrender" formula, the Free German Committee has been soft pedaled, and Ehrenburg has been given a free rein. His articles calling for vengeance on all Germans are prominent, not only in *Red Star* but in all the other important Soviet journals, and the government allots paper for printing hundreds of thousands of copies of his books.

His passionate admiration for France contributes to the poor view he takes of Anglo-Saxons, and in particular of the Anglo-American war effort of which, like most Russians, he has seen nothing. His articles led the Soviet journalistic clamor for a premature second front. When the Anglo-Americans finally opened their Normandy offensive, he explained the rapidity of their advance from the Normandy beachhead as being largely due to the effectiveness of the French Maquis.

A large English language publication recently cabled its Moscow agent offering Ehrenburg a fat sum to do an analytical article on Stalin, which would humanize the Marshal to the outside world. To anyone who knows Russia, this request was naive in the extreme.

I happen to believe that Stalin is a great man, who has guided Russia with an instinctive wisdom. But any Russian within reach of the NKVD who attempted in print to analyze the Marshal's motives or examine his character would be putting himself in real peril. Only abject oriental flattery is permitted, by comparison with which Carl Sandburg's admiring examination of Abraham Lincoln would look like an attempt at character-assassination.

Ehrenburg slid off this hot seat, at the same time salvaging considerable self-respect, by explaining loftily to the publication's Moscow representatives that he didn't care to do such an article because he hadn't always seen eye to eye with Stalin's political line.

Among these Soviet intellectuals were a number who have the privilege of deciding what English and American books are politically fit to be published in the Soviet Union. An attractive girl began to question me about Saroyan.

"How is he regarded in America?"

"Very highly. He is one of our important younger writers."

"But in the matter of his political line, what is thought of him?"

"I don't think he has any political line."

"But would not you say that it differs from the line of Steinbeck?"

I remembered an act of one of Saroyan's plays in which he satirizes Steinbeck's "Oakies." But I only said, "We consider Saroyan an important artist."

"Still there is a difference," she insisted firmly. So I would guess that while Saroyan may be enjoyed by a few Soviet intellectuals, he will not be translated in toto.

As they talked we learned that Walt Disney is more often than not in the Soviets' dog house since Mickey Mouse frequently deviates from the party line, which Charlie Chaplin never does.

Just as we sat down to the usual banquet, I was told that I would be called on for a toast, so as I ate and chatted with my dinner partner—the monumental mason who had done the statuary group at the Paris exposition—I began to formulate what I would say.

Ehrenburg was sitting just opposite me and I made some friendly remark to the effect that he was known in America as Russia's most popular writer. He nodded gravely. Then I asked him how many copies of his last book had been sold in Russia.

"Eight hundred thousand," he said. "But, of course, in Russia we have a paper shortage."

My brief toast was by now firmly in mind. It was to be a few sentences devoted to Ehrenburg. Now that I had formulated them I could forget them and discuss sculpture with my dinner partner. Eric spoke and then Averell Harriman arose. His toast was graceful. It was also brief. And to my horror it was devoted entirely to Ehrenburg. I would have to formulate a new toast. But why was everyone looking at me? Even the toastmaster.

"Mr. White," he said, "it is now your turn."

I got up, groping for a few polite sentences. It took me about ten seconds to think of the first. Then maybe others would come.

"I am here," I said, "not as a representative of American business" —I paused and the interpreter, a plump, raven-eyed German Jewess of about twenty-five, translated this into Russian "—but rather as an American writer"—again I paused and she repeated it in Russian—I was an Americanski something or other—"and representing her free press."

I paused. She didn't say anything. I looked at her.

"Go on," she said, sharply.

"But translate."

"Go on, go on."

"But translate what I just said."

"Go on, go on! I will translate."

But I couldn't go on. That second sentence hadn't yet come. In my head was only fury at the interpreter. What was the use of talking if no one understood? Well, just say anything and quickly sit down.

So I said, "I am most happy to be here to meet the writers, sculptors, and musicians of the Soviet Union," and sat down. I suppose it was abrupt. Averell Harriman helpfully leaned forward and said, in an extremely loud whisper:

"The toast—say something so they can drink."

Oh, yes, the damned toast. I struggled to my feet.

"It is a most happy occasion that we can meet with the creative people of this country," I said. And the interpreter translated.

"Say that in the future you look forward to closer bonds between Soviet cultural leaders and those of America," said Harriman.

"In the future I look forward to closer bonds between Soviet cultural leaders and those of America," I said. The interpreter then translated.

Then Eric leaned forward: "Say that cultural relations will cement the bonds of future business relationships," he said.

"Cultural relations will cement the bonds of future business relationships," I said. The plump interpreter translated.

Then, not to be outdone, Averell Harriman leaned forward again.

"Say that cultural bonds and business bonds are reflected by close diplomatic bonds of friendship."

So I started to say it, but as the alert interpreter already had begun translating, I didn't finish.

"And say that to a continuance of these three, and the perpetuation of cultural, commercial, and diplomatic relations between the Soviet Union and the United States of America, you raise your glass," said Averell, this time looking not at me but at the interpreter, who immediately began to translate. So I thought it would be a good idea just to raise my glass. It was, for everybody immediately raised theirs. Then I sat down, but I doubt that anyone noticed it.

I think there were a number of other toasts. As we were leaving the table, I almost bumped into the plump interpreter.

"Why wouldn't you translate what I said about the free American press?" I asked sharply.

She frowned. "You should know such a thing is *verboten* in the Soviet Union," she snapped. Then she went on ahead of me.

What might be called the American fifth column has never bothered to go underground, even during the war. Large sections of our people openly favored the axis before it began, and since we got in, powerful newspapers have continued caustic criticism of our British and Russian allies. By contrast with this, Russia seems a miracle of national unity, with not a dissenting voice.

But if Russians are contemptuous of us because all of our newspapers do not support Roosevelt with that degree of doglike devotion with which Russian newspapers support Stalin, we can retort that, so far, none of our generals has deserted to join either the Germans or the Japanese.

Moscow has not widely publicized the fact that General Vlassov, charged in the early days of the war with the defense of the Staraya Russa sector, went over to the enemy with his entire army corps, who were mostly Ukrainians. However, the Germans soon discovered that it was not safe to arm these men for combat on the Eastern front—for many of them would desert again to join the partisans.

We generously praise the high morale of the Red Army and sometimes complain that our boys do not seem to know what they are fighting for. But, for the record, we should remember that out of the many Anglo-American prisoners the Germans hold, they have failed to organize a single battalion willing to fight in Nazi uniform.

And if our people are sometimes influenced by enemy radio broadcasts, the fact that they are allowed to listen in itself reflects a healthy state of mind not to be found in Russia, where the government saw fit to confiscate all radios in the hands of private citizens during the first week of the war.

I don't say that American morale is higher than Russian. I only point out that we can hold up our heads in decent self-respect.

We have read many stories of the heroism of Moscow when the enemy was at its gates. Thousands of women left their homes to dig fortifications in the suburbs, saving the city to the embarrassment of our American experts who had predicted that it would fall. Such stories are true, and are typical of the great majority. But since they are the only ones we have heard I should like to give a few other stories which, although typical only of a minority, are equally well authenticated.

They were told me by a correspondent who had the ill fortune to be left behind in Moscow when other correspondents went to Kuibyshev. He is a very intelligent young man of twenty-eight, with one brown eye and one blue, and six fingers on his right hand. Since he is now living in the Hotel Metropole, I hesitate to disclose his name or nationality for fear what he told me might be embarrassing professionally.

So, however this may be, and whether this young man is one or many, the Moscow panic which he described for me began October, 1941, as the Germans approached the town. The foreigners had gone, the government had gone, and it looked as though the Germans might come any day. Long lines of Red Army troops were still marching through the city, the noise of their feet muffled in the snow, on their way to the front. As the fighting got closer rumors arose.

People began destroying all evidence which would prove they were ever sympathetic with the Party. My friend with one brown eye and one blue, says it isn't quite true that you could walk down the street and see the Order of Lenin lying in the gutter where someone had hastily torn it off. But they did burn up those pictures of Stalin, Lenin, and Molotov which are in many Russian homes, and they burned their Communist books—doing such a thorough job that it is still difficult to buy this type of literature in the book stores, since because of the paper shortage the government has not got around to replacing it.

The Germans were dropping leaflets—not only reprints of Winston Churchill's early speeches attacking the Bolsheviks—but also attacks on Jews. But German propaganda was not solely responsible for the rising anti-Semitism in Moscow; Russian propaganda also contributed.

For in an effort to arouse patriotism in the Russian people, the Bolsheviks had been turning to history, repopularizing the discarded heroes of czarist times, generals and czars who in the past had heaved out invaders in the name of Holy Mother Russia.

"We know," reasoned a prominent Bolshevik, "that the people are not fighting for Communism; they are fighting for Russia." It was true, and the Bolsheviks capitalized on it. But pride of race cuts both ways: if you convince a people that an unusual amount of heroism goes along with their possession of Slavic blood, they take the further logical step of concluding that something is wrong with anyone not similarly blessed. This popularization of the old medieval Slavic skull-busters resulted naturally in a rising contempt for Jews.

Perhaps the Kremlin miscalculated, or perhaps it estimated that the immediate gain in fighting spirit was worth its temporary cost. In any event, the anti-Semitism did not directly embarrass the Kremlin for, since the purges of 1937, very few Jews remain in high government positions. In any event, they have recently taken steps to correct the trend by soft-pedaling publicity about the Slavic skull-busters of antiquity. The czars often, for their own purposes, encouraged anti-Semitism, and one of the admirable things about the Soviet regime is its uncompromising attitude toward any form of race prejudice which it holds down with a firm hand; no small task in dealing with the Russian people, in whom anti-Semitism has been a tradition for centuries, and in whom a taste for pogroms seemed as deeply ingrained as their liking for cucumbers.

But the government has done a good job in keeping it down with the result that anti-Semitism is no stronger than it is in America, although conditions in this respect are not yet so good as in England, where the people have always preserved a high standard of race tolerance.

The people at the time of the Moscow panic were also sore at the army. For twenty-five years they had been sacrificing to maintain the biggest one in Europe, and they had been told it was the best equipped. But ever since June it had been kicked out of one defense line after another, and now had been beaten back to the outskirts of the capital.

The whole thing seemed hopeless to many, and since they were also frightened by the continual bombing, they felt the sooner it was over the better. My friend with one blue eye and one brown, had the habit of wearing in his button-hole a small replica of the well-known flag of his country in red, white, and blue enamel. It also happened that his country was then being highly praised in the

Moscow press for the aid which it promised to Russia, and the people were being assured that much more would soon arrive.

But my friend had to take off his little enamel flag because it got him into too many arguments.

Strangers would come up to him on the street or on the subway and say, "Why are you silly people sending help to the regime? Don't you know you're only prolonging the war? If you'd mind your own business, it would be over sooner."

And if anyone started making a patriotic speech, someone might remark sourly, "What's the matter with you, anyway? Are you a Jew?"

The people who lacked sufficient political importance or influence to be evacuated from Moscow, were understandably resentful of those who left. And what with the German leaflets, resentment crystallized around the evacuation of the Theatrical Commissariat which in Russia as in most countries contains somewhat more than the average proportion of Jews. Various groundless rumors circulated to the effect that they had evacuated both in haste and in considerable luxury, and the people argued that they should not have been evacuated at all, since they were hardly indispensable to the war effort and would have been of more use keeping up morale in Moscow. The Commissariat was, of course, acting strictly under orders, with the exception of the manager of the circus, who evacuated precipitously but with enough forethought to take along the week's gate receipts, for which offense he was later reported to have been shot.

However, about half the cast of the Bolshoi Theater was ordered to stay, and the ballet presently reopened. Other stages in Moscow were filled with ancient vaudeville turns of decaying actors who were delighted to come out of retirement.

In general, the evacuees were not popular. Rumors circulated as to the enormous prices they were paying for automobiles to make their getaway, and other rumors to the effect that peasants were stopping them on the highways to relieve them of hoarded valuables. In some apartment houses the inmates forcibly prevented them from loading their cars with food. "You're lucky enough to be going; at least leave those who must stay something to eat," was the argument.

As the Germans advanced, some, muttering against the regime, openly rejoiced. "Now the Bolsheviks are going to catch it!" But most, even among those who wanted the Germans to come so the bombs would stop, disliked them more than they hated the regime.

The great majority would be typified by the girl who had been exiled for two years for knowing a foreigner too well. At the height of the panic she showed up at the Metropole asking for my six-fingered friend. He assumed she wanted help in getting out of Moscow, but no: she was wondering if he could help her get a rifle, if any might be left in the empty embassies. With it she could go out to the near-by front and help kill the invaders.

The situation got worse. One morning my six-fingered friend noticed the militiaman on the corner had disappeared. Also those who guarded the vacant embassies against looting. It turned out that the previous day the levies of green troops hastily raised to defend the capital, had broken at Mojhaisk and run away. The militia had been thrown in to fill the gap.

Immediately there were near-riots at the food stores. Russians are not by nature an orderly people and as soon as they discovered the militia was gone, the slow-moving food queues became pushing crowds. There were many rumors that Jews were being beaten in the subways.

Three things stopped the Moscow panic. First, the government on October 17, ordered all stored food dumped on the market, giving people permission to buy in unlimited quantities. If the Germans were to take Moscow, it was better to have it in the cupboards of the people than in warehouses for the Germans. The people were so busy scrambling for this food that they had no time for rumors.

Second, on October 20, the government declared martial law in the city, which sobered everybody. But the thing which did most to bring back morale in Moscow was the fact that, when the government went to Kuibyshev, Stalin remained in the Kremlin.

The head of their nation was not running out on them, but staying to defend their city and share its dangers.

Moscow's panic was never publicized and was soon forgotten except for arguments between its citizens. Those who stayed accused: "You're yellow or you would never have left." But the others had a quick answer. "You're pro-German," they said, "or you wouldn't have stayed." Certainly, the disorder and dissension was no worse than would have been the case in either New York or London if the Germans had got within seventeen miles of the city. But the NKVD still has a watchful eye on those suspected of talking too freely during the Moscow panic.

Nine

THERE IS a whisper in Moscow that another party of correspondents may be allowed to go down to visit the newly-established American air bases in the Ukraine. When we arrived, one party was down there covering the landing of the Fifteenth Air Force on the first leg of its shuttle bombing mission, when it pasted Rumanian oil fields.

Incidentally, the boys tell me the Red Air Force, which almost never tackles either long-range bombing or high altitude work, was deeply impressed. Russian officers studied the photographs of the targets, which showed the accuracy of the bombs, and nodded with grave approval, handing them back.

Then they asked from what altitude. When told what that altitude was, they asked for another look at the pictures.

In the original agreement for American air bases in Russia, the Soviets laid down certain restrictions. The fields remained Russian fields, with a Russian commanding officer co-operating with the American commander, the Russians having entire charge of their defense. Under the agreement the number of Americans was limited to a few hundred which allowed only for administrative personnel, an American hospital unit, and provided about half the number of mechanics necessary to service the planes. The rest of these (as well as all the field guards, anti-aircraft gunners, and defenses) were provided by the Russians, and the boys say the Red Air Force combed its own personnel to send us their best.

Another part of the agreement provided that all American magazines and newspapers received by the troops should be carefully collected once a week and burned, which the reporters accept as routine in Russia. Although these American soldiers on Russian soil may read what they like, the Soviets don't want hundreds of American magazines being passed around the Ukraine.

The reporters point out that the Soviets have from their standpoint made a great concession by allowing even a limited number of foreign soldiers into the interior, where they must inevitably mix with the people, and where the American standard in uniforms and food must certainly arouse comment.

They say, however, that the American boys are getting along beautifully both with the Red Air Force and with the people of the Ukraine, and that this in itself is a great story.

I want to go because I am curious about the Ukraine. The Soviet Union west of the Urals alone is almost as big as the rest of Europe with nearly as many races. In the north live the Russians, and they are relatively tall and blond, in coloring like the north Germans and Scandinavians.

In the south the largest minority are the almost 40,000,000 Ukrainians. Their language differs from Russian about as much as Spanish differs from Italian (they can understand each other if they talk slowly). Like the Latins they are generally short and dark.

Russians generally build houses of wood—either log cabins or gloomy high-gabled ones like those of Prussia or Sweden. But in the south the houses resemble those of Italy and Spain—whitewashed stucco with tile roofs. The boys tell me of a town in Siberia settled ten years ago half by Russians and half by Ukrainians. In one end are the gay houses of the Ukrainians, with white fences, flowers, and shrubs. In the other are the gloomy, unpainted wooden houses of the Russians, with only potatoes growing in the yards.

There always has been an independence movement in the Ukraine, although the two races are now closer than they ever have been.

The Germans invaded the Ukraine in the first world war, and after the 1917 Revolution organized an independent state of Ukrainia which got considerable support from the people. For Bolshevism was not strong in the Ukraine, which tried to break away from Moscow and furnished many recruits to the White armies fighting the Bolsheviks. The Ukrainians were subdued only after several years of bitter fighting. They also resisted the collectivization of the land, and hundreds of thousands were arrested as kulaks and deported.

When the Germans came back again in 1941 they not only brought in priests, but many other tame Ukrainians, and again set up a separatist movement, recruiting a Ukrainian militia for which they found a fairly ample supply of anti-Russian or anti-Soviet Quislings.

They started breaking up the collective farms and re-established private business. The Germans made every effort at first to treat the Ukrainians well and compared to other occupied parts of the Soviet Union, they were pampered. Now and then the iron fist came through the velvet glove.

The Germans came to every village with recruiting appeals for their labor service in the Reich. It was supposed not to be compulsory, but if enough likely candidates did not volunteer, the Quisling Cossacks would then come around and see that they did.

Toward the end of the occupation, the people came to dislike the Quisling Cossacks more than they did the Germans. Then the Quislings presently fell out with the Germans, with the result that in some areas the Quislings were fighting both the Wehrmacht and the Red Army.

But out of all this confusion emerges the fact that a majority were loyal to the Soviet Union throughout—how large a majority is anyone's guess. The Red Army, when it re-entered, took a liberal attitude toward Ukrainians who had had to have dealings with Germans under the occupation. Many churches established under German occupation were allowed to remain, and even private stores survived for some months, probably until the Soviets got their own system of distribution under way.

However, many Ukrainians who had dealt with the Germans were given the third degree, with the result that many Quislings were shot and countless others given ten-year sentences without right of correspondence. For during the last stages of the mop-up, the Russians had captured entire regiments of Ukrainians in German uniform.

Furthermore, the attitude of the Red Army toward any of its

soldiers who surrender is not unlike that of the Japanese, and when any are recaptured, nobody pelts them with roses or lavishes sympathy on them.

During their visit to the Ukraine, the reporters found a number of Red Army soldiers begging from door to door for food. When they questioned them, the men explained that they had been captured by the Germans and later released by the Russians, but their cases had not yet been decided.

There is no doubt, however, that most Ukrainians hated the Germans. During their Ukrainian trip the reporters visited a village near Uman, which had been liberated so recently that two burned German trucks were still smoldering in a ditch, and the Foreign Office had had no time to organize propaganda, even if it were disposed to.

There they talked to two girls who said the Germans had mobilized them for "voluntary" labor service. They were loaded onto trains and spent weeks being shunted around, until they arrived in a big labor dispersal camp. In adjoining pens the Germans kept British and Russian prisoners of war. The girls said if it hadn't been for the bits of chocolate and biscuit from Red Cross parcels which the British and French threw over the fence to them, the Russian civilians would have starved. Finally, the British war prisoners started so strong an agitation that the Germans relented and provided the Russians with food up to the British standard. The two girls had gotten away ingeniously. One of them stuck her hand in a loom, and the other poisoned herself with nicotine tea from cigarette butts. So the Germans, declaring them unfit to work, had sent them home.

In the same Ukrainian village the girls led them to a house where a woman and her three children lay dead on the floor, their blood not yet dry from the bayonets of the departing Germans.

There is, however, no doubt that the Russians (as distinguished from other peoples in the Soviet Union) have borne the brunt of the war. In their territory the Germans behaved with much more brutality. Also the enthusiasm of the Russians for the war was greater than that of other Soviet peoples.

There are in the Soviet Union (as in the Czarist Empire) many nationalities and hundreds of languages, counting sub-dialects. But the Russian race is clearly the spark-plug of the whole. They are, to start with, dominant in numbers, and are the most enthusiastic Communists. As they fought hardest in war, so they work hardest in peace.

These little peoples resented Russian rule under the czars; the Bolshevik Russians are careful of their local prides. Newspapers are published in their own languages, which are also taught in their schools, and used in their theaters. Promising local boys are admitted to the Communist Party or given imposing titles in the local government.

Yet simultaneously Russian is spreading throughout the Soviet Union just as the French and English spread their languages through their empires and for the same reason; it is the speech of the ruling class, so the minority groups are eager to learn.

At about six o'clock at night the Foreign Office phoned the Metropole. Bombers from the Eighth Air Force on the first shuttle raid across Germany would arrive in Russia the next afternoon.

Tomorrow morning we could go by plane to greet them. Most of the correspondents had already covered the story when the Fifteenth bombed Rumania and did not care to go again. So I had no trouble in getting a place on the plane.

However, the Soviet Press, which had dismissed the first shuttle raid with a few paragraphs, had for some reason decided to make a field day of this one, for when we got down to the airport for the early five o'clock departure (the sun had been up for three hours) we found reporters from *Izvestia*, *Red Star*, and *Pravda* as well as the Soviet newsreels and photographers also waiting.

Then we found, having gotten up about four to dress and shave, that departure had been changed to nine.

Why hadn't they notified us the night before, so we could have had a normal night's sleep? Well, had they again telephoned the Metropole, some of us might have failed to get the message. The Russian correspondents accept this as either routine or reasonable.

Without even a shoulder shrug, they settle on the benches for a long wait.

Half an hour before departure our conducting officer arrives—resplendent in a brand-new Foreign Office uniform. His name is Okhov and the American reporters say he works in the censorship bureau. He is surprisingly young and seems a little shy. He has a pink and white complexion, is tall, and his slimness is accentuated by the tubular blue-gray overcoat of his uniform, which falls from his shoulders to his calves without a curve or wrinkle. Visiting the American Air Force, we will be in his charge.

We pile into a Russian-built Douglas, and what the country is like between Moscow and the Ukraine, I do not know, for I was asleep by the time the wheels cleared the ground, and did not wake until they bumped down again on the American air base in the Central Ukraine, a field on a flat plane of black dirt like Iowa or eastern Kansas. We step out into America. Here are our familiar steel matting runways, and at the edge of the field a square of khaki tents which might be any American air station in Wyoming or Guadalcanal, Scotland or Iceland.

Near it is a Soviet Pullman car, standing alone on a siding. I have attached myself to Eddy Gilmore, who knows his way around this base, and he says we are scheduled to spend the night in this, but if I will bring my duffel bag we'll sneak off from the others and go to the hospital area and he'll hit a medical major he knows for a couple of beds. More fun talking to the American boys there. And anyway, the damn sleeping car has bedbugs.

The medical major says it will be a cold night in hell when he can't find a cot for Eddy and maybe one friend—unless, of course, the planes bring in too many kids with flak in them. But we'll know about that soon; in fact we'd better get over to the control tower now; they're due in half an hour.

There we find a mixed crowd of high officers: General Walsh heading the Americans, and Lieutenant General Perminov, the field commander. Perminov is wiry, tall for a Russian, about fifty with slightly graying hair and a most efficient-looking officer. His staff also looks able—stocky, grave men, their uniforms a little shabbier.

By contrast the American colonels and majors look less impressive (it is summer and they are not wearing coats) and much neater. The reporters mingle with this small crowd; the Soviet movie and sound truck is near by.

An American gasoline re-fueling truck lumbers past, as the Russians stare at its bulk, its thick steel construction, its fat, new rubber tires. I am standing between a Russian colonel who speaks a little English, and an American colonel with the Eighth Air Force insignia sewn on his sleeve shoulder.

"There they come!" Very low they seem—tiny dots on the horizon. "Let's count them," says a reporter. "One-two-three-four"— they might be a string of geese flying south in the fall. But now more appear; a swarm of bees flying formation—"twenty-three, twenty-four, twenty-five—"

Now we can see that they have great altitude. Still another line appears behind over the horizon.

"—Thirty-seven, thirty-eight, thirty-nine—"

The ambulance has rolled out on the field and two nurses stand beside it. American girls with real stockings and clean dresses. And not top-heavy with bulging Soviet bosoms. The first formation is now approaching the field and we can see their four motors. It seems to spread out for miles, but on the far horizon other galaxies of tiny dots appear.

"—Fifty-two, fifty-three, fifty-four, fifty-five—"

The first formation is now over the field, with a deep organ roar of motors. The Red Air Force colonels and majors stand frozen, staring up at this blue sky, which thunders with twinkling propellers. The one next me turns, cupping his hand toward my ear.

"Even if they do not drop bombs now," he says, "it is still fearsome."

"—Sixty-seven, sixty-eight, sixty-nine—"

The caboose of the great sky train is now in sight, but the V of the lead formation having crossed the field, it swings wide in a huge turn. Now they are making their landings.

"Look at 'em!" says the Eighth Air Force colonel, "three on the runway at once! Boy, that's my old outfit!" Even at this rate, it will take almost an hour to bring them in. They taxi toward us—and the crews begin to climb out and stride over the field—husky boys with lean, Anglo-Saxon faces, pink-cheeked and limber—stuffed with vitamins—fresh milk, orange juice, and thick steaks. It shows.

And their uniforms—real, unscuffed, polished leather, real wool, and real rubber where these things should be. Lieutenant General Perminov is shaking hands with the first pilot and then a dark-eyed Russian girl in Red Army uniform hands him a bouquet of flowers, while the Soviet news cameras grind. The pilot takes it, and thanks her with an embarrassed grin.

It is a sad little bouquet, the flowers are scrawny and bedraggled. But then I remember that the town's greenhouse, if it ever had one, has undoubtedly been bombed. Someone must have laboriously picked these in the meadows.

The pilot is now working his way out of the crowd, still grinning with embarrassment as he holds the sad little bouquet of field flowers, when an NKVD man takes it from him with a quick tug and returns it to the black-eyed Red Army girl. The pilot looks bewildered. A second pilot is now shaking hands with General Perminov. As he turns, the Red Army girl hands him the bouquet. He also grins with embarrassment as the Soviet news cameras grind. So on with the third pilot, the fourth, the fifth—all have their moment with the town's only bouquet.

We walk over to the near-by plank desk where the American intelligence officer is questioning them. Soviet reporters also are taking notes. The pilots' stories do not vary. The total flight took almost nine hours and midway they smacked their target—a little town south of Berlin where the Heinies had either a rubber plant or an oil-cracker, the pilots weren't sure which. Anyway, they smacked this plant on the nose and got a fine black smoke column. Looking out to the north they could see the British working on Berlin—getting some good smoke columns going, too. No flak, except right over the target. And not a fighter until they were passing through Poland, just about where the ground fighting was going on. The opposition wasn't much, and their escorting P-38's had sure taken care of it—hit the Germans so quick they never knew what happened. They might have picked off a Fortress from the formation which came down on the other American air base—but none from this. They had met the Russian fighters about 30 miles inside the frontier, and here they were. A couple of fellows with minor flak wounds, that was all.

What did they think of Russia? They grinned. Pretty rugged, they told the Soviet reporters. And things were sure messed up. They hadn't thought there'd be that much bomb damage, but looking down at it through field glasses, even barns were destroyed.

Were they glad to have made this first flight from England to the Soviet Union?

Why, sure they were glad. Even the cooks were trying to get signed up for it.

Why were they glad?

Well, who wouldn't be? Wasn't it one of the longest missions the Eighth had ever flown? And across the toughest opposition in the world? And then, anyone likes to stretch his legs in a new country now and then.

The Soviet reporters tried once again. Couldn't they quote the captain as saying that the reason they had so little opposition from German fighters was because the entire Luftwaffe was probably engaged fighting the Red Air Force over Finland?

The captain looked puzzled. Hell, he didn't know anything about all that. They ought to ask someone who knew about it. He was only telling what happened.

What was the name of the town in Germany which they had bombed?

The captain couldn't remember. Soviet reporters exchanged knowing looks at such callow ignorance. The captain noticed and it ruffled him.

He'd glanced at it on the navigator's map, but to him it was just one more of those targets. And getting them there was a navigator's job, not the pilot's.

At this point there is a thundering explosion, then another.

We jump. "What's that?"

An American reporter laughs. "Only ack-ack. The Russian girls on those guns around the field probably noticed the newsreel truck, and figured they'd help out with one of those Soviet salutes."

"Hell, that's no salute!" said another reporter. "Look there!" He was pointing high into the sky. We could now see the ack-ack shells bursting in ragged puffs, forming a fairly regular line. Ahead of this line was the silvery streak of a vapor trail.

"German reconnaissance plane," remarked one of the American pilots, glancing up. "So they have 'em here, too. I've never seen one shot down yet—they're too fast. Come over us in England all the time."

I felt suddenly naked, with the enemy up there staring down.

"But don't the bombers follow?" someone asked.

"They try, but they haven't got a prayer. I mean we're really set up for them. Spitfires, night fighters, radar—they never get through all that. I haven't heard a bomb drop on our field since I came to England, and the Germans are only about 200 miles away."

I was ashamed to feel so relieved. Still it was nice to know we were at least 400 miles from the nearest German fields, with the Red Air Force in between. The last Forts were landing. The German reconnaissance plane, with pictures of our loaded field on his plates, turned homeward and was quickly lost in the high haze.

But what good would the plates do?

The group broke up. I went over to the administration building —a large, brick affair which might have been something in connection with a co-operative beet-farm, and ate cabbage soup and kasha at the Red Army officers' mess. Then I went over to the hospital area, they showed me my tent and I wrote a V-mail letter home, or rather one page of it, for just then an accommodating major turned up who had heard I wanted to see the town. If so, he had got hold of a weapons carrier and would be glad to take me. But if I wanted to see the town, I should hurry, for the sun would be setting soon.

I hastily signed the V-mail letter. I'd get this page into the box today—and it should be in New York in eight days—the second one could wait until tomorrow. The town was only half an hour away and was a wreck. There had been little fighting in the city but before they left, the Germans had dynamited everything, not only public buildings but also those big concrete apartment houses, which we find ugly but of which these people are so proud.

The Germans had been thrifty with dynamite—planted enough inside to blow out all the partitions, ceilings and floors, but not enough to push the outer walls into the streets and block traffic for the evacuation.

I asked the major what he thought of it all. He was a young lawyer from Chicago. He said you couldn't ask for better people, but this system they had—that was something else. That was something you kept running into all the time. And people back home who were fooling with the idea that we should have anything like it—they should come over and see it for themselves.

Yet there were certain things about it, not compared to us, of course, but to the rest of this end of the world. The way beggars and little Arab boys tagged after you all over Africa and the Middle East. None of that here. These people had real self-respect like we do. The thing you noticed driving over from Teheran, was that when you struck the first Russian town the begging stopped and the kids stood on the sidewalk and smiled, instead of following you. Maybe that came from the system, too—you couldn't tell.

Now, the major said, take that bunch of flowers in his tent. The day before a couple of kids had come past and he'd given them a chocolate bar. They took it all right, and this morning they came back with flowers they had picked themselves. Wouldn't take any more chocolate, because they said the flowers were to show their appreciation of the Americans. A thing like that couldn't happen in Africa or in Iran, the major said.

I asked him how the American boys were making out with the Ukrainian girls. We had got out of the car and were walking through one of the town's two beautiful parks. The gravel walks were full of strolling people, mostly girls. Now and then we would pass one of the Eighth Air Force boys with them, but they were mostly gunners or radiomen. The pilots were tired and had gone to bed at the camp.

The major said the G.I.'s were making out all right but reported that you couldn't get far the first night, which would go to show that girls are pretty much alike wherever you find them. He said they got along with very little language. For instance, if a G.I. were telling a girl good night on her doorstep and if it were Monday night, he'd say:

"*Zaftra?*" (which means tomorrow in Russian) but she'd shake her head.

Then he would say, "*Zaftra-zaftra?*" But she'd shake her head again.

Then he'd say, "*Zaftra-zaftra-zaftra?*" and she'd nod, which meant it was all right for him to come back next Thursday.

It was also helpful that many of the girls knew a little German as a result of the occupation for quite a few G.I.'s spoke some. The major said the Germans seemed to have treated these Ukrainians well, on the whole, and he found no bitterness against them as individuals.

He said the region was stripped almost bare of men. The Russians had taken some when the war began, then when the Germans came in they took more, and when the Russians returned, they drafted what was left. So the girls hadn't bothered much about how they looked. But then the Americans came in, and the first Sunday after this the girls all turned out to walk in the park in their beautifully embroidered peasant costumes, which they had washed and ironed. You wouldn't know they were the same girls, the major said.

It was by now dark, so we left the beautiful park and returned to the weapons carrier, but the driver was gone. The major couldn't understand it. The driver had said something about seeing some girl for a minute, but he should have been back long ago. It was half-past eleven when he did return, looking satisfactorily rumpled, and this got us back at camp at midnight.

As we stopped to get out, we found the officer on duty by the road.

"By the way," he said, "there's an alert on."

"That so?" said the major. I was trying, in the dark, to make out which tent in the alley was mine.

"How do you know?" asked the major.

"They phoned over from headquarters just a while ago. Said the Red Army up at the front reported to the Russians here that German planes passed over, heading this way."

"How long ago?"

"Maybe half an hour."

We went on down the alley between the tents. "We had one other, about a week ago," said the major. "Of course, nothing happened. Well, here's your tent."

"Thanks a lot."

"Got everything?"

"Sure."

"Sheets and a pillow case?"

"All made up."

"Guess they thought they'd fool the Russians—sneak in without being picked up and catch this loaded field before they could get their night fighters up. Well, the Russians'll probably show 'em."

"Have you ever seen a Russian night fighter?"

"Why, no, I haven't," said the major. "Guess they keep them on some other field. Anyway, with an alert on, they're in the air by now and maybe we'll hear some. We don't know much about how they handle the defenses, except for those batteries around this field, of course. They're strictly business, the Red Army is. Don't tell us a lot. Well, good night."

"Good night."

I went into the tent and turned on the flashlight just long enough to see where everything was. The other cot was empty. I took off my uniform and laid the pants carefully over the chair, using its back as a hanger for the shirt and blouse. Then I put on my pajamas. The camp was very still. I kept on my shoes because I was going to the latrine, which was only about four tents away. When I parted the flaps of my tent, I noticed, on the far flat of the horizon, a tiny ball of fire which rose above the rim only a little way, then curved over and winked out. As I stood there in my pajamas, another curved over and winked out. They looked like balls from a Roman candle but it could only be anti-aircraft fire. Now I heard leisurely footsteps coming down between the tents and saw the outline of a figure.

"Hello."

"Hello," said the figure and stopped. It was the voice of one of the medical officers.

"Just going to the latrine. Watching the fireworks."

"Where?"

I pointed.

"Yeauh, look at it," said the medical officer. "It's fire from the other field." Another figure came down the tent alley.

"Hey, look at that, George," said the medical officer. The other officer stopped.

"Must be trigger-happy over there," he said. "Damn silly thing to do. Because if a few German planes had slipped through, they oughtn't to light the place up and give away their position. Ought to lay low and let the night fighters take care of them."

"What are their night fighters like?" I asked.

"Never saw any of them," said the second officer. "And, of course, they never tell you much. But they wouldn't have them way back here. They'd keep them closer to the line."

"Don't know why they wouldn't," said the first officer. "What more valuable target would they have to defend than a loaded field like this?"

"Then maybe they do have. They saw that German recco plane this afternoon."

"Well, where are they? And why are they lighting up that target? Look—they've even turned on search-lights over there. Looks like a goddam birthday cake."

"Hell, they're just trigger-happy," said the second officer. "That recco plane this afternoon and then this alert have got the ack-ack girls excited. They want to show us how they can do their stuff. Hell, no German bombers could get through to here. This is further back from the line than any field in England."

"Listen," said the first officer, "I think I hear the night fighters."

We all listened. The camp was very still and there was no wind. Was that a high hum, or only the roaring of our ears?

"I don't hear anything," said the second officer. And then there was a bright flash and an explosion, and a tracer shell soared into the sky directly over us. We had all jumped. Now we all laughed.

"For Christ's *sake*," said the second officer. "Now our girls have caught it. Damn hysterical women!"

"Listen," said the first officer, "why don't we go down there by the slit trenches and watch this from there? We can see it just as well."

"Might as well," said the second. "But the girls'll have probably calmed down by the time we get there. You coming, White?"

"I'm going to the latrine. Where are the slit trenches?"

"At the edge of camp. But better let us show you first. Might have trouble finding them in the dark if you really needed them. Just take a minute."

"Okay." And since it would just take a minute, I didn't bother to step back into my tent for my uniform, although I was feeling a little chilly. In my pajamas I followed them through the dark, avoiding the tent guy ropes.

"Here they are," said the first officer, and he stopped. Then someone seemed to have turned on a very steady, brilliant white light in order to show me better. I saw the trench. I saw the parapet of fine black Ukrainian silt. I even saw the design on my pajamas, in a hard, white glare which lit up the leaves of distant trees.

"Jesus! A flare!" said the second officer. "Listen, we better get the hell down in this trench! There *are* Germans up there!" Like a sinister star of Bethlehem, the flare hung over the center of our field. By its light, we could see the silver wings of the fortresses stacked around the runways. There were so many you could not see the horizon—only the tilting silver wings. In the flare's light, they cast sharp ink-black shadows on the runway. We could see the brown tents of our camp and the black wrinkles where the guy ropes stretched the canvas. We could see figures from the camp running toward our trenches but their faces were in black shadow as this white light beat on their heads. The batteries were now thundering away at the flare but as the yellow tracers soared toward it, the blue-white glare seemed to put out their dull glow. It seemed nailed against the sky but because it got brighter, we knew its parachute was settling slowly toward our field. Above, we knew bombardiers peering through their sights, had us pinned down in this ever-brightening light. Our guns shook the ground. We kept waiting for the first whistles. The people running toward us from the camp were jumping in the trenches, and I remember feeling annoyed because any moving thing in that hard light might attract attention. Suddenly the whistles began—hissing, ripping, tearing the air apart along its seams and ending in a dull roar. Then for a few seconds the high hum of the fragments until they pattered down on the grass like gravel.

I remembered I didn't have a helmet. The trench was full now. The others were wearing them. On a wooden box in my tent there had been a helmet.

After the first whistle and explosion, I raised up. The flare had died. It was dark again, except there was now a dull orange patch out on the field which kept growing. Already one of our planes was burning.

Another flare, more whistles and explosions. When I raised up there were more dull orange patches and we heard crackling. At least four planes were burning.

In the trench with me were some of the young pilots from the Eighth and a few nurses and medical personnel. The lieutenants were a little more frightened than the others.

"Gee," explained one of them, "nothing like this ever happened in England."

It was clear they didn't know what to do. When they heard those interesting whistles, they would stand up in the trench to see where they came from. Only after they heard the roar of the bomb, would they drop down and hug the bottom of the trench. But soon they got the idea and began bobbing up and down with the rest of us—ducking for the whistles but raising up when the explosion signaled danger was past.

"I didn't have any idea it was like this on the ground," said the navigator. "When you're over a target, all you ever hear is your own motor. Sometimes the ship gets jiggled. You see tracers coming up at you or puffs of smoke ahead, but none of it makes much noise."

After the first fifteen minutes it got worse. We quit counting the fires on the field for the orange glows merged into one another. That whole end of the sky was shimmering. Heavy explosions were coming from over there which weren't German bombs and weren't our ack-ack. But we couldn't tell which were gas tanks blowing up in our planes, or which might be bombs in their racks.

I tried to think when I had been as scared. Three times in England it had been worse, when buildings I was in had been hit by bombs, but each time it was over in a few seconds, and when the ceiling didn't fall, I knew I was going to stay alive. This was continuous. And it was to keep up for an hour and a half. The worst thing was the shaking earth. When the whistles came, crouching face down in the trench with your knees hunched up to protect your guts and your hands over the back of your head to protect your skull, still didn't make you feel safe if the dirt beneath your face jarred or quaked from a big one. It reminded you that nothing was safe. That one might hit right in the trench. They were hitting everything else.

The nurses began to get hysterical and wanted to get out of the trench and run. This was the worst thing they could have done, but when a big one lands near by, everyone has the impulse for it seems sure the next one will land right on you. Any place else seems safer than where you are. Every time one would land, a nurse would scream. The boys farther down the trench were keeping them quiet.

Next me in the trench was a chunky little Ukrainian girl of about twenty, who washed dishes in the hospital mess. She had pulled on a dress and brought along an army blanket from her bunk. She was huddled down in the bottom of the trench, shaking and whimpering with her eyes squeezed shut and her hands over her ears—sick with fear.

Everything was confusion except upstairs, and that was as neat as an old maid's top dresser drawer. The sequence was like this— first a flare, then a pause, and you heard the bombers come in on their observation runs, to see what was left and pick their next target. Their motors would then die away and you knew they were circling to come in on the bombing run. When we heard the motors again we knew we would soon hear the bomb whistles, and it was time to stop staring at the fires on the field and huddle against the trench bottom.

It was like a page torn out of a textbook, telling how to bomb under ideal conditions. I doubt if anything was so like the book since the Italians bombed the Ethiopians.

The Germans seemed to be paying not the slightest attention to the anti-aircraft fire. I began watching its tracers. Most were directed at the flares. These are hard to shoot down but they succeeded in rocking one of them.

Watching this, I suddenly realized the Russians were doing the best they could with what they had. For it is impossible, on an overcast night, to hit a plane guided only by the sound of its motors. Without radar, you have no idea where the plane is at the instant you fire the anti-aircraft gun.

Now came a sharp short whistle and a terrific jolt. I thought our trench had been hit because the dirt came down on my neck. The little dishwasher screamed. When I looked up, she was crawling out of the trench but I got her ankle and pulled her back down to squat in the trench beside me. She smelled of bacon drippings and sweat and she chattered in Russian, whimpering and struggling a little to get away. To keep her from another quick break, I put an arm around her and she quieted down. The next time the ack-ack flashed, I saw she was smiling archly at me. Anyway this had taken her mind off the bombs. The main thing was to keep her in the trench so I would not have to jump out and drag her back.

Meanwhile I was quaking, and couldn't be sure whether it was from cowardice, which could not be helped, or from the cold, about which something might be done. For we were not far from my tent, where the uniform was hanging over the chair back.

So I decided to make a run for it, counting on the methodical orderliness of the Heinkels up above. After the flare dropped they had to make their observation runs, which allowed considerably more than a minute. I checked the interval on my stop watch to be sure I was right about the time. The next time a flare blossomed, I scrambled out and ran down the alley to my tent.

My uniform was exactly as I had left it on the chair, except that it was in tatters. A piece of shrapnel had even gone through the brass eagle on the cap visor. The wall of the tent nearest the field looked like lace. Through it I could see the glow of burning fortresses. I dropped the tattered uniform and snatched a blanket. That would do almost as well. I grabbed the helmet but when I tried to put it on I found that its owner had left it full of chocolate bars, which had melted in the summer heat and in the cool of night had hardened. I dropped it and only now noticed a sharp odor—not cordite smoke, or maybe that and something else. By my flashlight beams (the burning forts had ruined our blackout) I could see smoke from the other bunk. I pulled the covers back and found the mattress glowing—some white-hot bomb fragments had lodged there; so to prevent the whole tent from going up, I pulled it off the bed and out into the alley.

The field was very beautiful—flames sky-high in a dozen places and silhouetted against them were the wings of the other planes, but now I almost tripped over what I knew instantly was a man. He was lying in the shadow of my tent. I felt down in the dark. He was warm and wet.

A couple of medics had ventured into the next tent alley. I yelled to them and they brought a stretcher. But the boy was dead, so they rolled him onto it and set it down in an empty tent. Then I went on back to the slit trench. The medics followed soon with another stretcher and another body. There had been two boys, both of the Eighth Air Force. They had been asleep in the tent next mine. The bombs had wakened them but by that time everybody had left for the trenches. Not knowing where these were, they had foolishly crouched down behind the canvas wall of my tent instead of lying flat.

REGULATIONS

1. Find the call number in the card catalog, under the author's name, title of the book or subject. Write this number with the author's name and title of the book on the call slip, and present the call slip at the circulation desk.

2. Books may be kept for a period of two weeks, with the privilege of renewal, except for books in great demand, which are limited to three or seven days, and may not be renewed.

3. Borrowers who keep books overtime incur a fine of three cents a day, including Sundays and holidays. Lost books must be replaced.

4. Periodicals may be used only in the periodical room; reference books are to be used only in the reading room.

This one was still alive, so we made room at the end of the trench and helped the medics lower his stretcher. The boy was unconscious but he was breathing quietly. A doctor started working on him in the trench and it took him an hour to die. He must have had twenty holes through him—not one larger than a pea.

Now it started again. The two Eighth Air Force lieutenants were angry.

"Christ, if we only had some Spits!" one of them said.

"Just a dozen Spitfires!" said the other, looking up at the sky. "They'd clean out all that crap up there in ten minutes, and chase the rest back to Germany. They couldn't get away with this with Spitfires around!"

With the blanket I was warm but we were all irritable. When danger lasts too long it is like a boredom so intense you think you can no longer stand it. It seemed to me as the quarter hours slowly went by that it was the longest B-picture I had ever sat through. So far as I was concerned, this was where I came in.

Presently we could see a man running across the field. He was a technical sergeant who jumped into our trench and we got some news. He said that one big 500-pounder, landing just beyond our tent area, had wiped out an ack-ack battery, blowing all the girls to bits.

He said the Russian field guards had been very good. Practically all of them were staying with the planes, trying to fight the fires, which was, of course, hopeless, and that at least a dozen had been killed—a few by bomb fragments but most from stepping on butterflies.

A butterfly is a small mine the size of a hand grenade which parachutes down suspended from two flanged metal wings, hence its name. It doesn't explode when it hits the ground, but the jolt arms it, and the next person who touches it, gets only one leg blown off if he is lucky.

The technical sergeant said the Germans had dropped thousands of these little devils and we should be very careful until it got light.

We were talking about this when suddenly there was a flash high in the sky overhead. I thought maybe the ack-ack had hit a

German plane but Eddy Gilmore said it meant the raid was over, because it was a magnesium flash bomb, dropped to illuminate the airport for the final photograph. When it was developed, if the picture showed anything was left on the field, they might come back tomorrow to finish off.

Looking at the pink sky, I doubted that they would need to return. My watch, which I could read by the glow, said two o'clock. However, we couldn't be sure the raid was over. The explosions kept on. They might be German bombs or our own going off in the racks of the burning Fortresses. And ammunition in the planes for their 30-calibre and 20-mm. guns was going off like firecrackers. Yet we were relaxing. Now and then someone would leave the trench. I decided to make a dash to the latrine, for which I had started more than two hours before, keeping to the path, which I could see was free of butterfly mines. The latrine was undamaged except for a few bomb fragment holes in the canvas. I had been in there not more than a minute when there came one of the biggest explosions I had heard all evening. Automatically, I flattened out on the floor, fearing that this bomb was one of a chain. It turned out to be only the big gasoline truck, which had been parked near a Fortress and blew up belatedly.

Back in the trench they had news. More details of Russians who had been killed on the field during the night. The Russians had an improbable story about three mangled bodies they had found. Although the bodies were in civilian clothes and apparently Russian, the Russians themselves were sure they were disguised Germans— maybe a German bomber had been shot down. Where was the bomber? Nobody could say; they had only the three mangled bodies.

Dawn was coming and with its light the glare from the burning bombers paled. After all, the gasoline in a plane burns quickly and then there is little left to smolder but the electric wire insulation. We left the trench, hoisting up the stretchers of the wounded, and went back to the tents. My uniform was even more tattered than it had seemed but I borrowed another. Then I began wondering what was going on over at headquarters a mile away.

Since it was still half-light, and butterfly mines were thick, no one else was curious, so I started out alone, picking my way carefully along the path. Once it disappeared into a fresh 50-foot crater in the black Ukrainian dirt but tiptoeing painfully around its rim through the weeds, I picked the path up on the other side.

The planes on the field to the right were a grisly sight, but I was staring so intently for mines that I only glanced at them.

Just before I got to the building I saw General Walsh starting out in a jeep to survey the damage. The big building was untouched except, of course, all glass was blown out. Nobody was in the American wing, except a sleepy sergeant sitting at a telephone switchboard who told me that all our radio was blown up and all telephone lines were down, including the Red Army stuff. We were cut off from the world and no one but us knew what had happened at this field.

I went back down and at the door I had another idea. Why not look in on the Russians, whose headquarters were in the next wing? There was, for instance, Mr. Okhov, our conducting officer. What were his directives for the day? Where, in point of fact, was Mr. Okhov?

Russian headquarters seemed equally deserted. There was no guard at the door. I pushed it open. I called out. Then I started upstairs. Nobody was on the second floor. I went up the next flight in complete silence except for my footsteps echoing on the stairs. There was a large door marked Staff Headquarters, slightly ajar. I pushed it open. On the walls were the Stalin-Lenin-Marx pictures. In its center the director's table. But in the chairs were a dozen motionless Red Army colonels. A map had been spread before them on the table, but none of them were looking at it now. Some were sitting there with their hands in their laps. Some were leaning forward with their heads on their hands, elbows on the table.

But, all of them were staring at the table.

When they saw my American uniform, the three nearest the door sprang up.

With a smile and an apology, I started to back out.

But no, but no—what could they do for me?

It was nothing, I only wanted Mr. Okhov. Since he was not here, I would hunt elsewhere.

No, no, I must come in. And would I please sit down? They would find Mr. Okhov. They would have Mr. Okhov here at once.

But, I insisted, they need not trouble to. It was not an important matter. And they were busy.

No, no. No, no. They were not busy. And the name again, please —Okhov? If I would only sit down—just sit there and wait, just one moment. Already a major was on the telephone demanding Mr. Okhov. Impatiently snapping at the phone operator.

But when a minute of this did not produce him, I insisted firmly that I could myself find Mr. Okhov, bowed my thanks to the anxious Red Army colonels, and left them staring at the door.

Outside the building three correspondents trudged across the field from the hospital area, also after news, and they brought some of their own. They had gone to bed in the Pullman car. If it had any bedbugs, they were all stunned into inactivity shortly after midnight, when a bomb blew out all the windows. The reporters had scrambled out of the shattered glass and into the ditch beside the tracks, where they had spent the night. A bomb had hit uncomfortably close to the ditch and three of the Soviet correspondents had decided to find a safer place, which, of course, was foolish.

They had been killed not more than 100 yards away. It was these mangled bodies which the Russians during the night had mistaken for the crew of a German bomber.

I reported that nothing was to be learned here at headquarters.

"Why don't we walk out on the field and look at the damage," said one of the correspondents.

"The Russians will stop us, of course."

But I said I doubted that today the Russians would stop us. And I told them about the colonels who stared at the table.

"Well, anyway," they said, "we can start across, and if they don't like it, why, it's a free country and they can always throw us off."

So we started. Now we began to see many butterfly mines glittering in the weeds. We began wondering how many we couldn't see. So we formed a file, trying to walk in the footsteps of the lead man.

We took turns at the lead, as this was the position that really made you sweat.

The trouble with this procedure was that we stared so intently at the weeds ahead of each descending toe, that we could see nothing of the planes around us.

So we changed it. Without talking, we tiptoed slowly a hundred steps. Then we stopped to look around.

It was sickening. I had written the story of Clark Field in the Philippines as it was told me by a pilot who watched the Japanese destroy more than half our Flying Fortresses on the first day of the war. Now the dead words I had written of the Forts, crumpled on the ground with their backs broken, began to come to life. They were still good words. I did not want to change them, only now I knew what they meant.

I could not help admiring the workmanlike job the Germans had done. Sitting up there last night, the squadron commander had surveyed this flare-lit field as deliberately as a painter between brush strokes appraises his canvas, deciding which color to use. Where the planes were thickest, they had sprinkled incendiaries—exactly like the ones I saw them drop in London in 1940. Many had burned out harmlessly in the grass, but some had hit planes which had fired others. The burned planes were the story I had written before. Their heavy motors tumble from their melting nacelles to roll forward on the ground, their backs break in the middle, their running gear collapses and finally they lie flat on the ground like great dead birds with silver wings outspread. The charred insulation still smoldered.

In swampy places on the field where the planes had not been so closely parked, the Germans had dropped small anti-personnel fragmentation bombs—the kind which had made lace of my tent and killed the two pilots.

These planes looked intact until we got a few yards away and could see thousands of tiny holes in their aluminum skins, which meant that inside fuel lines, electric cables and oil tubes had been cut. It would take weeks or even months of repair and careful inspection before these planes could be flown. Many would not be worth repairing.

On the main runway strip the Germans had placed 1,000-pounders. There were great holes in the concrete. So that was out. Over the whole they had sprinkled these butterflies to make it hard to fight the fires or to get on the field next day to clear runway strips so that any intact planes could be put in the air. After this thorough, orderly night's work, they had taken a final picture and gone home.

We picked our way gingerly through the butterflies to the edge of the field. We had seen it all.

Now we saw half a dozen men in Red Army uniform walking toward us. In the lead was Lieutenant General Perminov.

"All right," said a correspondent, "let them throw us off now. We've counted them."

The general began calling to us in Russian.

"He isn't throwing us off at all," said one reporter. "He's only telling us the Germans have strewn many mines here and we should be careful."

"What in hell does he think we're doing," inquired the fat correspondent sourly, "playing leap-frog?"

The general now came over. He was a fine-looking man with real military dignity and assurance. He had one of his men point out a near-by butterfly so we would not fail to recognize them. We inspected it gravely and nodded our thanks. He was most courteous.

"The good ones always are," said the reporter who spoke Russian, and he said the general had told him they were starting to clear the field of mines. Even now the dozen men were spreading out in a long line, twenty feet apart.

"Then I wish he'd lend us an electric mine-detector to get back to camp," said the fat correspondent.

"Look," said the skinny correspondent, "that line is starting to move—see, they're going to sweep the field. But where are their detectors—and what's the idea of those long cane poles?"

"My friends," said the fat correspondent, after watching the line for a moment, "you will now see an example of mine detection as practiced in the Soviet Union, but you must first understand the basic principles of that branch of military science.

"Elsewhere in the world it is divided into two phases: first, the problem of detecting the mine and second, that of rendering it harmless.

"Here you will note they are combined in the following manner. They send a lot of Russians poking into the weeds with a lot of poles. Presently you hear a loud bang and see a Russian rising into the air on top of a column of smoke. This indicates not only the detection of a mine, but the fact that it has simultaneously been rendered harmless."

"Jees!" said the thin correspondent. "Well, I guess they've got plenty of Russians and plenty of cane poles."

Yet this was not what happened. True, the Russians lacked our elaborate electric frying-pan-type mine detector but as always, they handled their meager equipment with such skill and bravery that they got approximately the same results.

The line, holding its formation, advanced across the field. When a guard saw a mine he would call out. The others would then be ordered flat on the ground. After the soldier had inspected his mine he himself would lie down out of danger and, shielding his eyes, touch it with the pole, whereupon it would explode harmlessly in a twelve-foot pillar of smoke and dirt. The men would then rise and the line move carefully forward.

Fascinated, we followed the line and were coming abreast when General Perminov, courteously but firmly ordered us back. As guests of the Soviet Union we could share not even a small part of its army's dangers.

Back at the tent area, General Walsh ordered a new uniform issued to me and told us to get some sleep because they should have a runway cleared by noon, when a plane would take us back to Moscow. Having walked across the field, I presumed to doubt strongly that it would be cleared by noon but I said nothing.

Departure was postponed first until one o'clock, and then until three. As we waited at the control tower, where yesterday General Perminov and his pretty Red Army girl aide had received the

Eighth Air Force pilots, two big Liberators pulled up. One had a few small bomb holes in its aluminum skin, but the mechanics said they didn't think any vital wires had been cut, and that probably it would get us there. The other one was in fine shape except that its wireless was not working. They were the only two which could fly today.

Meanwhile the Red Army was working tirelessly. The bomb craters had already been plugged with sand and covered with steel matting. It was a curious race against time. It was only a three-hour flight to Moscow, but the ack-ack gunners there have orders to fire on any unidentified plane approaching after seven o'clock. Since all of our communications with the outside world were still down, Moscow didn't know what had happened at our base nor could we tell them we were coming.

However, if we tried to hurry the Russian mine sweepers, it was possible that our plane in the take-off might veer a few yards off the runway into a butterfly. With a full load of correspondents and 100-octane gas, we were not anxious for that.

Waiting with us were four boys of the Eighth Air Force who were also to go. Some time ago it had been arranged that they should broadcast the story of their flight across Germany to America from Moscow. They were looking very glum. Now much has been written of the feelings of a pilot who loses a beloved plane and some of it by me, so I thought I knew why and tactfully brought it up.

"Hell, no," said the second lieutenant, "they can make more of those. But when do we get home?"

"What do you mean?"

"Some of us have almost finished our fifty missions," said the second lieutenant.

"And after getting mixed up in a big stinkeroo like last night," said another, "they'd be afraid some guy would tell what happened at some Rotary lunch."

"After what we saw last night, I bet they keep us in the army until we're thirty," said the second lieutenant gloomily. I can truthfully assure the boys they are wrong; our army doesn't work like that.

Now the Red Army reports the runway is clear, they start warming the Liberators' motors, they count us. But where is our Russian conducting officer? No one has seen him all day. Ever since the bomb blew out the windows of the Pullman car last night we have been capitalist sheep without our Soviet shepherd.

But all of a sudden, just as we are climbing aboard to test the thoroughness with which that runway has been swept, Mr. Okhov arrives, still pink and white, still immaculate in the long, tubular sky-blue Foreign Office overcoat. In his arms he carefully holds a wilted little bouquet of field flowers, which we recognize as the one which the pretty Red Army girl yesterday presented to the Eighth Air Force pilots.

In war this country has little time to raise flowers but it loves them no less for that. Mr. Okhov undoubtedly has a wife or a sweetheart in Moscow. Nothing is wasted in the Soviet Union.

As a Postlude to the raid, I should here chronicle the fact that within a week Marshal Stalin promised us permission to bring in for the protection of these American air bases our own gun crews, our own night fighters, our radar and other detectional apparatus.

This request had previously been made both when the air bases were first established and immediately after the raid—but underlings had turned it down because it would have meant increasing the number of Americans allowed at the bases.

Ten

O̲N̲ ̲O̲U̲R̲ return from Leningrad, Eric had asked to talk to the head of the Soviet labor movement. He knows the top American labor leaders, gets along smoothly with the unions in his Washington plants, and like me, was curious to see how free labor is over here.

We talked to four of them—one a woman about sixty, in charge of building new housing for workers—but the head of the whole thing was a very smart man of forty-three called Kuznetsov. He was really keen. He'd lived in America, graduated from Carnegie Institute of Technology with a master's degree in metallurgy, and if you tried to point out that his labor movement here wasn't really free, he'd come right back at you with some American example trying to prove that ours was even less free.

Their set-up as he outlined it goes like this. All Soviet unions —representing 22,000,000 workers—send delegates to the All-Union Trades Congress. This he says usually meets every year or so but hasn't met for the last three due to the war.

This meeting corresponds to our AF of L and CIO national conventions rolled into one. It's strictly labor—no soldiers or farmers are in it. This big Congress elects fifty-five of its members to something they call the Plenum. These fifty-five elect eighteen to something called the Presidium. And these eighteen have elected him its secretary, which makes him head of the workers.

We asked him if all the workers belonged to trade unions, and he said at least 90 or 95 per cent. So we asked him who didn't belong.

"Well," he said, "some apprentices are too young, and then in the reoccupied regions, it takes a little time to convince all workers they should belong."

We asked him what the dues were, and he said 1 per cent of a worker's salary. There is no initiation fee, except that they sell you a book which costs only one rouble.

"Now, is this a perfectly free union movement," we asked him, "or is it directed by your government?"

It was perfectly free, he assured us. Of course, he said, anyone they elect to their Congress must be approved by the government, but we could see he considered this a very minor detail. It occurred to me that in America, if some carpenter's local couldn't send a delegate to their state or national labor convention unless the government approved him, our unions certainly wouldn't consider this a minor detail—but let that go.

We tried another tack. "Are you a member of the Communist Party?" we asked him; he said he was. "And the members of your staff?" He nodded. "Any that are not?" No, they all were members. Well, since the factory managers are all Communists too, and since the Communist Party controls both under very strict discipline, we felt that would leave very little to argue about between labor and management. So we said, "What do the trade unions discuss?"

"Working conditions in the factories, social insurance, housing, vacations, and things like that," he answered.

"Do they talk about wages?"

"Yes," he said, "particularly the pay for piecework. Most of these rates have been set during the war. Since we had no previous experience, sometimes the rates were set too high or too low. The factory bargaining committees discuss these with the management."

"But if they can't agree, what then?"

He insisted they practically always agreed. But if they didn't, they could appeal up to the Plenum or even to the Presidium, who could talk the dispute over with the vice-commissar who managed that particular trust. In that way, he said, amicable agreements always are arrived at.

"Always? Aren't there ever strikes?"

"Yes," he said, "in 1919 a strike in one steel mill lasted two days. And in 1923 there was another little strike in western Russia. We were changing over from the old czarist money to Soviet roubles, and it took time to get it all printed and out to the workers. As soon as the situation was explained to them, they went back to work. There have been no strikes since, and in the future there won't be any because our workers understand they are all working for each other."

"If a worker is discontented and gets discharged for any reason, would it be difficult for him to get a job some place else?"

"Very, very difficult," said Kuznetsov.

"Well, isn't this what the workers in America call an employers' blacklist?"

"No," said Kuznetsov. But he didn't say why it wasn't.

"Do you have any absenteeism?"

"We simply don't have it without reason."

"But aren't workers sometimes a little late?"

"Occasionally," he said. "The first time he is warned. The second time he may be fined. If it happens again, he is discharged. If a worker fails to co-operate, damages too much material or does anything else which we consider serious, he may be arrested and tried before a judge, and if he is unable to prove his innocence, sentenced to a number of years' penal labor. The rules in the factories are very strict and rigidly enforced." That gave us a clear idea of how they handle absenteeism and carelessness. And, apparently, the union officials encourage the workers to testify against a man guilty of these offenses—maybe they themselves bring charges against him. But we had other questions.

"Is joining the trade union in any plant voluntary or compulsory?"

"Completely voluntary," Kuznetsov said.

"How do you account then, for the fact that practically everyone who is eligible joins?"

"It is to their advantage in any country, and particularly in the Soviet Union, where the Trade Union Movement offers many benefits. Here a union member receives greater sick benefits than a non-union member. There is a housing shortage here and most factories own apartment houses which they rent to the workers. Union members receive first consideration. A non-union member would have trouble finding a place to sleep at night. He wouldn't have access to the factory recreation center, where they have dancing, games, movies and meetings.

"All workers are entitled to vacation with pay, but non-union members cannot spend their vacations in the rest centers maintained for workers. If a worker is sick, the physician may recommend an extra week's vacation, and he can go to a special type of rest center equipped to care for invalids. But non-union members are not eligible." We could see now why they joined almost 100 per cent and wouldn't need a check-off, either.

"Then, if a worker is dissatisfied with his job, can he quit and go somewhere else?"

"He may put in a request," said Kuznetsov, "but the decision will be up to the plant management. The head of the plant is a far better judge of a worker's qualifications than he is himself. So we don't have your 'migration of workers' except as we need it to increase production or evacuate plants because of the war."

"Will this continue after the war?"

"Why change?" he said. "We must all work where we are needed, to further the progress of the Soviet Union." That settled that.

"What per cent of an employee's salary goes for rent in these factory-owned apartments?"

"Usually about 6 per cent," he said. "Young apprentices live in rent-free dormitories. Older workers may live in them too, but they pay. Skilled workers, or those who exceed their norms, are entitled to better quarters. Because their pay is more, their rent is proportionately higher."

"What relations do you have with American labor?"

"None at all with the AF of L," he said. "We're very much disappointed. Also, their representative, Mr. Watt, criticized our Russian Trade Union Movement at the last meeting of the International Labor Organization in Philadelphia. He claimed we were not a free movement. You can see that we are. I don't understand why your government would permit this criticism of our trade unions."

"Well, you understand America, Mr. Kuznetsov, you've lived there. Our people have freedom of speech."

"Yes," he said, "but Russia is your ally. I can't understand why your government would permit it, and we simply don't understand the AF of L. It probably isn't the workers, but only the leaders who have these distorted notions. Here we are sure that your workers really want to co-operate with ours, only the leaders won't permit it. We do have some relations with the CIO—letters from Mr. Murray and several others. It is more sympathetic, and desires to co-operate, and more nearly understands the true position of workers in America and workers here. We hope some day we can co-operate with the American labor movement. After all, we are working for the same cause."

We thanked him for giving us this information and as we got up to go he said to Eric, "You are the first American businessman who has ever taken the trouble to call on me, and I want you to know I appreciate it. I know it is unusual for a capitalist employer to call on the head of the labor movement in a Communist country. And we want you in America to understand our trade unions and realize that it is a free movement here. I am highly honored that you should want to talk to me and I shall never forget your kindness in coming."

He seemed to mean every word of it. I don't know that I can agree with him, but I thought he was highly intelligent and completely sincere. From the Communist standpoint, I suppose their labor is free.

This evening I have a long talk with Jennie, our Intourist interpreter. To while away the days which we wait to see Stalin, they schedule another theater party for us. Eric has a slight cold and declines, so Joyce and I do the honors. Afterward Joyce, according to protocol, is taken home first and then I am dropped at the Metropole, where Jennie also gets out. She doesn't live at the hotel, which is operated by Intourist but in one of a tier of rooms behind it.

Since we leave Moscow soon, we won't see Jennie again, for another interpreter has been assigned to us for the Urals trip. So I ask her if she would like to walk across the square to the Moskva for a bite of supper before we go to bed. The government has recently opened its dining room as a night club—the only one in Moscow. Here prices compare with those in its new commercial stores.

I apologize to Jennie because I have only 600 roubles—at our cheap diplomatic rate of exchange this is $48—but she says that as an Intourist employee she gets a slight discount, and we should be able to get something for that.

The Moskva's dining room looks like Cleveland's Union Station if you put tables in the main concourse with napkins and cloths that had previously done a week's service in Billy's Okay Highway Lunch Wagon. It is crowded. The Red Army (which gets a 50 per cent discount) is there with its girls, all of whom are dressed in pathetic finery—handmade from old remnants, and ornamented with ribbon and ends of lace from the back of the top bureau drawer.

There are also farmers in to spend their free-market butter and egg money with their shapeless peasant wives who wear grisly calico and heavy work shoes. There is an orchestra and a central space for dancing. About one-third of the men are without ties but all wear coats. A recent culture drive proclaimed that it is an offense against People's Culture not to wear a coat in public. I wonder what they think of our neatly dressed army, in which blouses are not regulation for summer wear?

Jennie calls the waiter, we show him my 600 roubles and pose the problem. Since I am a foreigner, he is most co-operative. He brings us each a small serving of caviar and potato on a wilted leaf of lettuce, some gray bread and two bottles of beer. When we have finished these, there are two demi-tasses and the total is exactly $48 in our money.

It is little enough but having been gorged by Intourist, I am not hungry, and it is the least we can order as an excuse to watch the crowd. The orchestra proclaims itself a jazz band, and obliges with "Alexander's Ragtime Band." The sergeants and enlisted men are extremely acrobatic dancers and the officers wear their revolvers even on the floor.

I had been in Russia for several weeks, taking the impact of a system in every way alien to ours, smiling, being polite, saying what was appropriate and kind rather than what I thought, and I suppose this was why I presently began to unload on poor Jennie, who after all was only a nice girl, doing her job.

It started with some remark of mine about what a pity it was she couldn't travel abroad, because if she ever came to America, I would like to show her a night club there.

She said she supposed they were much finer. But that in peacetime a different class of people came to the Moskva. The peasant women in work shoes and the athletic dancers without ties were war phenomena. And I must remember that most Russians considered these war prices as high as I did—that only a few could afford to come.

"I suppose you are used to foreigners who try to tell you how much better things are in their own countries?"

"Even the Mohammedans," she said. "They try to propagandize me to become a Moslem. It is always the same."

"Because you've never been out, you don't understand why all foreigners do it. I wouldn't expect you to believe that your standard of living here is less than was that of our poorest on WPA."

"America, perhaps, yes. But it is not true of other countries. Our boys have told me that when our army goes into Rumania, the people there have welcomed them." Then she paused and went on a little defiantly. "Not the rich," she said, "not the upper classes—but the majority."

"Rumania is the most squalid country in Europe."

"But the majority welcomed us," she persisted. "Not the bourgeois, of course—"

"What about the Baltic States? Did they welcome you there?"

She stopped a minute. "But some Americans are glad to become Soviet citizens. I have talked with American comrades who have told me how delighted they are to be in a land where there is work for all. Many foreigners have become Soviet citizens."

"Do you know how many of them later went to their embassies to try to get their old citizenship back?"

"If there are many who do that, it is because foreigners cannot endure the hardships of Russians. You must remember that during the Revolution, everything was pulled down—all, all. I know myself that world that was destroyed—everything, so we must begin fresh. And have you ever read *Martin Chuzzlewit*, by Charles Dickens? He visited America when your country was young like Russia. He talks of America then as foreigners now talk of Russia —he says the people are crude, that they have no manners—"

"Have I complained of those things in Russia?"

"Perhaps not you, but others. And Dickens says America is all barbarous and slovenly, and that in America no trains are ever on time. You have read *Martin Chuzzlewit?* Then you should do so again when you are home. It will help you to understand Russia."

"Did Dickens ever complain that America was not free?"

"No," said Jennie slowly, "he did not say that."

"I have never objected to Russian manners. Did he ever say that in America people were not free to say what they thought and go where they liked and do what they chose? Of course, we were once a frontier people. But we have become great because we were free. And did Dickens complain he was not allowed to meet the people? Here you entertain us lavishly but we feel cut off from the country."

"But Russia has needed to be careful of foreigners," said Jennie, "because we never know when they will be on the other side."

"But it is not America which changes," I pointed out, "it is Russia which is first against Fascism and then allied with it and now against it. And did Dickens say that in America he saw always the same statues of always the same leaders? Did he say we had this idol worship in America?"

"But it is not our leaders who want such statues. The people themselves insist."

"Our people like their leaders as much as you like yours. But in all America I have never seen a statue of Roosevelt."

"But our people are grateful—to our leaders and to the system. Foreigners will never understand. It is because they are opposed to our system."

"I am not. If I were as patriotic an American as you are a Russian, I should start in America a Society to Keep Communism in Russia. If I were so patriotic I would say, 'So long as they have this system, in spite of their great country and fine people, they can never overtake our free system.' "

"But many of you like our system. And not only the American comrades I spoke of. When I was in Murmansk, British sailors tell me they would rather be in the Russian navy than in theirs. They do not like that they must salute their officers, and eat at separate tables."

"But since then it is changed, isn't it? Now your men also salute and eat separately, don't they?"

"It is still more equal. Even if what you say could be true, that ours is not so efficient, I would not like yours. Because," she said proudly, "my dress may not be so good as an American dress, but at least I know that no other Russian woman has a better dress! Under capitalism a woman is a parasite. All day they do nothing, or else play card games with each other. I would rather work than do that."

"So would our women. Most of them do. In our factories we have almost as many as you. If they do not work as hard in their homes, it is because their houses are better and they do not need to. And when you say no woman should have a better dress than yours, then I would answer that your system is founded only on jealousy. In America many people have better clothes than I and live in finer houses. But I am not so jealous that I would pull down a system which gives me good things just because it gives someone else something better. In America we are not so envious. Here, there are more differences between rich and poor than in America."

Then, Jennie said, of course there had been many changes in the Soviet Union, some which surprised even Russians, but that I should not argue with her for she knew little; I should talk with those who had more training and they would quickly answer the things I said.

I knew I had been foolish, overbearing and ill-mannered in talking like this and tried to apologize.

"Only do not talk as the Germans did," said Jennie. "They would say patronizingly, 'Communism is the best system—for Russia.' They try only to be polite but it makes me very angry."

Meanwhile the correspondents are seething. As soon as Eric sees Stalin, we are to start our trip across the Urals, into Siberia and then down into Turkestan, visiting cities which no American has been allowed to write about since the Revolution.

Several want to go along and Eric, who thinks Americans should know more of Russia, wants to take them. The Commissariat of Foreign Trade, which has charge of our trip, is willing (or tells us it is) but adds that they must get permission from the Foreign Office, which has charge of the movement of all correspondents.

And the Foreign Office suddenly says no. Why? Because, obviously, since we cannot take the entire foreign press with us by plane, the others would be jealous.

But the reporters who have been *invited* have an answer to that. They circulate among the others a pledge not to be jealous if the invited reporters are allowed to go on our trip. Although a few hesitate, finally they all sign and this document is triumphantly presented to their sinister enemy, Petrov.

The answer? Again no. Again why? Just no. The correspondents explode with rage. "Gentlemen, I must remind you that you are in the Soviet Union."

In anguish they come to Eric. Everybody is willing but Petrov. There is one man in Russia who can overrule the Foreign Office. When Eric sees Stalin tonight, will he ask permission to take them along? Eric ponders it. In all probability Molotov, head of the Foreign Office, will be there. And they can be sure Molotov knows that Petrov has refused.

Still, the correspondents insist, will he ask Stalin?

Eric says he is anxious to do so.

His appointment is set for nine o'clock at night, which is the hour that important Russian officials begin their business day. They work on until four or five o'clock in the morning and then sleep until noon.

How long will it last? The ambassador says that depends on

whether Stalin is interested. Maybe they will be out in a few minutes. With luck, they may stay an hour. Better count on half an
hour.

In point of fact the interview went off beautifully,* but the
big news for the reporters, when Eric returned at midnight, was that
Stalin himself had said they could accompany us. They had all been
waiting nervously, the "Field Marshal," who represented his syndicate, having decked himself out in his neatest correspondent's uniform for the occasion. Now they rushed jubilantly to the Metropole
to pack, as we were scheduled to leave at six o'clock. When we got
to the airport, we found Stalin's orders had gone thundering down
through the bureaucracy and there were on the field two planes instead of one.

Ours was a DC-3—a Russian-built plush job which made American versions look squalid. It had white silk curtains at the windows,
no safety belts (Russians don't believe in them), a strip of red
oriental carpet down the aisle. American DC-3's have a row of
double seats down one side and single seats down the other. This
had only single seats. Apparently, it carries fewer, more important
passengers, giving them plenty of leg-room.

Also with us were the patient Kirilov and Nesterov, president of
the All-Union Chamber of Commerce. What this body does I
never actually found out, but Mr. Nesterov was a most important
official in the Commissariat of Foreign Trade, a Communist from
boyhood and high in the Party. In dress and manner he constantly
reminded me of the late Andrew Mellon. He was quiet, perhaps a
little shy, and most intelligent. In addition there was a figure we
had come to know as "Nick." Presumably Nick spoke no English.
At least he spoke none to us. But he had always been a part of our
group in Moscow and Leningrad, eating obscurely at the ends of
banquet tables and traveling silently in the front seat of the car
when we moved. The reporters identified him as the NKVD
man. In America a plainclothes man is frequently assigned to dis-

* Eric Johnston has written his account of that interview in "My Talk
with Stalin," in the *Reader's Digest*, October, 1944.

tinguished visitors as a courtesy. Nick seemed to have charge not only of us, but of any Russians who had contact with us. Finally, we had as steward one of the two Intourist waiters who had always served us at banquets. We had hoped all this was behind us but ten minutes after we were in the air, he was climbing up the aisle, offering plates, caviar, and champagne.

The reporters also rode in a DC-3 but in an uncushioned bucket-seat job. With them was a hated censor from the Foreign Office, a wistful young Russian called Zemenkov whom they spent their time avoiding. Since he had never slashed any of my copy, I could approach the subject of Zemenkov with a detachment which irritated the other correspondents. I was to find he had a keen sense of the ridiculous and was good company. The others regarded me as a traitor to journalistic freedom. However, they were so overjoyed at having confounded Petrov that occasionally they could tolerate the lowly Zemenkov.

Until we reach the Urals, which divide Russia-in-Europe from Russia-in-Asia, the country we fly over is exactly as it was up from Teheran—the same thatched villages dominated by white churches with red-painted onion domes. We crossed the Urals, which are, in this area, not mountains in our Rocky Mountain sense, but low, rolling hills, wooded with birch, oak, elm, maple, but no pine.

In a valley not far beyond them is Magnitogorsk, the Pittsburgh of the Soviet Union, its huge blast furnaces vomiting smoke. As we come in for a landing we glimpse the usual patchwork quilt of workers' potato plots. We learn that this is no wartime phenomenon, although of course the gardens are now more numerous.

At this airport, as at all the others we are to touch, we are met by the local dignitaries and important Communists—the mayor of the town, the director of the steel plant and the Party secretary for the province—all grave, cap-wearing Russians, well-dressed by Communist standards. Zeeses take us across the city to the house of the plant director, where we will spend the night. To reach it we drive through teeming, unpainted slums which are worse than those of Pittsburgh although we keep in mind that Magnitogorsk is crowded because many industries have been evacuated here. Finally, we leave the slums and the road goes up a hill upon which, overlooking the slums and the blast furnaces, are the spacious homes of the executives—even as it is in Pittsburgh. We come into a paved residential street with gutters, sidewalks, and big yards. Except for architectural differences, we might be in Forest Hills, New York, or Rochester, Minnesota's "Pill Hill."

Our cars turn into one of the cement driveways. The big house is new and spacious, and the bathroom is, thank God, clean and in repair, as things usually are in Russia when the comfort of some reasonably important individual depends on them.

This is the first time we have been in a Russian home. It has hardwood parquet floors, and on the big mantel are busts of Marx and Engels. The furniture is dark, heavily varnished wood and seems to have been bought in a suite. The central piece is an elaborate settee with a plate-glass back.

In the dining room a long table is spread with cold mutton, jellied pork, sausages, and, of course, vodka and wine—but we seem to have left the champagne belt.

Now we get a closer look at the director, who runs these great steel mills. He is Gregor Nesov, a tall, stocky Russian, very much the engineer type, and only thirty-five. He tells us his father was a blacksmith in the Urals. We remark that he has a fine house but he explains he and his family occupy only the top floor, the ground floor being used for such ceremonious occasions as this.

Out in the wide garden we see three children playing with a bicycle: two boys and a girl evenly spaced between eight and fourteen. They are well-dressed and carefully scrubbed for this occasion. They are obviously curious about us but they stay in their part of the garden and self-consciously avoid looking at us.

When we sit down to dinner, an elderly woman in a white apron, standing beside the table, directs the two plump servant girls. We assume she is Nesov's wife and Eric, through the interpreter, passes her several compliments on the meal. But we are wrong; she is some sort of professional cateress. Mrs. Nesov never appears but later, butting into the near-by kitchen for a drink of water, I spot her—a pretty and well-dressed woman in her early thirties, running the show from behind the scenes. Although she is poised and most presentable, and although we eat several meals and spend a night there and frequently pass her in the hall, none of us is ever introduced.

At luncheon, Nesov tells us about Magnitogorsk. The town was started in 1916. There are now 45,000 workers in his plant, of whom 25,000 are construction workers, for it is expanding. Twenty open-hearth furnaces and six blast furnaces are operating, two of which were opened during the war.

The mountain which they mine contains an estimated 300,000,000 tons of ore which is 60 per cent iron, and another 85,000,000 tons which will run from 50 to 45 per cent—quite a stock pile! Eric tells me that we have only about 100,000,000 tons left at Hibbing, and are using these up at a wartime rate of 27,000,000 tons a year.

After lunch we drive back down the hill to the big steel plant. There are many workers on the road as this is apparently a change of shifts. I am riding with a correspondent.

Suddenly our car turns out to one side as we overtake a long column marching four abreast, on its way to work at the plant. Two things are remarkable about it. The first thing is that, marching ahead of it, behind it and on both sides, are military guards carrying rifles with fixed bayonets. The second thing is that the column itself consists of ragged women in makeshift sandals, who glance furtively at our cars.

The correspondent nudges me. Nick, the NKVD man, is riding in the front seat.

"Hey, Bill."

"Yeauh."

"Did you see what I saw?"

"Yeauh."

Every writer who approaches even a minor theme is confronted first with the problem of selection of material, and secondly with the decisions as to which incidents shall be expanded, and which he should merely chronicle, and the foregoing is a case in point.

I don't know how those women got there or where they were

going, so I leave them as material for some mightier talent with greater imaginative powers.

Entering the blast furnace section, the fumes almost choke us. We stumble along for miles through piles of slag, across precarious bridges over molten metal. The white heat of boiling steel pinches our faces. Amid the din, the director bellows two noteworthy statistics at us; the first, that on a 1,200,000,000 rouble business this year, he hopes to clear a 50,000,000 rouble profit. Secondly, that in this inferno, they have per month only eight injuries per 10,000 employees.

By any standard it is not a tidy plant. If the floors were ever concrete they have now been worn to gravel. Huge rusting chains and all kinds of bulky metal rubbish lie around. However, all six of the blast furnaces as well as the open hearth ones seem to be working furiously, turning out their 7½ tons of steel daily. This is processed into everything imaginable from tank armor down to wire.

The armament factory takes the prize for the most sloppily organized shop we have seen in the Soviet Union. Stockingless girls with crude sandals, lathing shells for the Red Army, stand on heaps of curled metal scrap from their machines. Occasionally they are protected from its sharp edges by crude duckboards.

Some attempt is being made to remove the scrap. We see two girls carrying out a load of it on a Russian wheelbarrow, which is a kind of homemade litter, with one pair of wooden handles in front and one behind. It carries a modest wheelbarrow-load but requires two people. They stumble along with it through the rubbish.

We watch them milling shells for the Red Army. There is no assembly belt but at one point they have devised a substitute. When one operation is finished, a shell is placed on a long, inclined rack, down which it rolls into the next room for the next operation. Only the rack is badly made and now and then a shell falls off. Instead of adjusting the rack, a girl is stationed by it to pick up the shells and put them back on straight. This may or may not be a waste of labor in this country where they have plenty of stout-backed girls, but a shortage of people with the know-how to build a proper rack.

We wonder how much politics has to do with the scarcity of skilled brains here. Suppose the Democratic party was limited to 4,000,000 members, and that no man could hold a responsible job whose loyalty to the secretary of its National Committee was in any way questioned? Many good men might have to be discarded because they were not politically sound.

Now we go through a brick plant, and here Eric is in his element, for he makes brick in his Spokane plant. After inspecting the product and the production line, he asks them how many workers they employ, and how many bricks they make per month. Then he figures on my reporter's pad and tells them that his plant, by using a different kiln system, turns out exactly three times as many bricks per worker. They have nothing remotely like it here; we watch the women laboriously moving bricks by hand after each processing operation. They have a great respect for our technique and tell Eric of their hope to install improved machinery. As we are leaving the plant, we see another long column of women marching under guard.

Back at the director's house we get a home-cooked dinner. The cold potato soup has a chicken stock base. Rice and meat follow.

Later we go to a theater which is new, attractive, and, of course, crowded, and here witness a fine Soviet soap opera having to do with difficulties between a king and queen which in the end are resolved to the satisfaction of all parties. The costumes and scenery are good, and the acting is spirited.

A few hours on the plane brings us to Sverdlovsk, before the revolution called Ekaterinburg because it was founded by Catherine the Great. It was here in a cellar that the hard-headed Bolsheviks shot weak-willed, well-meaning Czar Nicholas II, his wife and family, later changing the name of the town. Sverdlovsk is another Soviet Pittsburgh, bustling with a million people. This time we are quartered in a hotel near the town's central square.

The hotel makes me feel at home. It is exactly the kind of structure that we built in the 'eighties and 'nineties—high ceilinged, with tall, narrow windows, pretentious, of course, yet also airy. I remember several like it in little Kansas towns in which we used to spend the nights driving to our summer place in Colorado almost thirty years ago. They had been built on borrowed money in the days of the great land boom when every prairie village was sure it would be a city. And they stood dilapidated in those treeless dust-bowl towns.

In this, as in the others, the electric wiring was installed later, and the wires go up the sides of the walls and across the ceiling to the fixture. But then I get a big surprise for they tell me this hotel was built, not in the 'eighties, but in 1931 under one of the five-year plans. This open wiring is modern Soviet construction. I had thought that the cracked plaster came with age; this building, already falling apart, is not fifteen years old. Now a look at a typical Soviet bathroom. The toilet is of that ancient design where you pull a chain. I notice that the pipes were installed after the concrete had set. This is done by knocking a gaping hole in it with a cold chisel and hammer, pulling the pipe up through the hole, and then filling it in by dumping a little rubble and wet cement, leaving an uneven place around the pipe to catch dirt. Why, in 1931, they didn't set the plumbing before they poured the concrete, and wire the building before they plastered the rooms, is a Soviet construction mystery.

Probably the contract-pouring trust wanted to set a speed record and win itself a red banner, so it didn't wait for the plumbers.

In this typical Soviet bathroom, there is no hot water, nor in the basin is there a place where hot water can be installed. There is a single faucet of brass, set in the exact center. Hot water is not even a dim dream for the future.

By the toilet, here as always in Russia, sets what appears to be a covered wooden wastebasket. This is for used toilet paper, which cannot be flushed down with the other waste because *Pravda* and *Izvestia* would clog the line. About once every week or so, after the contents of this basket are thoroughly ripe, somebody usually comes around to empty it and burn the used paper.

Now we start out to inspect the plants. Sverdlovsk is the Soviet center for the manufacture of heavy machine tools. In one big shop we see a gigantic drop forge, made in Duisburg, Germany. I can well believe that there are only four like it in the world. It can apply pressure of 10,000 tons and we watch them pounding into shape a huge piece of white hot metal which will become the roller for a mill. There is near by a row of relatively tiny drop forges fashioning crank shafts for tank motors.

But the plant itself is the same old Soviet story we have so far seen—no light, dirty, bad floors, and in this one the roof leaks. Outside there is a summer shower and we watch the water pour down from the high ceiling onto the hot steel and get soaked ourselves as we walk through. But we notice they have mended the roof over the most important machines.

Now we start down a tank assembly line, and at the point where they are welding the frames, I drop back from the party and ask an old man who is a welder's helper where I can get a drink of water. Almost never do you see a drinking fountain in a Soviet plant. He starts to lead me toward a room which from its smell I recognize as a toilet, but thinks better of this and bids me wait. In about ten minutes he returns with a glass, and a bottle of carbonated water which obviously came from the director's room. Nothing less would do for a guest. The kindness of the people is touching.

I go down the assembly line to catch up with the others. The welding on the turrets is ragged and would never pass American inspection, but it is probably just as tough in battle. When we get to the end they have a tank ready to roll, and as we come abreast, it lumbers into the courtyard with an impressive rumble.

Now we go into the heavy artillery assembly room, which seems to be the busiest and the most efficient part of the entire Sverdlovsk plant, and hence on into the director's office where they tell us about what we have seen.

They were making a 48-ton tank and a 122-mm. gun. Before the war Sverdlovsk turned out every year 30,000 tons of machine tools. They have here both blast and open-hearth furnaces, plus power hammers, punching equipment and presses, and they have produced several 10,000-ton pressure presses for aviation plywood. Normally, they also make mine elevators, excavators and steam shovels.

Now their production is largely foundry parts for artillery. At the same time they are turning out steel castings to rebuild industries in the reoccupied areas. But in the picture is also much heavy machinery for plants such as Magnitogorsk and Chelyabinsk.

Since the war the production of Sverdlovsk, measured in roubles, has jumped almost sevenfold—from about 300,000,000 roubles to more than 2,000,000,000. They are turning out six times the number of heavy guns they made in 1941, and the fire power of the new ones is much greater. But since they had 6,000 workers in the artillery division before the war and 10,000 now, the efficiency has increased far more than the production.

Before the war only 15 per cent of their workers were women. Now more than half are. Another 5 per cent are discharged war invalids, and the average worker's age is thirty years.

Johnston asks why only young men are ever directors of such plants, and is told that older men are promoted to more important jobs—that they are heads of entire industries and cartels. Apparently, the Tom Girdlers and Eugene Graces of the Soviet Union are back in the Kremlin; and it should not be forgotten that in 1937 the veteran executives of entire industries were purged, thus giving these young men quick promotion.

Across the street from our five-year-plan hotel is the marble opera house. It is a little too ornate, but Russians like it that way. It seems to be the most substantial and carefully built structure in town. I inquire and find it is the provincial opera house, built in 1903 under the Czar.

We attend and the correspondents are eager, because maybe they will see Katya. Who is she? Once she was a ballet dancer at the great Bolshoi Theater in Moscow, but she got too friendly with a foreigner and last year was sent out here to Sverdlovsk in Siberia. The Sverdlovsk ballet is very good, but the boys don't recognize their old friend, Katya, and they don't go backstage to inquire where she is tonight. The NKVD probably wouldn't approve of half a dozen capitalist stage-door-Johnnies and it wouldn't help Katya.

Our Red Army pilot has us terrified. Yesterday we thought it was an accident but today, en route to Omsk, he did the same thing. Before you board an American air liner, they warm the motors so there can be no faltering on the take-off which could send the plane crashing into a fence. Then the passengers get aboard and buckle their seat belts. The plane makes its run, is airborne, and continues in a straight line until it has 500 or 1,000 feet of altitude, before the pilot attempts even so mildly risky a thing as the turn which puts him on his course. When he does turn, it is an almost imperceptible swing. Then he climbs to about 5,000 or 6,000 feet which gives him time to pick a safe landing spot in case anything happened.

Soviet air lines' procedure is as follows. You get aboard. There are no seat belts. There is no sign warning against smoking; if you prefer to burn alive in a take-off crash, that is a matter of personal conscience and no concern of the crew. Once the door slams shut the pilot starts the motors which have been cold since the night before. If they run at all he releases the brakes, guns the plane on down the runway. You gather speed and clear the runway by maybe ten feet. At this instant the pilot makes his turn by the process of tilting one wing up toward the zenith and the other down until its tip is digging potatoes on the adjoining farm. Once pointed on his course he levels off and if there are no mountains, he continues at this altitude of from 50 to 100 feet, scaring Kolhoz cows, Sovhoz chickens, and the passengers.

We recall that when this procedure left American pilots wide-eyed, the Red Air Force would ask them, "What's the matter, are you afraid to die?"

"The answer for me is 'yes,' " says Joyce. "Now if I had to live in Russia, I might feel differently."

The country below us is changing. It is dotted with lakes as round as pancakes, which look as tough as though they were craters made by a bombardment of giant meteors, they are so regular. These are fringed with pine forests but we are so far north that even this growth is sometimes scant, like timberline trees in the mountains.

At Omsk the delegation of dignitaries shakes hands with us as we step off the plane and tells us that our bags will be left at the airport, where we will spend the night. We inspect our rooms. They are spacious, yes. Clean, yes. But— Well, not a single but. The building is excellent, modern, simple and in good repair. Furthermore, it seems substantially constructed in contrast to the claptrap jobs we have seen. Joyce and I will share a bedroom with big French windows, and a sitting room.

Now off to the factory, but first the director. He is Constantin Zadarochni, forty-seven years old. His father was a carpenter, his mother a laundress. Before the war the Omsk plant had only 3,000 workers, and repaired locomotives. Now 15,000 make tanks. Zadarochni was formerly director of the Stalingrad Tractor Factory. Omsk before the war had a population of 320,000 and now has 514,000—evacuated workers, of course.

Eric goes into business figures. The director says that last year the plant did a business of 375,000,000 roubles but took a 7,000,000 rouble loss, caused, he says, by the expenses of capital investment. Apparently, there was no operating loss. But, he says, last April (1944) they got out of the red and will continue so the rest of the year. As sidelines the plant makes engines for fighter planes and optical equipment for the army.

We inspect the Mayor of Omsk—Kishemelev Kuzma. He is forty-four, and this is his second year in office. Before that he was Director of Automobile Highways, a title which is confusing to us, since the Soviet Union has few passenger cars and almost no highways.

We ask him how he got elected and he answers promptly that the people did it.

But how?

Kuzma goes into detail. There were in all five candidates, each representing one of the various trade unions. Everybody in Omsk could vote, he says, and of course the ballot was secret.

Is he a member of the Party?

Oh, yes.

Who were the other candidates and what were their platforms?

One represented the organized white-collar workers, and the other three represented unions in the Machine-Building Trades. He explains proudly that he led the field with 28 per cent more votes than the others combined.

Was he the only Communist Party member running?

No—there was one other.

And did this man run second?

By a coincidence, he did.

Well, just how does Kuzma explain his handsome majority?

That's simple—it was due to the discipline and authority of the Communist Party. He was its official candidate, endorsed by the Party organization. In addition he is a veteran of the civil wars of 1917. He has two orders and one medal—here he points to the ribbons on his chest.

Then we ask if, in any Russian city, any non-Party member has ever been elected mayor.

He thinks a minute. Then he says he doesn't know of any big city, but he has heard that occasionally in the villages men who were not Party members have been chosen mayor.

What we should have asked, but didn't, is whether in any town, large or small, any candidate endorsed by the Party has ever been beaten by someone it opposed.

How free can an election be when one party controls the press and the radio? I am sure they go through the forms of a secret ballot and an honest count. But if any candidate should attack his Communist opponent vigorously he runs the risk of being arrested by the NKVD as a political offender and hustled off to the salt mines in the middle of his campaign. Is the Party only letting the people play with the forms of democracy? Never having known anything else, they think they have the real thing.

We now inspect the factory where they are turning out eight

tanks a day. Sixty-five are on the floor as we go through—36-ton models mounting a little 45-mm. gun. On the whole the plant looks clean—well above the average of what we have so far seen in Russia.

A remarkable thing which I cannot explain but only chronicle: as we leave Moscow there seems to be a definite improvement in plant efficiency and also in girls. Their skins are better. The breed hasn't changed. But there is a definite sprinkling of pretty ones on the assembly line of this factory. Maybe it is vitamins or more sunshine. Whatever the reason, we all agree on the result.

A curious thing happened to me. Omsk boasted a very attractive female Tass correspondent who was covering our trip for the local press. I rode with her in a Zees from the airport to the plant, and since she spoke a little German, we got along well. She was about twenty-five, pretty, simply dressed, lively, and most intelligent. I was trying to find out something about Russian newspapers and she was making me promise to corral Eric for an interview. In the plant we were walking together, she translating for me ahead of the interpreter. It was all going well until I left her for a minute to speak to Eric. When I turned back, I saw that Zemenkov, our Foreign Office man, and Nick, the NKVD plainclothes man, had each grabbed her by an elbow and were hustling her along, lecturing her angrily.

Now there are so many possible offenses in this country that it did not then occur to me to wonder which one she had committed. I regarded it as an intra-party matter into which no tactful foreigner should intrude. Presently, they dropped her elbows and after a discreet interval, I walked up beside her, picking up the conversation where we had left it.

But she would neither answer nor look at me. After a couple of trials I fell back, trying to think what I could have said that offended her. Only she didn't seem offended. It was at least fifteen minutes before it occurred to me to wonder what Zemenkov and Nick had said. Then I discovered the correspondents laughing at me. They had seen the whole thing.

"Didn't you know? Hadn't anybody told you? You didn't think they'd let you talk to the people, did you?"

I was annoyed and decided to stop this foolishness. Up to now I had been able to view the Soviet Foreign Office with some detachment. But this time it had happened to me. No use tackling Nick, who was a dumb cop and spoke no English or pretended he didn't.

So I collared Zemenkov and asked him what the idea was in telling the girl she couldn't speak to me.

I was a little surprised that he didn't deny it but only laughed and looked sheepish.

Finally, he said he hoped I wasn't complaining of the quality of Soviet hospitality.

Not at all, I said, but if he came to America, he would find that nobody would be detailed to go around scaring people he tried to talk to. One of the reasons we were able to get things done was because we didn't have any army of able-bodied men tied up to spy on our Allies. Then I said I now understood the purpose of the new Foreign Office uniform: it was useful in frightening women.

Zemenkov did not like this. I had not intended that he should. All across Siberia I kept at him. Every time some battered old crone would hobble across our field of vision, I would cry out, "Zemenkov—quick, a woman! Do your duty—get out and warn her against us!"

By the time we were swinging down into Turkestan he was reduced to the point where he was humbly bringing up females for me to meet. I thanked him elaborately for these tender offices but spurned them all. I explained I was able to handle these matters without the services of a bureaucracy. All I asked was that when I did find someone I wanted to talk to that he refrain from scaring them away. In the end we became good friends. I found that he was an avid reader of Mark Twain and could quote comic passages from his most obscure short stories. When this bond became established, he either quit scaring people away from me, also passing out the word to Nick, or else they did it so discreetly that I was unaware.

But back to Omsk. The day reduced poor Joyce to a pulp and after the third factory he quit. Not ostentatiously, but quietly. When the cars would stop he would shuffle his feet as though about to get out and trudge through with the rest of us. But instead he would remain in the back seat, peering furtively after us but ready to break into a weakly guilty laugh.

That night they took us to a concert in a beautiful auditorium in a park. We should have enjoyed the concert more, for the performers were as good if not better than you would find in an American town of 300,000. The program was well selected. The people were enjoying it very much.

But we were enjoying the people even more. Between the acts we watched them promenade. It was a decently dressed, healthy-looking, friendly crowd, as curious about us as we were about them.

After all the champagne which had been crammed down us at the afternoon banquet I wanted a drink of water and so did Dick Lauterbach, so instead of going back into the hall we started out to locate a fountain. This should have been easy, because we were in a big culture park. We had gone three steps when a man in uniform stepped out and inquired what we wanted.

"Oh, hell," said Lauterbach, "there it begins."

"He's just a friendly Red Army guy."

"Red Army, hell. NKVD. You tell them by that blue hat band."

"Maybe he knows where there's some water."

Dick explained. The NKVD man beckoned very politely and we followed. And as always, the minute you get off the beaten track, things get interesting. He led us around back and opened a door, revealing a banquet table laid with the familiar pastry and champagne glasses. Only, mercifully, it wasn't laid for us. It was for the artists when the concert was over. Water? That they didn't have, and immediately offered us champagne which was exactly the last thing we wanted; so, following the NKVD man, we started out across the park. We walked along well-kept, winding gravel paths for perhaps a hundred yards until we came first to band music and then to an open-air pavilion where about 300 people were dancing.

After leaning over the fountain to drink, we stood watching the dancers. Except for a few overgrown boys, they were all girls in light summer dresses dancing with each other.

Every minute we expected the NKVD man would lead us back

to the concert but he didn't. Then he said something to Dick in Russian.

"I can't believe it!" said Dick. "Know what he said? Asks us wouldn't we like to go up there and dance with some of them."

"Tell him, sure."

"It just can't be true," said Dick, as we walked around toward the gate. "It would be impossible in Moscow."

"This is a good guy. He understands we'd like to know them."

"Sure, a country boy that doesn't know big city ways. He's so dumb, he's human."

The girls are very pretty. The first one I dance with is from Leningrad. The next was born here in Omsk. The third is also from Leningrad.

"You wouldn't believe," says Dick, "that some of these are the same grease-monkeys we saw in the factories this afternoon. Shows what a bath and a clean dress will do." The NKVD man is standing back by the entrance, looking on in a fatherly way. Every time the music stops the crowd, staring at us, very politely begins to edge our way and then one, bolder than the rest, tries out his half-dozen English or German phrases.

"Gee!" says Dick, "and with the NKVD man standing right over there. I suppose so few foreigners come through here that these people haven't learned it's dangerous to talk to us. A thing like this could never happen in Moscow."

The next girl is from Dnieprostroi, and the next from Tashkent, down on the Chinese border. She is studying to be a doctor and she dances beautifully.

But it is long past the intermission so, thanking the NKVD man, and telling him he is the most regular guy we have met in the Soviet Union, we go back to the hall.

When we return for the night at the airport, I watch Joyce taking his usual precautions against oxygen. He closes the bedroom windows tightly against the summer air. The sitting room door that opens into the corridor is already closed. But I am mystified when he shuts the door connecting bedroom and sitting room, since the air in both is presumably the same. Then I realize that when the small amount of oxygen in the bedroom is exhausted, he will not then be threatened by additional oxygen percolating in from the sitting room.

For some reason I couldn't sleep, and at about two I tiptoed quietly out and down the hall toward the empty airport waiting room for a cigarette. Only it wasn't empty.

Sprawled on the benches were two khaki-clad figures who sat up, blinking sleepily. One of them asked me something in Russian. Before I could explain I didn't speak it, the other one said, "Hell, Tex, he's no Russian."

"No," I said, "I'm an American. You guys Americans too?"

"I should hope to kiss a horse we are," said Tex.

"Who are you and what are you doing here?" said the other. "By the way, what's the name of this burg?"

I told him what I was doing here and that this was Omsk.

"Omsk," he repeated sourly. "Well, good place to wait for a plane as any. Time is it, Ed?"

Ed looked at his watch. "'Bout two."

"'Nother hour," said Tex gloomily.

They told me they'd been assigned as technical advisers on a big war construction project.

"A mine up north," said Tex. "And now we're going out."

"How was it?" I asked.

"Not bad," said Ed. "Of course at this little burg, they set up a whole Intourist Hotel to take care of us, because we were foreigners. Brought in a supply of wine, cheese, cigarettes, candy, noodles, and dried eggs. For the rest, we were supposed to scavenge off the country. Of course, they sent in a cook and an assistant cook, a bookkeeper—in all about ten people taking care of us."

"How did you get along with the Russians?"

"Very friendly the first day. Said next week you must come over to dinner. But that was all we ever heard of it. Although one or two apologized. Seems word had passed out it was against government policy to have anything to do with us. On the job they were nice guys, though. We would help each other with Russian and English lessons, but that was as far as it could go."

"Had a Russian-English primer that was a honey," said Tex. "The first sentences were, 'Miners in America get very low wages,' 'Great Britain is a capitalist plutocracy,' and 'The Soviet Union is surrounded by enemies.' There was stuff like, 'Ivanov invented electricity,' or 'Petrov first harnessed steam,' names you never heard of. Certainly gives them a cock-eyed picture of the rest of the world."

"We went to a movie one night," said Ed. "They had an American film—Deanna Durbin in '100 Men and a Girl.' Only by then we knew enough Russian to read the sub-titles they'd put on it. These had it that poor old Deanna was the victim of capitalist exploitation, her old man was jobless and on the bum. Then in that place where she gets something to eat, they're only giving it to her to watch her make a fool of herself so they can laugh at her bad manners. It was all we could do to stay in our seats."

"Even if they had been allowed to ask us to dinner," said Tex, "not many could have done it. Home life is pretty sketchy. Except for the top guys, most of them eat in community kitchens and sleep in dormitories, even in the villages. And sometimes the kids live together in a pile. At least there was a little town near our project which has a normal population of about 3,000. They had some kind of school or orphanage with 1,200 kids. I assumed their parents had been killed in the war. But they said no, only a few. Mostly they seemed to be just kids nobody wanted. Whether that's typical of the whole country I don't know."

"We didn't really get to know many Russians," said Ed. "Except it was different with the girls. They have some fine girls and nobody seems to mind if you take them out. We suspect they might have been assigned to us. Or anyway had to tell the NKVD whatever we said."

"We know they gave the hotel employees a lecture," said Tex. "Said we were foreigners, and anything we did they must report. Very suspicious."

"Now, of course," said Ed, "if you are out from under supervision of the NKVD—like for instance you're on a train headed some place—all the people are friendly as hell. You couldn't ask for better. But once you settle down in some place to work, they let you alone."

"How do they run their mines?"

"They sure do things different from what we do," said Tex. "Instead of having big construction firms, they call them trusts— and most of them are branches of one big central trust. Whether they bid against each other for a particular job, I wouldn't know— anyway they're supposed to show a profit."

"Now you take any ten-year-old American child with a Meccano set," said Ed, "and he'll start at the bottom and build up. But these Russians always start at the top, build the roof first and then raise it."

"And work like hell, so they can throw up some kind of a framework that they can hang a red flag on the tip of and make speeches," said Tex.

"Oh, but first thing," said Ed, "they always put up a tribune to make those speeches from, and hang big pictures of Stalin and Lenin. And, of course, those big boards for the names of what workers have done the best. You've got to wait until those are finished before they'll even let you break ground for the foundations."

"All those pictures and speeches are because Russians are not steady workers," said Tex. "Or maybe it's part of their system. Anyway, they diddle and putter around about nine-tenths of the time, telephoning each other and nothing gets done. Then all of a sudden they hop up on those platforms, and make a lot of big speeches about Stalin, get themselves worked up under a big head of steam, pitch in and get it cleaned up in record time. Except for the weeks they wasted talking. They call that Socialist competition."

"But we wouldn't know why," said Ed.

"The worst thing is they've got no respect for materials," said Tex. "Never owned anything themselves. It belongs to the state so what the hell do they care? They have no conception of how much work has gone into making them. I've seen them unload valuable pipe from a flat car by just rolling it down an embankment—smashing hell out of it. And fire brick for smelters the same way. It's cut very accurately and you can't use chipped ones. The way they'd heave it off, about 25 per cent would be damaged."

"When we'd try to stop it," said Ed, "they explained they had a law in Russia because of the freight-car shortage, that they had to be unloaded within two hours after arrival. No one seemed to see it would take more cars to bring more material. Or maybe they didn't care."

"We were only consultants," said Tex, "and if they got tired of us hollering, they'd get around it by not supplying us transportation out to the job. They'd say our chauffeur couldn't be found. Which was nonsense, because he was picked by the NKVD, and if he took a five-day vacation, he'd be shot."

"They don't understand mechanical stuff," said Tex. "They put things up out of plumb and then blame this trouble on poor American design. So they take it down and start all over. Once we saw them assembling a complicated steel frame out in a field, instead of on its foundation. When we asked why, they said they wanted to be sure it would fit.

"One of the mines needed more air so we designed a fine ventilating system. They redesigned it. We protested, but they went ahead anyway. When it didn't work, the poor architect committed suicide."

"We would explain to them how to do a job," said Ed, "and they'd listen attentively and then do it their own way."

"We were always asking for conferences—not they," said Tex. "If the work was to be kept rolling, we had to know their plans. Now and then we'd get the top director out of his fancy office, and he'd see what was wrong. Things would go better for a while. But their system is unwieldy. Sometimes he would pick up one of the four telephones on his desk and issue a lot of orders. But then nothing would happen.

"The top director and his engineer were sincere and capable, but their system bogs them down with detail and paper work. They even have to sign warehouse receipts—things that in America we leave to an underling. It's like civil service back home. There's a hell of a lot of conversations—we'd complain, they'd listen and make decisions. But definite instructions often don't get out to the men in the field, and the top men haven't time to get out of their offices. The trouble with the whole country is there aren't enough capable men to carry out orders."

"I think it's their system," said Ed. "It doesn't give them the drive, the personal ambition, the incentive that ours does. And it's so complex—they have to talk to so many people before anything gets done. The Communist Party has a set-up which duplicates everything in the industry. In every organization the director is a Party member and the engineer sometimes is. Party members are the only ones who can ever get anything done in Russia. But even they are slow. Yet on our job they really wanted to work with us. But in general, they could never be a competitive threat to America. We can always build in a year and a half anything it takes them ten to do."

"Are their engineers well trained?"

"Some," said Tex. "The best engineers were the NKVD."

"But isn't that their secret police organization?"

"Sure. You see, in Russia they don't have our penitentiary system. They herd prisoners into labor gangs, and the NKVD, which has charge of them, has developed a fine engineering staff. They bid on construction jobs, supplying both the engineers and prison labor. Often the engineers are also prisoners."

"On our particular project," said Ed, "there were about 70,000 workers, and half of these were prisoners. Mostly women. The prisoners were assigned to separate huts. But on the job the only way you could tell them from the others was that they were under guards with fixed bayonets."

"Prisoners are a subject in itself," said Tex. "You see, in this country there are so many ways to do things wrong or talk out of turn, that somewhere between thirteen and fifteen million are always in prison. They put them to digging canals, or building railroads, or on jobs like ours. Then there are a few million more who are arrested and found guilty, but only sentenced to keep on working at their old jobs with reduced pay. Those are the lucky ones.

"The others, when they're arrested, just drop out of sight. If your wife is really fond of you and works hard, maybe in three months she can find out where they've got you and what the charges are. Then, if she hires a lawyer, she may get the right of correspondence, which means she can write you once a month, and you can write twice.

"Usually no letters are allowed, particularly for political prisoners. But since the food shortage, his wife can send food parcels. If the prisoner dies, they always send the food parcel back with a sticker saying the guy is dead. So then she gets to eat the food."

"Which is only fair," said Ed.

"I didn't say it wasn't," said Tex.

"Politicals get the roughest deal," said Ed. "They have NKVD spies in the markets and hanging around the store counters, waiting for someone to pop off. They usually get ten years chopping wood with no correspondence, and 500 grams of bread a day. Of course, if you are husky and can work hard, they'll give you more."

"If you miss getting typhus and live out your sentence," said Tex, "they turn you loose, but your passport has a red line through it. That means you can never get a house or a good job—you've got to keep moving."

"Or you may not get sentenced," said Ed, "just arrested and investigated. If things don't look quite right, then you get a passport with letters in front of the numbers. This means that you are under some suspicion, and can never hold a key job."

"Only about half the workers on our project were prisoners," said Tex. "The rest were what they called free labor. Various kinds. Some were draft-age men with physical disabilities who had been classified for limited service and assigned to labor duty there. Some were evacuees from suspected sections—maybe they'd lived near the frontier or else in Poland or the Baltic States so they didn't trust them."

"Tell him how they were housed," said Ed.

"Oh, yeauh. They dig a pit about 10 feet deep, 20 feet wide and 100 feet long. Then they make a peaked roof of pine logs over this. The mattresses lay on the cold dirt."

"How did they work?" I asked.

"They were supposed to work twelve hours a day. They'd work about an hour and sleep the other eleven."

I suppose I looked incredulous.

"Isn't that right, Ed?" he asked.

"Well," said Ed, "some of the women were better. Worked from 30 to 50 per cent of the time."

"Didn't get enough to eat—any of them. We used to watch them being fed," said Ed. "Each prisoner was supposed to provide himself with two American tin cans that he fastened to his belt by a wire. They'd haul out one kettle of soup, and one of kasha. Some days the food truck would have dried fish on it, and they'd toss this out over the tailboard like you'd throw fish to a bunch of seals. We couldn't see that the food of the free labor was any better. Nobody gets enough to eat, and they hardly had the energy to walk around."

"Some engineers weren't getting enough to eat, either," Tex pointed out. "Of course, supervisors live in town, and their ration cards vary. They go to different commissaries, run by whichever trust employs them, and some trusts rustle better grub than others. But all of them have to buy extra food at the free market. Trade their clothes and extra possessions until they are stripped."

"You see a mining engineer gets about 1,800 roubles a month," said Ed. "They get one room for which they pay about 30 roubles. All they can buy on their ration cards amounts to 400 or 500 roubles a month. Then they must go to the free market for enough butter, eggs, meat, or fish. A rabbit will sell for 300 roubles there. Two eggs are about 25 roubles. So you see a salary of 1,800 roubles a month doesn't go far. But if you have an extra pair of stout, used boots, it might bring 3,000 roubles and you could buy food with that.

"The chief metallurgist was a Party member. His wife could go to a special store and buy perfume, American soap and canned goods, butter and clothes. She even got one of those American Kodiak windbreakers with the removable lambskin linings they like so much in Siberia. But this store was reserved for the top people in the metallurgical section. They really ate better than we did."

"Most Americans have the idea that our stuff goes to poor, unfortunate Russians," said Tex. "What they don't understand is that under the Soviet system, everybody may be somewhat unfortunate but no one is outstandingly poor unless the government wants them to be that way—like their political prisoners. You'd hardly expect them to pamper prisoners with American canned goods. So it goes to the ones who are doing the most important jobs—the army and the Party members. Don't you agree, Ed?"

"That'd be it," said Ed.

"How did you eat?" I asked.

"Now and then," said Ed.

"They gave us the best they had, except maybe for the top Party members," said Tex.

"Once they sent down 200 kilograms of frozen sturgeon—that's more than 400 pounds—for the two of us. Of course, it's a great delicacy in Russia but we began to get pretty tired of it, and before we could eat it all, it began to rot."

"But then they sent the potatoes," said Tex.

"I'll never forget them," said Ed. "While they lasted we had potatoes three times a day, including breakfast. When they were gone we had only this fish and some goat meat until the middle of May."

"About that time, word came through that the big boss was coming down on an inspection trip," said Tex, "and the next day they produced half a side of beef. The day he was supposed to come, they even killed two chickens, but he was delayed so we got to eat the chickens."

"In order to keep eating decently, we had to raise hell," said Ed. "For instance we were tipped off by a Russian engineer that our trust had got in a carload of tangerines for their commissariat. We hollered to Intourist and they finally came through with a crate. The same way when we learned they had eight barrels of concentrated lemon juice for their hospital—we managed to talk them out of a couple of gallons. It's good against scurvy."

"You mustn't ever back down in dealing with Russians," said Tex. "As a people they're heartless. They've had to shift for themselves since childhood, and they don't ever seem to have close friends. I guess under their system, you can't trust anyone. Whatever makes it, you've got to be tough and realistic in your dealings with them. They've got no sympathy whatever. Remember that red-headed girl?"

"She was in our organization," said Ed. "She got sick, and could hardly drag around. We mentioned it to the boss, trying to get him to lighten her work. He just looked blank. 'What does it matter?' he said. Couldn't understand why it was anybody's business but hers."

"Do the top Communists push the workers around?" I asked.

"No," said Ed slowly, "they don't."

"I'd say it was just the other way," said Tex.

"When one of the top directors does get out of his fancy office and onto the job—which isn't often—he shakes hands with everybody and calls them by their first names."

"Another thing," said Tex. "In America a corporation will sometimes nurse a man along if he isn't delivering, but it's true here to a greater extent. They'll scold him, fine him, and try to get him to do better, but they rarely fire him like we do in the States. Of course, it's no punishment to a man to be canned here—he just goes to work somewhere else. You see, he can't leave his job unless he is fired."

"It almost looks like the director was afraid to crack down for fear he'd get in trouble with the people," said Ed.

"The workers have that air of emancipation like our Negroes," said Tex. "They've been downtrodden for centuries and now they can talk back to the boss. They're not afraid of him. Now the NKVD is something else."

"Machinery is Greek to them. All they understand is hand-labor," said Ed. "They've been doing it for centuries."

"All their labor is green," said Tex, "and I don't know why. We can take hill-billies out of Kentucky and make machinists out of them in Detroit but I guess their system lacks the incentive.

They'll take a dull handax to prepare concrete forms, and they will be full of weepholes big enough to throw a cat through. Then they'll let their reinforcing rods stick out where they're doing no good at all. It's like building with sheep-herders," concluded Tex disgustedly. "And I can't explain why."

"Tell him what the girl said," suggested Ed.

"Oh, yes," said Tex. "Maybe she had it. She was a political prisoner. But she was smart as hell—had a college degree in engineering. They had her in charge of the inventory of mine explosives, which is how we got to talk to her. She said—"

"Wasn't she one of the ones that died?" asked Ed.

Tex paused a minute. "Believe she was," he said. "The last month we were there, 2,600 of the 70,000 workers on that job died of typhus. Of course, it was mostly the prisoners. Believe she was one of them. Anyway she said—"

"Hey, listen!" said Ed. From outside came the roar of motors.

"By God, there it is," said Tex. They both rose and picked up their bags.

"Well, White," said Ed, "looks like you're going to have a nice trip."

"But some day you ought to come over here and see Russia," said Tex.

"Wait a minute," I said. "What did the girl say?"

"Her? Oh. Take too long. But she sure hit the nail on the head. Some other time." They went on out to the plane. I went back to Joyce. I had finished my cigarette at Omsk airport.

Now for a note in this Russian suspicion of foreigners. Russia does not yet trust the outside world. Diplomats are just as closely imprisoned in Moscow as are correspondents. At the time of our visit the current British ambassador had been unable to secure permission to travel outside the capital. One of the Allied countries which has in power a left-wing government adorned its diplomatic staff in Moscow with a special labor attaché, and appointed to this post an important union official. He came to extend the hand of fellowship from the toilers of the West to their fellow workers in

Russia. He complains now that the Soviets gave him countless banquets but have let him see nothing. This lack of freedom has so warped his viewpoint that he now insists that the Soviet system of unions is only a scheme to get the last ounce of work out of labor.

By contrast the 1,500 members of the Soviet Purchasing Commission in America are free to get on any train at any time and go to any part of our country. As trusted Allies they are welcome to inspect our war industries. No American should object to this, but Americans should understand that hitherto it has been a one-sided arrangement. On our trip we were taken to any factory we wished to visit and questions were freely answered but foreigners as a rule are treated as spies, and Soviet officials withheld from their Allies even the location of their war industries back of the Urals, while permission to visit them was unthinkable.

Although Russian suspicion has decreased since Teheran, it is still strong. It has roots both in the Communist Party and in Russian history.

In earliest Russian history the monk Nestor chronicles the fact that the Russian merchants of the Dnieper trade route, harassed by Tartar nomads, from Asia, sent word to the Northmen of Scandinavia, "Our earth is broad and rich, but there is no order in it. Come and rule us." So came the Rurick dynasty of czars. Later Asia swept in, and Muscovy paid tribute to Genghis Khan. Under Peter the Great Europe seemed to prevail. European craftsmen were invited to build her capital. Czarina Catherine imported Germans into the Volga basin to teach the *moujik* to farm, and French had become the language of the court and literate classes. Under Czar Nicholas I foreign tutors were discouraged, Western ideas and literature suppressed by rigid censorship. After the Revolution, Lenin invited foreign concessionaires to help get Russian industry back on its feet. Later they were thrown out. Stalin invited foreign engineers to build the great factories and dam rivers, but later put some on trial for espionage.

During the German invasion when the government was leaving Moscow for Kuibyshev and various departments were burning their files, *Pravda* published an editorial suggesting that screens be put on the chimneys, so that charred fragments of documents might not escape to be pieced together by foreign embassies.

The basis of the mental disorder called paranoia is a deep, subconscious hostility toward the outside world. In its second step, the patient reverses it and comes to believe that not he but the world is hostile, that he is surrounded by intrigues, poison plots and spy rings against which he must defend himself.

Of course, Bolshevik hostility aroused bitter counter-hostility. A *cordon sanitaire* was built around Russia. France supported Poland in a war against the Bolsheviks in 1921, and Russia was for over a decade excluded from the League and denied diplomatic recognition. So their suspicion of foreigners came to have some basis in fact.

This warped view of the world held by the Kremlin is slowly yielding to reality. After Lenin's death, Stalin won power and supported the thesis—gingerly at first—that socialism in one country was possible and Russia could dare to devote her energies to building up her own economic structure. World revolution, he explained, was desirable, and he pledged himself to bend all efforts to bring it about. But for the immediate future, it was not indispensable to the Russian Bolsheviks.

In recent years there has been a further change. For publication the Kremlin has announced that world revolution is neither necessary nor desirable from the standpoint of the Soviet Union. And the ablest foreign observers in Moscow agree that these protestations are sincere. They point out that Russia has been terribly weakened by war and needs desperately a few decades of peace. They say she now realizes that Europe does not want to be "liberated" from capitalist democracy, and that this could be accomplished only by a further bloody struggle involving sacrifices which the Russians are both unwilling and unable to make. Russia wants, they insist, only a stable and friendly Europe.

These observers do not pretend that Russia has any enthusiasm for either democracy or capitalism in Europe. She accepts them only because for the next few decades they promise to give Europe that peace and stability which Russia needs. However, if they do not bring stability—if there are disorders and unrest which create a power vacuum anywhere on the continent, the Russians are not stupid, and they will move a Communist government in to fill this vacuum. But if America and England act firmly, both diplomatically and economically to preserve real democratic order in Europe, these observers think Russia will be well satisfied to accept the decent compromises which we should insist on.

I would qualify this with an angle of my own. Such an optimistic picture of Europe's immediate future is based on the assumption that Russia will follow policies which are to her self-interest. Although the Bolsheviks have a clearer view of world reality now than they had in the 'twenties and 'thirties, they are still plagued with suspicions and there is no guarantee that they will not stumble into policies which might provoke another war which nobody wants, least of all themselves.

Eleven

WE FLY eastward over a country of tundra, cold swamps, and pine trees resembling the Hudson Bay region. It is dotted with round lakes.

Our destination is Novosibirsk, Siberia's capital, which lies in the center of this chill roof of the world, about midway between Berlin and Tokyo.

The next two days, spent at Novosibirsk, were dominated by one of the most vivid personalities I have ever met, but it was several hours before we began to be aware of him. Certainly he did not stand out at the airport. The group which greeted us there looked like all the others except that perhaps it was less formal, and more like a picked bunch of town boosters and community builders who might gather at an airport in Kansas City, Denver, Salt Lake City, Wichita, or Los Angeles to welcome a visiting celebrity and show off their town.

Their faces were grave like the others who had been lined up below. But the spirit somehow became freer. The feeling of this big, sprawling boom-town was like that of the West where the robust town-builders are proud of their city. West of the Urals, Bolshevik civilization has taken over ancient towns and palaces and their new structures rise on the ruins of things they destroyed. But here in Siberia, as in our West, they have chopped and blasted and dug their cities out of a virgin continent. And they have something to be proud of.

Novosibirsk has almost a million people, but we see little today for we are whisked across the town and through 6 or 7 miles of wooded countryside which looks like Minnesota to our quarters. Tiny potato patches are along the highway shoulders and others are back in forest clearings. Women bend over to clear them. Big hand-some girls, often barefoot, walk erect down the road with scarves around their hair and farm tools over their shoulders. Occasionally the road passes through a cut in a little hill. Even on the cut's steep clay sides, potatoes are planted in close, even rows.

We are told that the patches have been assigned to workers in the city. Some factories maintain busses which take the workers out on weekends to hoe the patches. But most must trudge out from town, as we see them doing now.

Presently we ride along the banks of a river as wide here as the Ohio at its mouth, but as yellow as the Missouri. We are told that it is the Ob, of which none of us have ever heard, and that it is the fourth longest river in the world.

It drains this vast plain, comparable to the Mississippi valley and flows almost straight north to empty into the Arctic Ocean. We marvel somewhat at this, but more at how little we know of this huge country of Siberia, as vast as a continent and in many ways so like America.

We come to the *dacha*—a Russian word meaning country resi-dence for someone who normally lives in the city. It gleams new and white against the great trees which surround it and overlooks the yellow waters of the Ob sliding greasily toward Arctic ice-bergs. The house would be indistinguishable from the great estates of the wealthy New York families which line the Hudson. It has an equally large staff of servants. The rooms are as large, as clean and as luxurious.

I have written much about Soviet sloppiness, and the fact that Russians build pretentiously and then seldom repair anything. This is probably an Asiatic characteristic rather than a Communist one. But whatever the answer, we find that whenever the convenience of a high Communist is involved, these people can be as clean and tidy as the Dutch or the Swedes. So it is in this *dacha*.

A doctor, summoned for Joyce, pronounces him without fever—sound in wind and limb, hale if not hearty. There is no schedule this afternoon and we are to rest and amuse ourselves. Below the *dacha* a private bathing pier extends out into the Ob. Down the hill we see through the trees a well-kept tennis court, with flood lights for night games. To the right is a volley-ball court. Eric immediately suggests to his hosts that after we have eaten (the usual banquet is waiting) and slept, we have a volley-ball game—Russians versus Americans.

At about four o'clock it starts, although the Russians slip in an extra hour's practice. I watch from the *dacha* balcony. Eric and the correspondents are in one court. Opposite are Kirilov and the Russians who met us at the airport.

Both sides play reasonably well, and as in all such games, there is considerable shouting, as players call back and forth. But presently I notice that on the Russian side only one man does any shouting; the others play in grim Slavic silence. The Russian shouter is an undersized man in his forties, with wide cheekbones and a shock of curly hair—quick as a fox terrier—who keeps up a running fire of command and encouragement to the Russian team.

He is strikingly un-Russian. Some odd combination of chromosomes has produced out here on the steppes a quick-minded, tough little Irishman. He could be Jimmie Cagney—complete with wiry hair and jutting jaw. He even talks out of the corner of his mouth.

Clearly he was used to giving orders and the other Russians accustomed to taking them in silence; yet I wondered idly why he had been selected captain of the team, for his size kept him from being a good player and he guarded a relatively unimportant position on this court.

Dimly I remembered him at the airport with the local dignitaries. We had met the mayor, the chairman of the local Soviet, the leading factory director. If this little Irish type had held an important title I surely would have remembered it. When the game was over I asked who he was.

His name was Michael Kalugin and although he turned out to hold no office in either the local government or its industry, it was easy to see how he had acquired the habit of command. He occupied the unobtrusive position of Secretary of the Communist Party for Siberia.

We remark how curious it is that so perfect a Tammany Irish

type as Mike Kalugin could be repeated out here in the middle of Asia, running another party. Not only does Mike's Russian slide out of one corner of his mouth, but he looks at you hard and raises one eyebrow skeptically when he talks.

I want to send a telegram to America so I get a car to take me to the post office, which gives me a closer look at Novosibirsk. Most Asiatic towns, judged from their central district, look smaller than they really are. This town of almost a million has a shopping district about the size of Wichita's with public buildings comparable to those in Kansas City.

In the central square there is a beautiful new theater, comparable to Kansas City's WPA-built auditorium, with some fine buildings around it. It is used, I learn, for the ballet, but Moscow artists also occasionally perform there. Near by, a somewhat smaller theater is devoted to operettas, and plays are given at a third—this being the standard set-up in every large Soviet town.

We pass a markedly well-built and spacious apartment house and I ask who lives there. They tell me it is reserved for the artists and actors who perform in these theaters, and that doctors and professional men occupy a similar one. In Kansas City it wouldn't be the best apartment house, but it certainly would be a decent class B one.

In the post office I climb a flight of stairs to the telegraph desk. Here we are back to the usual Soviet shabbiness. The building is pretentious but the linoleum is worn through. In the halls, tiles are chipped and missing—not just a few but more than a square yard at the doorsill.

On the way back we pass the railway station, from the outside an impressive modern building, and on a sudden impulse I tell the driver to stop. It is in size midway between the Union Stations at Kansas City and Wichita. The architecture is dramatic—high ceilings with sweeping vistas, but the materials look second-rate. The Kansas City and Wichita stations will last centuries if they are not pulled down for something better. This Novosibirsk station is shopworn already, but the effect is beautiful.

The crowd is fascinating. One great hall is roped off for women with babies and small children. There are no seats, but the children play happily around their mothers who sit on the clean-swept terraza floor. But there are the usual polished wood benches in the spacious main waiting room—only this is reserved for wounded soldiers who sprawl on every inch of the space, their crutches leaning on the benches beside them or lying on the floor. The soldiers are either sleeping or trying to. They look patient and weary beyond words.

In an American station USO girls or Red Cross nurses would be fussing over them, handing out magazines, pillows, or hot coffee. There are none here—which does not prove that they don't exist in Russia. At least the soldiers get the station's only benches. There must be between 500 and 1,000 of these weary men, most of them with an arm or leg missing. So far as I know this is a normal hour of a normal day in Novosibirsk station. I stand here, looking at this quiet eddy in the great sewer of war, where the waste material of an army, used, broken, and rejected, is being poured back onto the vast Siberian earth.

Wandering back toward the main hall I am again struck by how much this is like a new Union Station in any big city of our West. They even have Indians—the same copper-yellow faces with high cheekbones and straight, black Mongolian hair. These, of course, are from Kazakstan down on the Chinese border. But I see no racial difference between Uzbeks or Kazaks and our Osages or Navajos, except that these Soviet Indians are not so well-dressed as ours. Like ours, they were fighting nomad Mongolian tribes until the Russians tamed them.

The station restaurant is closed, but the usual long, patient queue of Russians is lined up waiting until the doors open.

Leaving the station, we go back to the car. There is a parking area but it is much smaller than that of an American station. Yet in Russia it is adequate for here there is only one other car—a big, black, carefully polished Zees with a uniformed chauffeur in the front seat, and in the back, an extremely well-dressed middle-aged woman. In Kansas City she would be the wife of a bank president, waiting to pick up her husband after his trip to Chicago. Here she is probably the wife of the factory director or some other important Party member.

For one paragraph I must get ahead of my story. The next day Mike and the other Novosibirsk boosters took Eric on an official tour which included this station. They gave him a dramatic glance down onto the waiting room from a high balcony. Mike was plainly annoyed when Eric, at my suggestion, insisted on going down onto the main floor to walk through that forest of Red Army crutches, past the queue at the restaurant and through the women and children squatting patiently on the floor.

Maybe a committee of American town boosters would be annoyed if a visiting dignitary threw a tour off schedule by insisting on a quick trip through a slum area. Any such group wants to show off its best, without necessarily denying that unpleasant things exist, but I think Mike found our interest in the seamy side dangerously morbid. He saw me whispering to Eric and I felt he had a not too friendly eye on me after that.

Back at the *dacha* the minute I step out of the car it is clear things are beginning to happen. A Red Army band is tuning its instruments down by the water front. As it strikes up a military march a second band appears, in even smarter uniforms, and begins tuning up.

As we go in to dinner, a gleaming white river steamer ties up at the wharf. We are told that after dinner we will go for a ride on the Ob. At dinner there is a curious incident. When it comes time for toasts, Eric pays tribute to their hospitality. Then Mike Kalugin rises and, squinting his eyes down the table, tells us of the pleasure it gives him to have us in Novosibirsk. Joyce, who has by now recovered, then gets up for the American team and amplifies the theme of Russian hospitality, saying that it overwhelms us. After this the tall, thick-set, imposing Russian mayor of Novosibirsk stands. Mike had been leaning over, whispering with Eric. When the mayor rises, the table falls silent. The mayor, as is customary, picks up his glass. Then he opens his mouth to speak. At this point Mike glances up, sees the mayor, frowns and quickly jerks his thumb down. The mayor closes his mouth, drops back into his chair as though he had been butted in the knees from behind by a goat. Then he remembers to put his glass down, and silently picks up his fork. It would seem that Mike does most of the talking for the Russian team. Also that Party discipline out in the Novosibirsk region couldn't be better.

After the dinner Mike ushered us down the river bank and aboard the steamer. The sun was shining brightly and would not set until ten o'clock. On our way up to the deck, we passed the dining salon. We had just got up from one meal in the *dacha*, but a table was laid with wine glasses for another.

Mike waved us expansively to a row of deck chairs just forward of the bridge. The better of the two bands, lined up on the bow facing us, struck up as the boat moved out into the current. The cold arctic sun was burning the tawny waters gold between the green trees that lined each shore. No wonder the band was magnificent, for it was the official band of the Red Army—musicians selected for their skill from all of Russia's millions. Their uniforms were spotless. Half of them played instruments and the other half was a perfectly drilled male choir of perhaps thirty voices. The big river rang with gorgeous Red Army marching songs and heartbreaking old Russian folk tunes.

Whenever they stopped for breath, the other band, out of sight on the stern of the boat, would play. The first band was really made up of stage artists and musicians in uniform. The second one, however, was a standard army band in well-worn uniforms, whose marching tunes made up in volume what they lacked in precision.

"Did you *ever* see anything like this?" a correspondent whispered to me. "What American millionaire could put us up in a summer house like this, give us such food and entertain us on a big yacht with not one band, but two? Do *you* know anybody who could?"

A couple of Red Army boys now advanced to give a sword dance, the rest of the band playing background accompaniment. They danced wild, barbaric Cossack dances, sitting on their heels and kicking high. Swords flashed out and steel clashed against steel —sparks flying as the two men leapt high in the air.

Eric leaned forward. "Now notice Mike," he said. "A minute ago when those two sword dancers were jumping around, they got close to the rail. Immediately he motioned two over to stand by that rail so they wouldn't go overboard. He looks out after his people. A real leader always does that in any country. And he's one."

The choir, with woodwinds and brasses soft in the background, was now singing a fine old army song of the yearning of a soldier for his home village. It somehow had in it all the strength and resigned sadness of the Slav peoples. The sun had just set, and the river had turned from gold to dull yellow. The trees along the distant shores dropped from fresh green to black. The band now played a waltz. Two pretty little waitresses who had been brought along from the *dacha* to serve our supper were on deck listening, and the Field Marshal, who had his eye on the brunette with the blue eyes and snub nose, invited her to dance. At everybody's urging Eric danced with the other.

When it was over dusk had fallen, and Mike advanced with what appeared to be a blunderbuss pistol.

"He says," translated Kirilov, "that he will now fire salute."

Mike pointed to the darkening sky, and pulled the trigger. There was a soul-shaking bang, a shower of sparks, and a hissing rocket leapt from the gun's mouth and spiraled its way toward the zenith, where it burst in a beautiful pale green star which slowly settled toward the river and then winked out.

Mike was bending over to reload the gun from a large box of shells on the deck. He handed it to Eric with a lordly gesture. As this star bored into the sky, Eric's wrist wobbled under the kick. Mike now took it and sent a purple star skyward, reloaded and handed it to Eric, who took it with a trapped look. There were at least fifty shells in the box. For variety he pointed the gun toward a small island out in mid-channel and his star luckily fell among the weeds on its shore where we watched it burning out. Mike immediately took the gun and placed a second flaming star on top of Eric's. This was precision shooting in any army. It occurred to me that Siberia would not be a healthy place for any Party member who did not see eye to eye with Marshal Stalin.

When two dozen of the fifty shells had been fired, Eric called for help.

"Joyce—Bill!" he called, with an effort at vivacity, "wouldn't you fellows like a turn here? Come on—do!" Joyce prudently bowed out but I falteringly volunteered. The pistol kicked like a mule and I knew Eric's arm must be pulp. I handed it to the Field Marshal.

When the box was empty, Mike proudly ushered us down to the dining salon and the boat turned around, heading for our dock. Eric and Joyce sat down with Mike and the Russians at the big table. I sat at a kind of children's table which had been arranged for the correspondents. There were the usual polite toasts between Eric and Mike honoring Marshal Stalin and Gospodin Roosevelt.

When the boat returns us to the *dacha*, we find half a dozen women in evening gowns. We are introduced; they are artists from the local opera. In the next room another staggering banquet is laid; they are to dine with us. Dinner is not easy for they are distributed among us at table and they speak only Russian but do their best to make polite small talk with gestures. Bob Magidov, who represents the Associated Press, is particularly helpful. He lived in Russia until he was fourteen but came to America with his parents then. His Russian is perfect.

Eric has discovered he is a far better translator than the Intourist girl and uses him constantly.

"But, Bob, don't you get tired, translating all this after-dinner guff back and forth?" a correspondent whispers.

"Not Eric's," says Magidov. "You guys've got no idea how good his stuff is—how smooth it goes over in Russian. I tell you, it's marvelous."

In the middle of dinner, one of the opera stars went to the grand piano in the adjoining room and a blonde one of about forty rose to sing the Russian version of a blues song—it could have been Helen Morgan singing "Just My Bill." Such a singer always selects from her audience one man to whom she sings directly, and this Soviet blonde selected the Field Marshal—probably because he was nearest, possibly because of his American war correspondent's uniform, or maybe because he was bald and middle-aged.

With unusual zeal the Field Marshal entered into the game; although the words were Russian their import was clear, and he would respond to the song's emotional climaxes by appropriate gestures. We all enjoyed it and saw nothing unusual in the fact that the Field Marshal, when at the end the accordion players swung into a waltz, should ask her to dance.

We watched with measured envy. Although the singer was no child, she was easily the youngest and prettiest of the artists, and had but one visible gold tooth. They danced down toward the end of the room. Just beyond were French doors leading to a spacious and well-lit porch, plainly visible from this room.

It was not remarkable that on a warm night they should open the door to continue the dance out on the terrace. At this instant the music stopped. This would not have been unusual except that it broke off, not at the end of the tune, but in the middle of a bar. Then we saw Mike. He had risen. With a quick gesture he silenced the orchestra. He was staring at the blonde. She was already halfway back to her seat. The Field Marshal proceeded to his more deliberately, with some attempt to compose his dignity, and amid dead silence. When he sat down the music started again.

"Anyway," whispered Harrison Salisbury of the United Press, "now we know which chick is Mike's."

"Except why should it be just one?" argued another correspondent. "I'm letting them all alone. I've got dependents. A situation like this is more risky than any front trip."

But Mike was now making us a brief talk.

"He says," said Bob Magidov, turning to Eric, "that there are now two alternatives to the entertainment, and it is for these honored guests of the Soviet Union to choose. Outside on the tennis court a motion picture machine is set up, ready to show the great film "Volga-Volga." Or, if we prefer, these stars from the Novosibirsk opera and ballet would be proud to give more vocal and musical numbers.

We had once suffered through "Volga-Volga" and Eric handled the situation with great tact, explaining that it is we who would be honored if these representatives of a great artistic nation would favor us with its majestic songs. And after a decent interval, Eric and Joyce excused themselves and went upstairs for some much-needed sleep.

Meantime the Field Marshal was recovering his dignity.

"Just to show old Mike there's no hard feelings, I'm going to make him a *Katusha*," he said. "Anyway, I was just being polite to his girl. The cutest one here is that little brunette waitress. Where are the bottles?"

A *Katusha*—named after the man-killing Soviet secret weapon— was invented by the Moscow correspondents and consists of a large water glass, filled half with vodka and half champagne. Few can drink it and survive.

Tiptoeing over to Mike with the two brimming glasses, the Field Marshal summoned the interpreter. Explaining why this drink was so named, the Field Marshal offered him his choice of the glasses.

Mike appraised his quizzically, lifted his eyebrows as though asking "why not," clinked his glass and drained it as though it had been milk. The Field Marshal, beaming, was starting back to his seat when Mike raised a hand.

"Another," he was insisting, this time mixing them himself. These were downed. It was a triumph for the Field Marshal, but again Mike plucked his sleeve.

"Yet another." The Field Marshal's smile had dwindled to a sickly grin, but he was caught. Mike smacked his lips over the third but as the Field Marshal started away he put a firm hand on his shoulder. Good friends, he told him, should not part so abruptly. If he insisted on going back to his seat, he should have a final one to cheer him on his way.

At this point the blonde with the single gold tooth tried to interpose; Mike brushed her aside. The room was now in an awed silence as they drank. Excluding the champagne, each had had the equivalent of a pint of raw alcohol. Something must give; perhaps not immediately but soon, as the liquor took hold.

The Field Marshal came back to his seat and told us now at last we were seeing Russia—out here meeting swell guys like Mike who really had power and authority, and what they said went, instead of those little second-rate squirts you had to deal with in Moscow, all afraid to make a decision. But a guy like good old Mike, well, you were really talking to somebody who counted in the country.

Then the Field Marshal rose for a toast. He told the Russians how glad the correspondents were to see Russia—they were here at the express invitation of Marshal Stalin—before this various underlings hadn't allowed them to come to Novosibirsk, but Marshal Stalin had ruled otherwise, and since the correspondents were, it could be said, almost the personal guests of Marshal Stalin on this trip, since Marshal Stalin had wanted them to see Russia, he was raising his glass to Marshal Stalin.

The Russians drank but seemed most uncomfortable, except for Mike. He was relaxed in his chair with his eyes closed; the blonde with the single gold tooth was getting down him a glass of strong hot tea.

There was another musical number and after it people got up from the table. We looked around; the Field Marshal had disappeared. We found him on the brightly lighted porch. On the bench beside him was the pretty brunette waitress with the snub nose. He was holding her there by the wrist.

"She looks like she could take care of herself," said Bill Lawrence of the New York *Times*.

The Field Marshal knew about eight Russian words. These he was trying most earnestly to arrange into a sequence which would convey his meaning.

"Maybe he's asking her to join the Red Cross," said Dick Lauterbach.

The pretty waitress kept shaking her head.

"I guess she doesn't like the Red Cross," said Bill.

"Or she could already be a member," said Dick.

"Maybe we ought to break it up," said Bill.

"She's not in any trouble," said Salisbury. "She's handled drunks before."

And even as he said this she slipped away, and with a friendly grin to us went in and began clearing off the table with her friend the blonde waitress.

The Field Marshal approached us unsteadily. He was annoyed.

"Listen," he said. Then he paused. "If you want something in this town, no use fooling around. Just one guy to ask. If he tells 'em, they do it. I'm going to ask Mike. What's use having friend, if you don't use 'em? If he tells her, the argument's over." He went on through the door.

"Maybe we'd better stop him."

"Mike'll handle him."

"Mike's pretty tight."

"Mike's not that tight."

Mike was tottering uncertainly but with great dignity under the arch which led into the hall. The other Russians had gathered around the piano and were singing. The two waitresses were clearing the table.

The Field Marshal approached. He put an arm around Mike. Mike nodded with grave contentment. With the other hand, the Field Marshal pointed at the brunette waitress. Both waitresses were watching this out of the corner of their eyes as they worked. Then the Field Marshal tapped his own chest and pointed to the bedroom floor above, looking gravely at Mike.

Mike considered, then slowly and emphatically, as one who has come to an important decision, he nodded. He beckoned to the brunette waitress. But before she could cross the room, the blonde one appeared, bearing two water glasses she had hastily filled from a vodka bottle. Automatically, each took one. Automatically, they drank. Then the Field Marshal lurched through the archway and up the stairs toward the bedrooms.

Again Mike beckoned the brunette waitress. He stood for a minute talking to her just past the arch. We could not see her face or whether she was still shaking her head. Then Mike beckoned again, this time toward the front door, where the NKVD man was stationed. He gave him some kind of orders. Then he lurched off down the corridor to his own room.

Now the NKVD man was talking sternly to the girl. This time we could see her shaking her head firmly.

"My God, are they really going to do it?"

"I don't like to watch this."

"But remember, Mike was drunk. They were both drunk."

"Where I come from you don't get that drunk."

"Listen, don't get hysterical. It could happen any place. Have you ever been to a clambake?"

"No, and I don't guess I like clams. I don't want to even watch it. Let's step out for some fresh air."

"But you haven't watched anything yet."

"Let's just stand here. To see if it's really that kind of a country."

The brunette waitress was still shaking her head when the NKVD man gripped her by the upper arm. As they went upstairs he was still holding her firmly.

"All right. Now you've seen it. I suppose at the clambakes they grab them by the arm and lead them?"

"Lot depends on what kind of clams they're having."

"Well, I want some fresh air. I don't like the smell of clams."

Just below the lighted porch was the tennis court. On it was the motion picture screen. Two operators were patiently waiting on a near-by bench. It had been about eleven o'clock when Eric decided he did not want to see "Volga-Volga." It was now almost four. As we came to the edge of the porch, a switch snapped and the screen lit up. They thought we were coming down.

"Hey," shouted Dick in Russian. "It's all right to go home!"

The figures only stirred.

"But who are you? They're waiting for Mike to tell 'em they can go. Unless he remembers, they'll still be here next Wednesday."

"No cinema tonight!" shouted Dick in Russian. "It's all right to go home. Everybody's in bed now."

This time the figures switched off the light and began packing the gear.

"And I suppose that's where we'd better go," he added in English.

We walked back across the porch. Just as we entered the dining room, we saw the brunette waitress come down the stairs alone. She had been gone less than a minute. She went into the dining room. She was smiling. And she was completely unruffled. So was her neat hair and her clean starched apron. She quickly whispered something to her blonde friend, and they went briskly about stacking the dishes.

"Well, what do you know! Is that how it is at the clambakes?"

"If they really make up their minds, that's how it always is, any place."

We went over to the waitresses, and said it had been a fine dinner. They thanked us, and hoped we had been well served. We said we had been very well served, and thanked them again.

Then the brunette, with a perky smile, said it was a pleasure to serve us at the table. Anything we wanted. At the table.

Then we said she was an extremely nice girl, that in our own country we didn't know any nicer.

She thanked us again, and said she had a fine, two-year-old baby and a husband in the Red Army.

We said we bet he was a brave soldier.

She said he was and also handsome.

We said we were sure of it, and went on upstairs. As we thought, the Field Marshal was lying across the threshold of his room, out cold.

"I'd just as soon leave him there."

"Don't be romantic. Maybe some day you'll get tight."

"Or get as old and silly as he is, so you'll have to fall back on your political pull."

So we undressed the Field Marshal, all but his shorts, and put him to bed. But we didn't hang up his uniform. Then we went to bed.

The next morning we start out, none too bright and unreasonably early, to visit Lenin Optical Plant No. 69, which now makes range-finding equipment for artillery and tanks. Its director is Alexai Kotliar, a sober Russian of thirty-six, who has been director for four years, before that production chief and before that an engineer. He was originally from Leningrad but was evacuated with this factory, arriving here November 16, 1941. Sixty per cent of its 15,000 workers came with the machinery; the others volunteered to remain and defend the city, so their places have been filled from the local population.

The factory is clean, well-lit and apparently very well-run, for no one is idle at the benches. Walking down the assembly line, Kotliar explains the process to Eric, but Mike lags behind, talking to the workers, a wave of the hand to this one, a pat on the back for that—a ward-boss patrolling his precinct.

"Get a load of Mike!" says a correspondent. "Isn't he wonderful? Strictly Tammany!"

"What's he saying to them?"

"Ask Dick: he's been back there listening."

"That last little girl—the cute one that he patted on the head—he called her by her first name, said he noticed on the board she's overfulfilled her norm, and why hadn't she joined the Komsomols? She said well, she didn't quite know why, she was working pretty hard and all those meetings took so much time. Then he said she ought to think it over. That the Party needed smart girls to work hard for Russia. She said she would."

The director here is proud of his precision work. We ask him if it is as accurate as the great Zeiss plant in Germany—admittedly the best in the world before the war. He says it is now as good, but only recently and there are two reasons. One is that they have been bringing up the standard here. A second is that Zeiss standards are deteriorating, to judge by the latest trophies captured.

Then they take us into the testing rooms where optical equipment is subjected to cold—50 degrees below zero—and then past benches where the glass is precision-ground.

At this point a pretty Komsomol presents Eric with a bouquet of flowers and a speech, to which he must reply in kind. During the pause we get some information out of Mike. First we ask him about restrictions on traveling; and he says here there are none. Back in Moscow, Leningrad and in the war zone region, yes, of course. But on this side of the Urals travel permits are not hard to get.

Then we ask what happens if a married couple are working in the same factory (most of them do) and the husband is mobilized, sent to the front, and later discharged and assigned to another factory. Must the wife remain where she is?

Only if she prefers it, Mike tells us. If she applies to work with him in the new factory, it is usually granted. They don't separate families.

One of the correspondents is disgruntled. A famous Russian fighter pilot is convalescing here in Novosibirsk with his wife and family. The correspondent had asked and received from Zemenkov, our Foreign Office chaperone, permission to interview him. It would be wonderful to get into a Russian home for some real atmosphere.

But now Zemenkov tells him this would be entirely too much trouble, so that the pilot will be brought to the *dacha* for the interview.

"And you know I think they really mean well, but that's Russian hospitality for you. Drop a hint you'd like to go fishing, and they break a leg to bring you a bucket of whale meat."

"Have you heard what happened to Magidov?" asks a correspondent.

"No—what?"

"Of course, you know how good Magidov's Russian is—born here and all that. Well, it seems last night when Mike was tight he backed Magidov into a corner and said, 'We know all about you. In the last war you were a czarist officer and fought against us; we've been keeping track of you—you were a bad boy. But that was a long time ago; we're willing to forget and you can come on back. You'd look pretty good in a Red Army uniform, and three stars on your shoulders wouldn't look bad, either, would they?'"

"Wha'd he say?"

"Said no, no, they had it all wrong; he'd left Russia when he was a boy and certainly had never been a czarist officer. But Mike said, oh, yes, he had; they'd kept track of him. That if he didn't want to come back, that was his own business but he might never get another chance. Said he'd fought in the civil war himself and considered it a poor afternoon when he didn't kill two of those bastard czarist officers. Poor old Magidov, I don't think he slept much."

In the factory dining room each of us is presented with a fine pair of 8 x 30 Red Army field glasses, with our names engraved in Russian characters, and, of course, there is another banquet. Eric handles the toasts smoothly and then we go back to our cars which will take us to the *dacha* where we can catch an hour's rest before the next banquet there.

On the way to the cars, a correspondent overtakes me.

"Had a little run-in with Mike," he says.

"What happened?"

"Guess I kind of blew up at him. You know, all these banquets and everything. So I finally just told him: 'You haven't got Marx and Lenin here at all!' I said. 'You've got the damnedest inequality I ever saw!' Asked me what I meant. 'Why, look at all this food you give us!' I told him. 'We can't eat half of it—it must be thrown away! And then all these starving people! We have nothing like that in America!' I told him. 'We don't have that inequality! I've read Marx and Lenin and they certainly weren't for that!' "

"Wha'd he say?"

"Said I was all wrong. That Lenin had never been for equality. Said equality was only a dream they hoped to realize in the far future. That now, people were paid on the basis of what they produced. But I guess I got him pretty sore."

Back to the *dacha* for a brief rest before the evening banquet. A part of Novosibirsk hospitality to foreign guests is a comely female barber who arrives in your room wearing a spotless white surgical gown. You sit in a chair and she does the rest. Joyce has the works first and then she goes into Eric's room while Joyce lies down for a nap. I read a magazine waiting my turn, while Joyce dozes in the next bed.

By the time I had been shaved and was in my seat at the banquet table, Mike Kalugin had risen for the first toast. He was talking slowly and looking from face to face with narrowed eyes. Magidov was translating.

"Mike says," said Magidov, "that this will be our last dinner together, that we have been good friends, that he has tried to show us Novosibirsk and the hospitality of a Siberian, and he hopes we have enjoyed ourselves."

Mike continued with measured words, his eyes narrowed to slits.

"He says parting with friends is always sad, but on some occasions it is less sad than on others. On such occasions guests who have pretended to be friends of the Soviet Union after they have left have become traitors—writing and saying bad things about the Soviet Union. Parting with traitorous friends like this is not very sad, he says."

The room was in complete silence. But when Mike began again, his eyes were not quite so narrow. There even seemed to be a grim smile on his lips. Through the ferns, I could see Eric at the other end of the table. His face was stern.

"Mike says," said Magidov, "that he is sure our friendship is not like this, so our parting is truly sad, and he invites us to drink that our friendship may forever endure."

Then we rose to drink the toast, but after it Eric remained standing. He filled his glass, and raised it, looking first at Mike and then at the interpreter. His jaw was very firm.

"We have enjoyed your generous hospitality," he said, looking now at Mike, "and when I was invited to the Soviet Union, it was agreed that I would be free to say and write exactly what I thought when I got home. While there are many things that we admire about the Soviet Union, I must be frank with you; there are some things I do not understand. When I get back to America I shall feel perfectly free to say exactly what these are.

"For instance, I have never understood the policies of the Communist Party in America, although it is not strong there, and has fewer members today than it had twenty years ago. But the Soviet Union should understand that if the American people feel Russia is interfering with our local affairs through this Communist Party, then co-operation between America and the Soviet Union will be impossible.

"As you know," he said, "in Moscow I saw many of your important people, and only four days ago I saw Marshal Stalin. I talked with them and with him as frankly as I am talking to you now. And, therefore, I also want to raise my glass to a toast for the continuation of Russian-American friendship."

We drank. Mike rose rather slowly to his feet. For a minute he stared at the tablecloth. Then he looked sharply across at Eric and began to speak.

"He says," translated Magidov, "that from the days of the Civil War, when he fought with the Red Guards, he has always followed the discipline of the Communist Party, as he follows Marshal Stalin today. He says the Marshal now tells us that we should not interfere in the affairs of other nations. That we should get along with foreigners. That's all he wants to know: it will be done. So he raises his glass to the health of his great leader, Marshal Stalin."

That finishes the toasts. The artists of the opera are here to entertain us tonight at last, and a plump one rises to sing. Mike dances with her while the next is singing, and this reduces to jealousy the slender blonde with the single gold tooth who had, the previous night, restored him with hot tea. But when he sits down between them, talking impartially with both, tranquillity is restored, at least on the surface.

We are tired, departure for Alma-Ata tomorrow is early, so very soon the Americans excuse themselves.

But there is at least an hour's champagne left on the table, so we hear the piano until almost midnight.

Breakfast next morning was in the same room, and as we sat down the mayor of Novosibirsk, apparently having first obtained Mike's permission, rose for a toast.

The mayor said they had found Americans to be good and warm friends; he could assure us that Russians were also warm friends. But if a friendship is broken, Russians can be terrible in their anger. Russia's friendship with Germany had been so broken, and to her great sorrow Germany now knew the weight of Russian anger. Then the mayor wished to Mr. Johnston and to those with him a pleasant journey on through the Soviet Union, and that they would get safely home.

We finished the caviar, Russia's breakfast substitute for scrambled eggs. We nibbled at the French pastry, trying to pretend it was buttered toast. We drank the glasses of tea, longing for just one cup of coffee. Then we rose. The correspondents were bringing down their bags.

Then the ten servants of the *dacha*, including the two pretty maids and the cook, lined up alongside the dining table and in true baronial style, each was given a glass of vodka to drink our health. Outside five cars were waiting to take us to the airport. We had seen Novosibirsk.

And now, while we are on the plane, headed south out of Siberia and down into the country of the Tartars and the Mongols, whose nomadic emperors Tamerlane and Genghis Khan once ruled all Asia and threatened Europe, let us consider this Communist Party whose rule here is no less absolute.

In 1917 when it seized power after the collapse of the Romanov dynasty, the Bolshevik Party was a handful of Marxist theoreticians. Russians only fleetingly enjoyed freedom and the Party then assumed the autocracy of the Autocrat of all Russias. The heritage of this Party is in almost equal parts of Marx and of Genghis Khan.

The small hereditary ruling class from whom the Bolsheviks seized power did little to justify their privileges. Lenin was able to outwit the gabbling lawyers of the Duma because Russia was not ready for the liberal democracy they hoped to establish. The greatest indictment which can be brought against Stalin is that, because of his iron rule which suppresses freedom of opinion, Russia is still less ready today, in spite of his paper constitutions.

In America, a Republican can be anyone—white, black, rich, poor, drunk, or sober, who has decided he likes the party's principles or candidates. But becoming a member of the Communist Party is as difficult as joining a yacht club. The usual first step is to join the Komsomols or Young Communist League, which works under the direction of full-fledged Party members. After some time in this, the aspirant may apply for Party membership. For a year he is watched carefully. Everything about him is investigated—from his work habits and political opinions to his sex life.

The Party wants only intense workers who will subject them-selves completely to a discipline as rigid as that of any army. It also tries (with less success) to exclude those who may not have strong convictions about its principles, but see it as a necessary step on the ladder to success. It does not want "careerists" although in Russia membership is indispensable to a career.

Once the coveted membership is gained, the man is less closely watched, but any slackening in zeal, any deviation from the Party's political line, or any signs of "personal ambition" are punished with expulsion. These admissions and expulsions are controlled by the Party's secretary, and in the early days this was put in the charge of an unobtrusive Bolshevik named Joseph Stalin. Only after Lenin's death did the more prominent Communists like Zinoviev, Kaminev, Bukharin, and Trotsky come to realize that the man who controls the Party's membership controls not only the Party but all Russia.

The high Party members, who now wield the power of the Ro-manovs, have moved into both the palaces and the privileges of the old aristocracy, and are drinking quite as much champagne. But no one can argue that they do not justify their existence by hard and useful work for the state, and by taking leadership and responsibility.

Class distinctions are rapidly springing up in Russia. But, for the present at least, these distinctions are based on achievement and hard work—even though the achievement may sometimes be only political skill necessary to climb to the top of the hierarchy.

"He's got everything a Commissar should have," the correspond-ents once said, "a motor car, a peroxide wife with gold teeth, and a *dacha*." But at least, he got these things by hard work, presumably (and usually) in the service of the people and the state. The privi-leged class in Russia is full of the rich sap of hard work. There is in it so far none of the rotten dead-wood of hereditary fortunes, piled up by useful men with vision but handed down through generations of weaklings who yet retain the privileges.

The Communist Party had about 5,000,000 members until Stalin's purges beginning in 1936 reduced it to about 2,500,000. After the war began the base was broadened and membership raised to 4,500,000, many from the army. But since responsibility for leadership goes with Party membership and Communists are supposed to (and do) set an example of personal courage, an unduly large number of them have been killed and nobody now knows the exact membership.

One of the Party's functions is to provide the Kremlin with accurate reports on the state of Russian public opinion for of course this exists even as it has under both Mussolini and Hitler. In the field of foreign affairs, of course, the people have no facts other than those provided by the government-controlled press. But in domestic matters the Russian people have definite ideas as to what they like and do not like. The Party is sometimes unable to check a trend in public opinion. If it is a real ground-swell they do not fight it, but divert it into proper channels.

They remember 1917, when they themselves rode into power on the crest of a tidal wave of unrest which the old autocracy failed to recognize in time, and was too stupid to handle. They expect similar unrest after this war, and are sure they will be quick enough to canalize it before it gets out of hand.

American correspondents in Russia who are most warmly sympathetic with the dictatorship say that it amounts to a government by the Gallup Poll, which is much too rosy a view of the facts. The dictatorship is, of course, acutely concerned with public opinion. But most of this is created by the government's own press; another portion may be directed into safe channels—and there remain a few instances where the government finds it must abandon, reverse, or postpone policies because they are too unpopular.

Only in foreign affairs does the dictatorship have a completely free hand. Since no Russians may travel abroad except on official government business, the people know nothing of the outside world except what they learn from their controlled press, which is of course only what their government wants them to know. Lacking any independent basis for judgment, they must accept wars, allies, and peace treaties as these are handed out from the Kremlin.

Some observers in Moscow think even this will change. They say that the top Bolsheviks realize what they have lost by not permitting their people to travel abroad, for Russia has always sorely needed foreign help. But always they say—even if it grants this concession—the Party will control.

On one side of the picture this is a slave empire. On the other side it is a vigorous, dynamic empire—moving on.

"Hey," said the Field Marshal, "the Intourist interpreter is certainly off of me."

"What happened?"

"Oh, some crack I made. Probably shouldn't have."

"Wha'd you say to her?"

"Oh, just that she was pretty lucky, having this soft job with Intourist which lets her have all those nice clothes and all this food with us, while the other girls go around, some of them, without any shoes."

"Wha'd she say?"

"Flared right up. Said those clothes went with her job. And that for ten years she'd worked as a hotel chambermaid, swabbing out cans and cleaning bathroom floors, and she guessed she'd earned the right to nice things. So I couldn't argue."

Twelve

𝒲E ARE FLYING south out of Siberia, down into the ancient Oriental peoples now ruled by the Soviet Union. For the first few hours the country is still Siberia—lakes, chill swamps, marsh grass, and forests. Slowly the lakes disappear and presently the forests dwindle. We watch the checkerboard patterns of the collective farms.

Suddenly we are crossing a huge blue lake. It is so big that when land drops away behind us we still cannot see the shore ahead. When it does appear, we see the beginning of a rolling desert. On our left a chain of blue, snow-capped mountains rises like a fence. Geologically, they seem about as old as our Rockies. On the east side of this fence is China.

The desert below is not scorched sand like Africa or Arabia, but its thin yellow grass obviously can support little human life, although we see an occasional collective farm huddled along a water course.

We have entered Kazakstan, of which Alma-Ata is the capital. A word on the Kazak people. Eric, who knows the Orient, says they look exactly like the Chinese of Manchuria. I have never been there, but I can't tell them from our Southwest Indians.

They are part of the savage nomadic tribes who for a thousand years have pressed against Europe and once formed a part of the armies of Genghis Khan and Tamerlane and Atilla's Huns.

When Europe invented the rifle, they sank from the status of a terrible menace to that of a constantly harassing threat.

In the past few centuries the Russian people have been pouring through the Urals to colonize Siberia as our settlers crossed the Alleghenies to civilize the West. Like them, the Russians had to struggle with these savage Mongolian nomads, whose culture was only a little higher than that of our American Indians. They can duplicate our wars with the Iroquois, the Sioux, and the Blackfeet. They have battled the equivalent of Geronimo and Sitting Bull and they have their Custers who made valiant Last Stands, but who finally, after a series of border wars, opened the continent to the White Man. We penned our Indians up in reservations. The Russians found another solution as we shall see.

We come in close to the mountain range, losing altitude for our landing. We step out onto Alma-Ata airport at the base of the foothills into a country exactly like that around Boulder, Colorado, or Colorado Springs. The trees, the scenery, even the weeds are the same: I can hardly believe I am on the other side of the earth, and that across these snow-capped Rockies lies not Utah but China.

Again as in Colorado the June sun beats down hot through the thin air, and it is so dry that in the shade it is almost chilly. The group which greets us at the airport is about two-thirds Russian and one-third Mongolian Kazak.

"What the hell are those?" demands the Field Marshal suspiciously.

Kazaks, he is told.

"Hm. Kazaks. For my money they're Comanches." He rubs his scalp nervously. "Many of those fellows around here? They're all right, aren't they?"

Both the prominent Russians and the prominent Kazaks wear immaculate white raw silk suits. We shake hands and climb into cars for the drive into Alma-Ata, which, like Denver, is on an irrigated plain with mountains rising in the background. We pass through cornfields, where sun flowers grow along the irrigation ditches— again exactly like Colorado. The farm houses are of sun-baked brick, made of clay and straw—the adobe of our Southwest.

This Soviet Denver is a sprawling Russian town, which before the war had 180,000 people and now has 400,000. Take away Denver's automobiles, its new residential district, its business section blinking with neon, fill it up with shabby, hard-working Russians and equally shabby Kazaks, and you have Alma-Ata.

We are taken to a clean, modern hotel, where our party occupies one entire floor. We have the afternoon free, except that Eric who is very tired mentions a sun bath, and around here his slightest whim is not only law, but apparently a part of the Constitution of the Kazakstan Soviet Socialist Republic. They bring out Zeeses and we are driven for half an hour up a mountain canyon following a stream, which boils down over boulders. The water is yellow so the creek must be up and I say they must have had rains on up the canyon. Eric guesses it comes from glaciers melting in the hot June sun, and he proves to be right. Along the road where the canyon is broad enough, we pass a few farm houses and patches of cultivated land and Kazaks wave as we pass. Finally, we get out and climb 50 yards above the road to a big rock which is the site for the sun bath. On up the canyon the blue snow-caps rise; back down it we can see the heavy haze of the plains.

My feeling about sun baths is that when I need vitamin C it is simpler to eat a slice of lemon than to let ants crawl over me. But Eric is entitled to hold a contrary view.

That evening after the customary banquet we go to the local opera, where they give a performance based on an old Kazak folk tale. The actors are all Kazaks as are the words, music, and costumes. It is a beautiful show, and gives us a vivid idea of what these people once were like. The costumes are clearly derived from the Chinese and a musician picks out a haunting Oriental tune on what looks like a Chinese banjo while a pair of twin Kazak boys sing.

All of their culture came over the mountains with them but today it is preserved only here in the opera, for the clothing of those we see in the streets is not picturesque, but is a drab composite of clean patches indistinguishable from the rest of the Soviet Union.

Next morning they take us for a drive out through the irrigated river valley, past pink adobe houses indistinguishable from those of New Mexico (lacking only the strings of red peppers) to a great Soviet experimental station—one of four in the Kazakstan Republic. Kazakstan, by the way, is four-fifths the size of all Europe exclusive of Russia, but it is largely arid like our American dust-bowl.

We meet the Russian director of the station, Andrei Pruss, who shows us around. This is a fruit farm, where under irrigation they are raising apricots, peaches, cherries, and plums. They are keenly interested in the performance of a plum which they recently brought here from Canada, and which is already producing more than twenty-five pounds of fruit per tree. In this particular orchard they are using the most modern system of subterranean irrigation. Pipes are laid under the ground. But they are proudest of their vineyards; in 1914 they had 3,000 hectares of land in grapes. Now they have 30,000.

Workers on this state farm get only 300 roubles a month in salary, but at the end of the season they get a produce dividend of about 700 kilograms (roughly 1,500 pounds) of vegetables, which includes corn, melons, and pumpkins. Then each has his own irrigated garden plot—about a quarter of an acre for each worker. If they wish to sell the produce dividend on the free market, they get such prices as 50 roubles per kilo for raspberries, 5 roubles per kilo for sugar beets, 3 for watermelon, and 12 for apples. These are low compared to the Moscow free market prices—as they should be, here in the heart of the fruit country.

We ask the director about himself. He gets 1,700 roubles a month and pays monthly 35 roubles for two large rooms in a big house which he shares with someone else. The rent, he says, is figured on the basis of 1 rouble, 30 kopeks, per square meter of dwelling space. In American figures, this is about 10 cents a square yard.

The farm, the people, and their methods look good. Russians are born with green thumbs.

Now they take us back for a tour of the movie studios, which at the beginning of the war were moved out here from Moscow. Overnight Alma-Ata has become the Hollywood of the Soviet Union. But best of all we meet the great Soviet director, Sergei Eisenstein. He has worked in Hollywood and knows the leaders of the motion picture art all over the world.

Eisenstein is, as his name indicates, of German-Jewish origin. He is a short, fast-thinking, friendly little man, whose curly gray hair is not quite so bushy as Einstein's. He and his staff wear colored polo shirts with short sleeves in the Hollywood manner, and Eisenstein wears a well-cut white linen suit.

He begins to tell us of his present great work filming the life of Ivan the Terrible, of which we have already heard much in Moscow. Ivan is one of the newly resurrected Soviet heroes. Eisenstein speaks fluent English, with a slight but agreeable accent.

"All the things that had previously been done on Ivan the Terrible," he says, "were in the wrong line." They were about his personal character and underlined the cruelty of his later years. Now, however, Eisenstein explains, the "line" on Ivan the Terrible has been changed. (He seems to accept this philosophically, as every Soviet artist must.) "This time," he says, "we are bringing out the fact that in his earlier years he was a great builder of Russia—quite a normal czar, in other words."

Ivan's life will occupy three full-length motion pictures. The first part was finished in October, 1943. The second was scheduled to be done by January of 1945, and the final part would be completed by the following October, 1945. Of course, we are anxious to see shots from the picture but only the day before the film was shipped to Moscow, and all Eisenstein can do is to take us through one of his sets. It is a replica of a great medieval throne room—in one end of which a table is set for a traditionally staggering Russian banquet. Only this time we don't have to eat. The wine jugs and plates are papier-mâché and the jewels which adorn them are colored glass.

They now announce we must go to the provincial capital, where we will meet the president of this Kazak Soviet Republic. It had been scheduled for the following day because the president has a cold with four degrees of fever. But on hearing Eric's decision that we must leave tomorrow morning, the president of Kazakstan has risen, dressed, and gone to his office where we are now taken to meet him.

It is in the administrative capital building—an impressive, new white edifice with simple decorations inside which are dominated, of course, by the usual Soviet pictures. At the windows are immaculate, pongee curtains, and the officials sitting around the table wear white suits of the same silk.

The name of the President-Premier of Kazakstan is Nutras Undasinov. He is a pleasant, kindly old Comanche or Sioux, who except for his European clothes, might be the dignified tribal chief you would meet on any Indian reservation. Most of his cabinet ministers are also Kazaks, but there are a few blue-eyed, blond Russians present. The Russians, however, are in the background.

We ask the Kazaks about the early history of their country. They tell us the people racially belong to the Turkoman-Mongol group, and were fighting for independence as early as the twelfth century, when the southeastern part of the present republic was under the rule of the Chinese Seventh Dynasty. Later they adopted the Mohammedan religion. The title of the hereditary ruler was the Khan—as in Kublai Khan and Genghis Khan. The Mohammedan religion is still popular—many people go to the mosque.

But Kazakstan is now one of the republics which make up the Soviet Union, and has a great measure of independence; recently it was given the right of a separate foreign minister, they tell us proudly.

But Joyce is irritated by this line of questioning. He whispers to me, "Never mind all that stuff—get it out of any encyclopedia." Then turning to the premier, he says, "You say now this is an independent republic; well, tell us about some of the conflicts you've had with the central government."

This is translated but the premier is baffled.

"Now in America, there are lots of conflicts between the various states and the central government. Tell us about some of the conflicts you've had with Moscow."

The premier says there haven't been many conflicts, and lets it rest at that.

"Well, now, you say you have the right to send ministers to other countries; who will you send them to? Will you send one to America?"

A big Russian down at the end of the table, who has hitherto kept silent, now tactfully leans forward and suggests that such ministers will be sent to those countries most useful to them commercially.

Joyce turns back to the premier. "All right then, are you going to send one to America or not?"

The premier doesn't believe that has been decided yet.

"Well, who will decide it?"

Of course, that would be decided in Moscow, the premier explains. But Joyce is not satisfied with this triumph.

"Give me one instance of your past differences with the central government; you must have had them."

The premier goes into a long dissertation. For centuries, he explains, his country was the gateway for invasions from the south, and these destroyed and impoverished the people. At the time of the 1917 Revolution the people were 93 per cent illiterate, and the few who could read were either Russian priests or civil servants of the Czarist government. Today illiteracy is gone, and the Soviets have built many theaters and schools. Naturally, the people are grateful, so why should there be any disputes with the Moscow government? The Soviet Union is a united whole. Of course, there are disagreements; a few years ago there was one between Kazakstan and the neighboring Soviet Republic of Uzbekistan over the use of water for irrigation from the river which divides them. Finally, each republic appointed a committee and they ironed it out. Kazakstan is rich in agriculture; Henry Wallace, when he stopped here, took back some seeds to try out in America.

But Joyce will not be put off. "Now, I want to understand your political system here," he says to the interpreter. "Ask the premier how he got his job."

The premier explains that the people elect delegates to a regional Soviet, who send delegates to the Kazakstan Soviet, who chose him as premier.

"All right," says the Field Marshal, "now ask him how Stalin got his job; we want to understand it. Ask him that."

There is an awkward pause, and then the handsome Russian down at the end of the table leans forward and explains smoothly and briefly the intricacies of the Soviet electoral system. He did it politely and there was no feeling that he was brushing the premier aside; only helping him over the hard places.

In 1926 I visited the Osage reservation in Oklahoma. Oil had been struck on their land and the tribe was rich. We had an interview with the chief in his ceremonial feathers. He was a fine old Indian, but when our questions got too hard, there, as here, they were politely answered by the reservation agent, a bright young man sent out by the Coolidge Administration.

Likewise when we ask how many refugees are here, it is the alert and friendly Russian who tells us that a million are still here, although many have already gone back to the reoccupied territory.

If this alert and handsome Russian occupied any official position in the cabinet of Kazakstan, we missed it. Possibly he was only the local secretary of the Communist Party.

They now present Eric with a complete Kazak costume which consists of a gold-embroidered robe more gorgeous than anything I have seen this side of a Shriner's convention. But its crowning glory is a hood of red velvet, with ear flaps the size of soup plates, and the whole, including the ear flaps, is lined with silver fox fur.

Eric is both grateful and taken aback, and having donned the robe, is about to put on the hood when Joyce suddenly clutches his arm, with a wild gleam in his eye.

"Watch out, man! Don't do that!" he whispers hoarsely.

"But why not, Joyce?" asks Eric, holding up the silver fox and velvet.

Joyce leans closer and grins. "Bedbugs!" he whispers. However his fears are groundless.

I don't know why the party they gave us at the hotel that night was the most pleasant we attended in the Soviet Union. Perhaps because it was the most informal. The dinner was elaborate as usual, but for some reason, it wasn't stiff. The local notables were at hand, but they were easy, friendly notables.

There was, for instance, the local Foreign Office representative, who attended in full uniform. We were surprised to find one so far out in the back country, but he explained that Alma-Ata is on the frontier—the main Soviet Port of Entry from China—so he has to be here. But he was obviously homesick for Moscow, which was his home—lonely and hungry for any tidings of the great capital.

There is an attractive girl—she teaches dancing at the local academy and has been included for the obvious reason that she speaks good English. It is fairly fluent but curiously awkward. She explains she has learned it all from books and until now has never spoken with an American or an Englishman.

There are vice-premiers, councilors, and members of the local government, some Russian and some Kazak. There are also half a dozen stars from the local opera—all Kazaks. There are twin boys in their teens, who sang last night, now resplendent in twin Tuxedos, of which they are very proud. There is a Kazak girl of about twenty, who danced the role of the Oriental princess with the cruel father. She could be any of the pretty Indian girls who, when Indians had oil money, were sought after by sororities at the University of Kansas.

Then there are two older artists—women in their forties, who, except that they look like sisters-in-law of Madame Chiang Kai-shek, could be any of the Russian artists who have entertained us in the other towns. Their evening dresses are just as good, they have as many gold teeth, but in addition they wear beautiful Oriental jewelry set with precious stones—old Kazak workmanship worthy of a museum.

I wish I could write that they sang and performed well; alas, they did not. At best they were only fairly good, verging on down into the frankly terrible. But they had worked hard, and it was clear that they sang and danced better than any other Kazaks, and were proud that the Russians had chosen them to represent their people in the arts.

Most of all, we liked them as people. They were gentle and friendly, and obviously had never been warned against foreigners. Almost the same thing could be said of the Russians. That invisible barrier of tension and suspicion which separates Russians from all foreigners had been slowly dissolving since we left Moscow. Here in Kazakstan, it disappeared entirely.

In proof of this I submit the fact that for the first time since we arrived in the Soviet Union, no toast was offered to Stalin. Of course, it was not deliberate. But we were having such a pleasant, easy time that everybody forgot these compulsory formalities. Likewise no one remembered to drink to Gospodin Roosevelt. Possibly, the day after we left, these oversights were noted and several people may have been shot in atonement. If so, I am sorry, but at least we had our golden moment.

First the little Indian princess sang. She was only fair but a nice child, so we applauded. Then the twins sang. They were worse, but so anxious to please, we gave them a big hand. Then they wanted to hear some American songs.

Eric, who did a stretch in the Marine corps, led us with, "From the Halls of Montezuma to the Shores of Tripoli." Then we insisted the Russians sing one of theirs, so they obliged with "Volga Boatman," singing it magnificently, letting it die away at the end, as Russians always do and no American singer ever does.

When they wanted another from us, Joyce obliged with "Three Blind Mice" which delighted them, and they came back with an ancient Russian rondel, which translates as follows:

> There was once a priest
> And he had a dog.
> He loved her.
> But she ate a piece of meat
> So he killed her.*
> He gave her Christian burial,
> And on her tombstone he wrote:
> There was once a priest,
> And he had a dog.
> He loved her.
> But she ate a piece of meat—

And so on, far into the night.

We came back with, "My Name is Yon Yonson, I come from

---

* In czarist times it was believed that a dog if fed meat would become savage.

Wisconsin, I work in the lumber yard there." And after that Eric led us in "I've Been Working on the Railroad."

The Russian girl who taught dancing told me it was very nice to find that we Americans had so many songs about working, that it made them realize we too were a nation which believed in hard work, even as they did, even if we were capitalists.

Then it was my turn, and since my repertoire was completely exhausted, the only genuinely American song I could think of was "Pepsi-Cola Hits the Spot!" which they applauded as loudly as the others, although they said such a wine was unknown in Kazakstan, and inquired from what grape it was made.

One of the Russians got up for a little toast to the Kazak artists. He said he hoped we had enjoyed them and told us that the Kazak artists were taking their place in the great artistic world of the Soviet Union; that Kazak artists had gone to the front to entertain Red Army soldiers, so we toasted Kazak artists.

Relaxed and at home for the first time in weeks, I was enjoying these friendly, hard-working people, and thinking how little they were allowed to know of the war outside Russia. My toast was long, certainly sentimental and probably in bad taste. I paraphrase it here only because of the curious effect it had on the Russians and Kazaks.

I started by saying I was both surprised and pleased to learn that Soviet artists entertained at the front and regretted I had known so little about all they were doing in the war.

Since I had not known this, I thought perhaps there were many things American artists were doing which they did not know. For our artists were taken by plane thousands of miles out into desolate Pacific Islands, or across the great Atlantic into camps in Italy and France, to sing to them the old tunes of our homeland.

I told of the English artists during the 1940 blitz, when both Russia and America were neutral. And of how the little island that had stood alone against Hitler was saved by a handful of boys in her air force. (At this point in the translation, Nick, the NKVD man from Moscow, frowned a little and shifted uncomfortably in his chair, but no one paid much attention to him.) How terrible their losses were only the boys themselves knew at the time.

But in those months when they were going up to almost certain death, their artists had come out from London to give them the best that the English people had.

I explained that we had in the American army a morale problem, which did not exist in the Soviet Union. For Russia was invaded and every Red Army soldier knew he was fighting for his own home soil.

But no invader had set foot on American soil, and yet we were sending our boys thousands of miles away to oppose the fascist aggressors in a war which many had thought we need not enter. Small wonder, that sometimes these lonely, homesick men asked themselves why they were being sent to die capturing islands and cities whose names they had never heard. And all the more need to give them our best to cheer their loneliness, to prove that their own people had not forgotten. Then I offered my toast to the artists of all Allied nations.

We drank. There was a silence, but not an uncomfortable one. Then a Russian got up and said they had been most interested to learn what English and American artists were doing. And he would now tell me more of what Soviet artists were doing—not to boast but only because I myself had said I was sorry I had known so little. Soviet artists, he said, followed the Red Army into battle. They went up to the front in tanks. They sang in trenches and in dugouts. Many had been killed, but they gladly died to bring cheer to the men.

I thanked him for telling me, and we toasted the bravery of Soviet artists.

There was another thoughtful silence, and then a very nice and spontaneous thing happened. One of the Russians started to sing "*Lubeme Gorod*" and they all joined in. It is a sad, magnificent war song, but there is no class hate in it. It is only the song of a little sailor of the Red Fleet who in the morning is going into battle. He sings of his home village for which he will die, and the good people in it, and the good Russian earth. We Americans, of course, did not know the Russian words, but we could join in singing "la—la—la" for we had heard it several times before but never as it was sung tonight. We could sing—beating the table, some of us with tears in our eyes—for the homesick boys of all countries. For the moment nobody cared whether Nick, the NKVD man, might think Russians were getting too friendly with foreigners, or whether Eric Johnston, on his return, would recommend that American business grant long-term credits to the Kremlin, or any of the troubles that normally occupied us. We were singing for the homesick boys of all countries, and hoping that the fighting would soon be over, and that they would come safe home.

After this we get up, one by one, from the table, talking in groups. One of the Russians at the dinner is a plump young man who represents the Soviet news agency, Tass, in Alma-Ata, and who speaks a little German. The two young Kazak artists bring him up to me to translate for them into German, which I understand.

Very earnestly they ask me if I enjoyed the singing and, lying a little, I say I certainly did; particularly theirs.

Then they shyly ask me if I find them cultivated.

I answer yes, and then lying a little more, say that this does not surprise me, for even before I came I had heard fine things about the Kazak people. Then I ask them if they find me cultivated.

This question surprises them greatly. They say but, naturally, I am cultivated, for after all I am an American.

Then I say this does not follow, for there are many who say Americans are not cultivated. This they do not believe, but they are now less worried about the problem of how cultivated they are.

At this point, the plump Tass correspondent beckons them aside and talks for half a minute, while they nod their heads in agreement.

Then they come back to say that if I write of this trip when I return, they hope I will not forget the young Kazak artists, or the Kazak people for whom Stalin and the Revolution have done so much. Because before it, the Kazaks were a poor and fearful people, hiding in the high hills.

But the government coaxed them down into the valley, and there built dams for them and gave them irrigated land, and showed them how to plant orchards, and how to build for themselves many schools and this beautiful theater I have seen. And they have taught the young Kazaks to sing and play their own songs and stories in their own speech. So today the Kazaks are no longer a people huddled in the hills, frightened of others and ashamed of themselves, but a nation proud of itself. And if I write of the great Soviet Union, will I please not forget the small Kazak Nation?

The Tass correspondent then plucks the Tuxedo sleeve of the twin who is talking, and whispers something in Russian, and the twin adds that all these things they owe to their great leader, Stalin, and will I also write this?

So I assure both twins that I will remember to write all these things.

Then the piano in the next room starts, and a pretty little Kazak girl in Spanish costume begins an Andalusian dance with a young Kazak partner in bell-bottomed velvet trousers. But the music is far away, the girl falters, makes a misstep, bursts into tears and, covering her face with her hands, runs off the floor, ashamed at having disgraced her people before these mighty foreigners. We all try to comfort her, and someone suggests the piano be brought into this room. But this can't be done, because the Comrades whose duty it is to move pianos have gone to bed.

Whereupon the correspondents pick up the piano and bring it into the room so the girl may finish her dance. This causes much wonder, that such dignified and well-dressed foreigners should so casually pick up a piano, and someone suggests that it is an example of that Amerikanski technique of which they hear so much.

Then the Kazak girl asks me if we still build skyscrapers in America, and I say not since the war. Then she wants to know if they were ever really useful or were they not built only as exhibitions of this great Amerikanski technique.

I start to tell her that, unlike Russia, nothing is ever built to exhibit technique, but only in the hope that it can be sold or used to the profit of the builder. But this would only confuse and perhaps offend her. So instead, I urge that she now finish her dance, which she does this time without a misstep. And because it is now late, we say good-by to the Kazaks and go to bed.

The thing I liked best of all about the Soviet Union, and it is one we would do well to copy, is the intelligently decent Russian attitude toward minority races. They are helped without being patronized, and they have developed self-respect and an understandable gratitude. If they have no real freedom, neither do the Russians.

While this Soviet racial-colonial policy may not be so good as our handling of the Philippine Islands, it is infinitely better than our bungling and thoughtless treatment of the Negro.

Thirteen

*A*LL MORNING we fly south again, paralleling the Tien Shan Mountains. It is like following the Rockies down their eastern slope, Cheyenne past Loveland and Boulder and Denver and Colorado Springs, in the direction of Raton pass toward Santa Fe.

On our left is the towering wall of the Tien Shans, separating us from China, India, and Afghanistan. They rise to more than 20,000 feet—much higher than the Rockies and geologically they are newer—their crags are steeper and there has been less time for erosion, although they are not so new as the Alps.

On our right is dry rolling country, with collective farms on the plateaus and along the water-courses of the winding streams. In America such country would be dotted with great herds of red Hereford cattle—like the semi-arid grazing lands of Colorado, New Mexico, and the Texas Panhandle. I see none here. We are now approaching a mountain pass and struggle for altitude. It is relatively as high as Raton, which separates Colorado from New Mexico.

Beyond the pass, rolling, grayish black hills stretch away to the horizon—as dry and barren as the mountains of the moon. Here and there a little river rises from nowhere, struggles through a valley just far enough to nourish a collective farm, and then loses itself in the sand. We fly over many lakes—greenish white with crusted salt—or gray-white patches which are dry salt marshes or old lake beds. We have now left Kazakstan and enter the neighboring Socialist Soviet Republic of Uzbekistan, whose capital is the ancient Mohammedan city of Tashkent. Ahead we sight the broad blue coils of a great river winding through yellow desert sands, its banks green with the irrigated plots of collective farms.

Today I am riding in the caboose plane with the correspondents. The bucket seats are rugged, but the buffet service is as good as in the plane ahead. It even includes fresh strawberries, taken on at Alma-Ata. Dick Lauterbach pays a visit to the toilet and returns shaking his head.

"I'll never get used to them. Five thousand feet above a howling desert they serve us strawberries, caviar and champagne, and then I go back there and find nobody has remembered to empty the chemical bucket for three days."

As we begin losing altitude for the Tashkent airport, we see roads over the sand converging toward the city. On one is what appears to be a line of marching spiders. Coming lower, we discover it is a caravan of heavily laden camels.

The first thing we remark about Tashkent, while the plane's wheels feel for the runway, is its scorching heat. This desert is no less blistering than Egypt, and the green strip of river bank does nothing to break the heat. Next we see the crowd of airport-greeters. As at Alma-Ata they are wearing white silk suits. Again half are Russian and half local Orientals. Since we are now in the Soviet Republic of Uzbekistan, the local boys are known as Uzbeks. A sartorial note here; the jackets of all Russian white silk suits button up to the collarbone and have high turned-down collars like the Chinese. With them they wear, not Panama hats, but caps made of the same white pongee silk.

The cap, incidentally, is a relic of revolutionary days and was symbolic of the working class, since only bourgeois exploiters wore felt hats. Recently, the government has begun making felt hats, explaining that in the new Russia, they need no longer be regarded as a badge of shame. I notice, however, that all the old-time Bolsheviks still cling to caps. Nesterov, who was a Party member when he was sixteen, always wears one. Mike Kalugin wore one. And, of course, Stalin, in all his pictures. As a hall-mark of the old Bolshevik aristocracy, the cap is probably politically safer than the hat.

But now for the Uzbeks; racially they are a mixture. They resemble the near-by Afghans, and others might have Persian or Arab blood. Occasionally we see a Mongolian face which has strayed down from Kazakstan.

We have hardly shaken hands when they hurry us into cars and across the town to our first factory. Tashkent is an enormous sprawling city of cracked and peeling stucco with wide, hot, dusty streets not unlike Teheran, except for its empty, dingy Soviet shops. But we are by now so used to this we hardly notice. Finally, we arrive in the clean, comfortable office of the director of the Stalin Textile Trust of Tashkent.

What with the heat we are frantically thirsty. They start to open champagne but we stop them, pleading for water. So they bring out bottles of that warmish, pink soda pop which Russians always proffer their guests instead. Mercifully, there are on the table half a dozen fresh peaches. In half a minute the plate is empty and in another half minute it contains six peach stones. Ordinarily, I don't care for peaches, but nothing ever tasted so delicious. Only now do I realize how starved we have been for fresh fruits and vegetables.

We get acquainted with our new hosts. The plant director, Nikita Ryzhov, is a thin-faced Russian production man, friendly but serious. He tells us a few facts and figures. The plant was built in 1934, and all of its equipment is Russian except for one division, which has some American machinery.

Since we crossed the Ural mountains we have seen little American machinery—indeed, few foreign machines of any kind.

There are now 14,000 workers in this textile plant, the director continues, and 80 per cent are women. The raw material is cotton, grown under irrigation in this valley as in that of the Nile. But they also weave silk, which they import.

The war has shrunk this plant. In 1941 it had 16,500 but now they have less work and most of it is for the army—shirts and underwear.

They tell us the plant's total production is, in terms of money, half a billion roubles.

The director explains that, unlike England and America, they don't count their production in square yards or meters. They figure in running meters, and on this basis, they turn out 260,000 meters every day, the cloth being about 89 centimeters wide.

Profits since the war began are hard to estimate, he tells us. But in the last peacetime year their net was 60,000,000 roubles.

Patterns? The director doesn't know how many thousands they have on file; he only knows they can fill any order they get. They matter little now, since 90 per cent of their work is for the Red Army.

Now for the workers. Their hours run from eight to ten daily according to their age, and they average more than 1,000 roubles per month, although some crack ones make as high as 4,500. In addition each worker averages between five and six meters of cloth per month as a premium. They can make this up into dresses and underwear, trade it for food or sell it for whatever price they can get, just as the farmer on the co-operative may dispose of his food dividend.

With us in the office is the mayor of Tashkent. He is a dark little Uzbek, a friendly but rather timid Oriental. His name is Sadik Khusaynov.

Before the war, he tells us, Tashkent had 700,000 people and more than 50 per cent were Uzbeks. At the peak of the evacuations, there were 900,000 but now it is back down to about 850,000. Of course, many more were cleared through Tashkent, staying only a short time.

Many machine-building industries were evacuated here with their workers—mostly the light and medium but a few heavy machine industries as well. They also have aircraft production here.

At this point a big, handsome, full-faced Russian with very blue eyes—who reminds us of Wendell Willkie—moves up and sits down by the mayor. More precisely, the big Russian tells us, they have here a plant making Douglas planes. Also a light machine tool plant which is converted to turn out arms and ammunition for the Red Army.

The big Russian adds that they also have shoe factories and garment industries here, plus a plant for making emery stones needed by heavy industries.

The handsome young Russian is Rodion Glukhov, and he is vice-premier of the Uzbekistan Socialist Soviet Republic. Now and then he interrupts—always picking up for the mayor if he falters. He isn't obtrusive, he has put his arm on the mayor's shoulder in a most friendly way, yet somehow the little Oriental looks ineffectual.

It is Glukhov who tells us that Uzbekistan had a total of 2,000,000 evacuees. About 60 per cent of them settled in cities; 90 per cent of these have now returned to their homes.

However, other evacuees came with their plants, and, of course, these will stay permanently. Where had the plants come from? From Moscow, the Ukraine, and the North Caucasus. And from Leningrad they have many skilled workers and engineers. He tells us with a smile that, of course, Leningrad is anxious to have these engineers back, but Uzbekistan is anxious to keep such valuable men. It will be for Moscow to decide.

But, we ask, what about the people themselves? Where do they want to live? That seems to be a matter of little importance. The workers would want to live wherever Moscow decides they are most useful.

He tells us that Uzbekistan before the war had 6,200,000 people, so the addition of 2,000,000 refugees was a big task. But when we ask him how he managed it, he politely refers us to the mayor.

The little Oriental explains that the first problem was to receive and house them. They made a survey of dwelling space, and squeezed in all they could. Then they built many new one-story houses. In Tashkent alone tens of thousands of square meters of new living space were built for evacuees.

Then there were the industries. They needed hundreds of thousands of square meters of factory space. The big Russian breaks in to tell us that all had to be improvised quickly, for before the war they had had no plans for receiving refugee plants. And from here on out it is the big Russian who answers our questions.

The evacuations began in July of 1941 after the bombing of Moscow. The industries began arriving in October.

He tells us they had only two weeks' notice before the first trainloads arrived. And then it was only a month before they were settled into their new factory and production had started.

There were many problems. For instance, a huge munitions plant evacuated from Rostov-on-Don had left its foundry behind. Back in Rostov it had taken two years to build. Here in Tashkent they finished one in twenty-eight days. A great aviation plant was moved from Moscow; within a month it was up to 80 per cent of its former production.

The second big problem was food, but in this, Uzbekistan asked no help from the Central government. Every factory got a grant of land and all of its workers cultivated the soil after hours. The Uzbekistan Republic furnished horses for the plowing and arranged for the arms factory to turn out a little agricultural machinery. The Central government in Moscow sent in seeds.

The big Russian is vividly re-living the struggle for us. In 1942 crops were poor because of lack of experience. But in 1943 they were better; this year they are excellent. It has been a good year for fruits and vegetables, and the factories expect to raise all their own fruit. For instance, this particular textile plant will harvest, on its farm, three times what it raised last year.

There was a second means of raising food—the individual victory garden. Although each factory had its farm, workers would come to the mayor asking for individual plots, with the result that there are now fifteen times as many plots as before the war.

The first wave of refugees and refugee plants came from July, 1941, to February, 1942. Then there was a lull, but military reverses in the North Caucasus brought a second wave, from July to December of 1942.

We now start through the plant, entering a huge, clean, well-lighted building with endless rows of looms all turning out heavy sheeting. At first I assume this to be the entire plant, but it is only one small section. Others are making different weaves and weights for uniform linings or women's dresses. The designs—similar to those used for calico—are etched on copper cylinders. The dress fabric is considerably heavier and coarser than we use in America, which is only sensible considering Russia's colder climate and the harder wear these dresses get.

They explain that the factory has only recently started making print goods for civilian consumption. For three years Russian women have been wearing their old clothes. And who will get this limited new supply? The shops maintained by those factories or farms which have over-fulfilled their norms. Again we see how little money means in the Soviet Union. If you don't work in such a lucky factory, it is almost impossible to buy such a dress at any price.

In still another section they are weaving parachute silk for the army. We see only women workers and they wear ragged home-made sandals. Many are barefoot. They are practically all Russians —with now and then an Uzbek.

Eight thousand people work in this mill, which has 250,000 spindles. Another 6,000 work in the electric plant, machine shop, and motor factory which are necessary to keep the looms in re-pair. They are proud of their product. When we ask what their highest thread count is, they tell us 70 to the inch, which is good by American standards. They say they are duplicating the output of the best British mills.

I know nothing of cotton mills, but this one was clean, orderly, bright and seemed well-managed, although one of the correspond-ents who watched carefully insists that 25 per cent of the machin-ery we passed was idle. But threads break in all mills.

We are driven several miles out to the *dacha* where we will stay. It is as comfortable and spacious as the one at Novosibirsk. A natu-ral American question is to ask who owns this rural mansion. Here we have learned to ask what it is used for. This particular country place is a rest home and summer vacation place for members of the Uzbekistan cabinet.

Now another character enters the scene—a plump, middle-aged woman called Nona. She has large, warm blue eyes which she swivels this way and that. She seems to have been called in as a hostess. She is the kind of big, friendly, jolly girl who makes herself useful on picnics.

Nona was probably assigned to us because she spoke excellent English, which she had learned in a most curious way. Not too long ago she had been "the mother," as she explained it, to a number of American pilots who had been forced down on Russian soil after Aleutian bombing-raids. They were scrupulously interned by the Soviet government which is neutral in the war with Japan. They had been housed under guard in a *dacha* similar to this and Nona was in charge. She was fond of them all, and they had brought their troubles to her.

Nona was born in Leningrad, where she married an architect. Not long after their marriage they had been sent to Tashkent where seven years ago he died. She is proud of him and later points out a co-operative apartment house which he designed. She has not re-married and what her job is we never learned. She is by Soviet standards remarkably well turned out, with plenty of afternoon and evening gowns. Yet I have noticed that under all systems in all countries, good-looking, hard-working, intelligent girls are invariably well-dressed.

That evening Nona goes into town with us to the local opera house (new, and well-done with Oriental decorations copied from ancient Uzbek designs) for a concert. They give, especially for us, one act of an opera based on an incident in Uzbek history. This is followed by a couple of vocal numbers and then by a "jazz band" which is on tour from Georgia (U.S.S.R., not U.S.A.).

About half the crowd in this theater is Russian and half Uzbek. Watching the act from the Uzbek opera I begin to realize that the most admirable thing about the whole Soviet Union is what we might call its colonial policy—its relationships with the smaller and sometimes backward races. This is partly accounted for by the fact that Russians historically have few race prejudices.

Instead of Jim-Crowing the weaker peoples, the Russians lean over backward to give them titles and offices which, if anything, are rather beyond their capacities. At first, I jumped to the conclusion that the native office-holders were stooges, dressed up and provided with fancy offices but with little real power. This is in the right direction, but it is possible to jump too far. For we learn that the premier of this republic is an Uzbek and a smart one—an old-time Bolshevik with a steel-trap mind, highly respected in the party councils. We are assured he is no stooge. He is apparently as powerful here in his own right as was Manuel Quezon in the Philippines. He is now in Moscow conferring with the Kremlin, and the less important matter of entertaining visiting firemen is relegated to his handsome Russian vice-premier.

Returning to the *dacha* we have our nearest approach to a row with our Russian hosts. Our route takes us near the ancient Oriental cities of Bokhara and Samarkand, where Tamerlane is buried. These names out of Arabian Nights have fascinated me since childhood; I have been curious to see the clash between Bolshevism and the world of Kublai Khan. Can they really mix commissars and camel-caravans?

Eric is as excited as I am. Like a litany Kirilov has been repeating, "Well. Perhaps. We will see. Maybe I call Moscow."

But tonight he announces there is no airfield at Bokhara or Samarkand big enough to accommodate a Douglas. We can go up one day by train (it takes twelve hours), see Bokhara on the second and return the evening of the third. But as Kirilov well knows, Eric does not have that much time. The Russians talk heatedly among themselves about our request. Are they hiding something down there in the Arabian Nights country?

Since I am so keen on ancient cities they offer a brief tour in the Oriental quarter of Tashkent. We drive through the broad streets of the new Russian town to the old city, which is a labyrinth of winding alleys like those in the Arab Medinas in North Africa, the old quarter of Jerusalem, the Cairo bazaar, or the cities of Afghanistan across the border. But just outside this old city are two beautiful new white buildings, both ornamented with Uzbek designs—the post office and a huge cinema. The Russians have put their two most beautiful modern buildings in the native quarter instead of in the center of their own section of Tashkent.

I stop the car to take a picture of the cinema when still another car—a dilapidated Zees—which has been behind us, pulls up at a respectful distance and waits. There are five men in it—the local NKVD. When we go on it follows.

When we stop to walk through the ancient city it also stops. At first there seems nothing to see but adobe walls enclosing cobblestone streets—with here and there a carved doorway. There are no windows in the walls; Uzbeks don't believe in them. There are only a few of us—two American reporters, Nona, who is translating, and the plump Tass correspondent who has been riding with us since Alma-Ata.

Finally we engage a shabby old man in conversation who offers to show us his house. We gladly accept. With an ancient, six-inch iron key he unlocks a door under a pointed wooden arch, and we step out of the drab alley into a gem of a garden with a fountain in the center. At one end of this patio is his home—two clean, white-washed rooms, some low furniture. On the floor is a mellow Oriental rug which he says was his grandfather's, and a polished brass samovar. He apologizes that his wife is not home to offer us tea.

We admire his rug and garden, thank the courteous old Uzbek and, after I take a final picture, are about to go when the Tass correspondent who has been talking to the old man, beckons me back.

The old man now tells me, as Nona interprets, that if I write any of this in America, I should understand that he is an old man, who has seen many years go by, and well he remembers the days when the emirs ruled this land. And that in those days he was not a man. But now he feels like a man, and is treated like a man, and for this he has to thank the Revolution and Comrade Stalin. I thank him, and I particularly thank the Tass correspondent, and then we go out. But for all of the Tass man's helpfulness, I think it may well be true.

All Soviet streets are clean—even the crooked alleys of this Oriental town which elsewhere in the east would reek of garbage. But I must for the record tell Hal Denny's story of the eager professor.

For years Hal was New York *Times* correspondent in Moscow, and we first met in Helsinki during the Finnish war. Hal had just come from Moscow, of which he was unutterably weary. One of his afflictions there had been the numbers of eager tourists who came every summer to spend the few weeks necessary to study the marvels of the Soviet system and become authorities on this Land of the Future.

One such gusher, a professor of municipal government in a mid-western college, arrived to spend a month studying his specialty. After two weeks in the library he showed up at Hal's room, break-ing in on a party of homesick correspondents, and began to talk about the marvels of the Soviet town-planning system. Because here at last was perfection! Here finally was order out of chaos, everything anticipated, all problems solved!

Hal at this point always adds that all Russian plans are marvelous, provided you study them in the Lenin Library and don't bump into the results.

All, all was marvelous, the eager professor insisted; their methods of police protection, taxation, utilities, elections, and administration! Yet on the rather unimportant topic of sewage disposal there seemed to be no literature. Soon he would find the proper book, but in the meantime could Hal tell him what they did with their garbage?

The answer, instantly given by that roomful of correspondents, rose in spontaneous chorus: "They eat it!"

Perhaps this is why even the Oriental alleys are clean in this hungry land where there are no dogs, cats or cockroaches, where tin cans and carefully straightened nails are sold in the market place.

In passing let it also be on the record that we saw no beggars, although I am told they sometimes hang around church doors. But in a country where there is work for all but everybody is a little hungry, and more than a little shabby, no one in his right mind would give anything of value to a stranger, and most of them have too much self-respect to ask.

From the Old City we hurry across town to the airplane factory, still trailed by that battered Zees-load of NKVD plainclothes men. Why? I am not irritated, only curious. In this busy country it takes the time of five men and an automobile to spy on me while I take pictures. No wonder they keep our party herded together; it would take scores of cops and cars to tail each one if we scattered out through the city.

Travel in the Soviet Union is expensive for the foreigner, but his tour must be even more costly to the government, which must hire spies to follow him.

We arrive at the airplane plant a little ahead of time and are taken to the director's room to wait for Eric. I am half choking with thirst and my eyes light up as I see a bottle of water sitting on the big table.

I reach for it—but too late. One of the Russians has whisked it out of the room.

I would like a drink?—it will be only a moment. The champagne is ready for Mr. Johnston's arrival. Perhaps I would like a glass now?

"Thank you, I'd much rather have water."

Water? But certainly and here it is. They produce a bottle of the familiar syrupy sweet carbonated soda pop.

"No, thank you, not that. Just a glass of plain water from that bottle which was on the table a minute ago."

Oh, but that was left there by accident. It was old water, left from yesterday.

"But I'd really prefer it."

Well then, of course, they will put it on ice, and as soon as it is properly chilled, I may have a glass.

I give up.

When Eric arrives, the forty-year-old director, Afanasy Yarunin tells us this plant, which builds Douglas airplanes, arrived here from Moscow in November of 1941 with 7,000 of its workers, and thirty-five days later was in production. Now they have 14,000 workers building a Russian modification of the DC-3 and they turn out six planes daily.

With us this model Douglas is seldom used for anything but transport or cargo; for other needs we build special models. But the Red Army has modified the Douglas so that it can be used as a combination transport, paratroop ship, hospital plane, and night bomber.

Because it sometimes goes into battle, a huge transparent gun blister bulges from the top of its fuselage, creating a wind-drag which must cut at least 50 miles per hour off its speed. They also use wood in the floor-braces, partitions, and doors. The director insists it is as good or better than aluminum and easier to work.

Perhaps in Russia, where both aluminum and tools to work it are scarce. But aluminum is stronger and wood, under machine-gun fire, dissolves to flaming slivers.

Russia pays no royalties to Douglas, having paid a flat sum in 1939 which the director believes was $2,500,000. Before that, his chief engineer, Boris Lisunov, worked in the Douglas Long Beach plant for two years, so they needed no American help when they set up production in Moscow. Only about 5 per cent of the machinery is American; the rest was made in the Soviet Union.

The plant is in good shape. We estimate that they are turning out at least as many planes as a similar number of workers would produce in America. Remember also that our man-power shortage is not so great as theirs and our workers include no twelve-year-old boys such as we see here. It is the best Soviet plant we have so far seen.

Now we are taken out into the desert to visit the Stalin-Chirchik Electro-Chemical Trust, which, when it is unscrambled, turns out to be a Soviet Muscle Shoals. They have dammed the Chirchik river, providing the 100,000 kilowatts of electric power necessary to run a huge nitrogen-fixation plant, which makes 80 tons of ammonia every twenty-four hours. Before the war it turned out 600,000 tons of fertilizer per year.

This is an impressive plant, likewise orderly, clean, and apparently efficiently run, but we see most of it through blinding tears, since our eyes aren't used to the escaping ammonia, confined here under great pressure in gigantic tanks and boilers. They show us compressors which bring the pressure up to 600 atmospheres, and miles of stout tubing connecting the huge tanks. For a stunt, they bring out a pail of liquid ammonia, infinitely colder than ice and boiling merrily at room temperature.

All of this complicated equipment was made in the Soviet Union, they tell us, although some of it was designed in America. And at

the noon banquet they have the usual outlay of wines, but we remembered for days the deliciously cold beer and water, chilled
by the liquid ammonia.

Without a minute's rest (because eating is the most grueling
part of our work) we are packed into cars and after a half hour's
drive unload at a "fruit factory," an irrigated valley.

They walk us down an incredibly long arbor where grapes hang
so low they knock our hats off. At its end we arrive at a pavilion
where (Oh, Heaven! Be merciful before these well-meaning people
kill us!) a long table is set for another banquet.

They tell us they are experimenting with cotton. This sovhoz
(state farm) raises seed for all the kolhoz (collective farms) in the
region.

This particular experimental station was started by an ancient
Oriental with the jaw-breaking name of Rizamat Musamukhamedov,
who is brought out to meet us. He is now sixty-three and started
working in the vineyards as a boy of thirteen. He is an Uzbek of
a peasant family, a thin, dreamy man with an Uzbek skull-cap (or
tubeteyka) and a scraggly beard out of Arabian Nights. His work is
known all over the Soviet Union. He has on his coat the ribbons of
many state decorations.

Most of the information we get from the Russian director, Abram
Maltezeb. The big struggle since the war, he tells us, has been for
sugar. Russia has been without it since the Germans moved into the
Ukraine. Four refineries were evacuated from there to Uzbekistan,
still others to Kazakstan. The four plants exiled to Uzbekistan are
training local workers; when they are finished the Ukrainians will
go home and new plants will be built for them.

Since the Germans seized the sugar beet fields of the Ukraine,
Uzbekistan has planted 35,000 hectares in beets for sugar, with this
year another 15,000 hectares for seed for the liberated Ukraine.

Irrigation is responsible for the heavy yield of the seventy-five
kinds of grapes grown here. At this point the grizzled old Uzbek
scientist, who has given fifty years of his life to grapes, picks up
the theme.

Uzbekistan, he tells us, can grow every kind of grape in the world. The average yield is 22 tons per hectare, with water supplied three to five times a season so the yield is steady. But they have produced as high as 40 tons and he hopes to live to see 50 tons per hectare. Samarkand is an even richer grape country. And, as here, the little hand-work done is on the grape collectives—most of it being done by tractor. The possibilities here, he says, are unlimited, because "we have the skill, we have the good land, and we have the will to work."

What we have seen of Soviet agriculture has been uniformly good. Since I come from a farming state I could not be badly fooled. True, they have shown us their best. But it is at least as good as our best.

We are returned to the *dacha* in time to change our shirts for the local opera. We'd like to beg off but this big, blue-eyed vice-premier is a slave-driver. It is his duty to show us his booming new province and the opera is an important part. We see something called "Ulug-Beg" which was one of the titles of Tamerlane, and its story is of his times. Between acts we are taken into the banquet room (Yes, God help us, the usual table is laid.) to meet the composer, a slender young Russian intellectual who has arranged these primitive Oriental tunes for a beautiful ballet. His wife, a handsome but worn-looking girl, who has written the words—not in Russian, mind you, but in Uzbek—is here to explain the plot to Eric.

Her English is fluent and beautiful. If she hadn't told us she learned it in America where she spent a few years as a child (undoubtedly during the Revolution) I would have guessed she had learned it at Oxford.

We are fascinated by them both. The opera is a lovely thing. Here are two young intellectuals, interested in the theater, who in any other country would gravitate to its metropolis. She tells us casually that once they lived in Leningrad.

What brought them down here to the ends of the earth?

"Do you like Tashkent?" I ask.

"Yes," she answers, a little wearily, there is much material for her husband's work in the old native songs, and, of course, she is busy, for she had to learn Uzbek in order to write the verses. When they first came they had a lovely old house down in the native quarter, with an ancient garden. Small, but lovely. Now they have been moved into an apartment. They left Leningrad for Tashkent seven years ago.

I count back. That would make it 1937, the year of the purges. People were exiled for knowing foreigners. This girl, with her beautiful English and her cosmopolitan manners, surely must have known many.

"Why did you leave?"

"For various reasons," she says.

"Were they political reasons?" I ask.

"No," she says.

"And are you happy here?"

"We have our work. And in Russia one should go where one is most useful. Here there are many themes—much to be done."

At this point, the vice-premier and Kirilov come up to talk to Eric. After a few minutes Eric breaks away and suggests to the girl that they stroll in the foyer with the crowd. Kirilov and the big vice-premier, ever attentive hosts, get him between them for the stroll.

And this, almost the last vivid glimpse into the Soviet system, was perhaps the most revealing. Personal happiness counts for little. Loyalty to the Party, to the leader, to the cause are all. You go where you are sent. If you should find yourself in Tashkent, you may then be most useful for the rest of your life down in the baking heat, writing beautiful operas which only Uzbeks hear, in words which only they understand, to do your small and quickly forgotten part in giving self-respect to what was once a half-savage tribe.

At first I thought Kirilov and the big vice-premier didn't want us to know this. Thinking it over I realize that they probably would not care, or see reason to apologize.

Now for a personal story; I had a secret motive for wanting to go to the near-by city of Bokhara. In the early twenties a hard-headed American businessman went to Russia under the New Economic policy and as a concessionaire did so well that the government owed him a considerable sum in roubles. He made a deal under which they paid him off in glittering finery from the attics and storage closets of the murdered czar—some of it gaudy, bejeweled junk, but there were ancient Byzantine things of real beauty. I saw them on sale in New York and one thing fascinated me: a long robe of old burnt orange velvet lined with magenta and heavy with gold and silver embroidery. Covering the shoulders was a gleaming medallion of Oriental design.

It was on sale with an elaborate parchment certifying it as a coronation present to Czar Nicholas II from his vassal the Emir of Bokhara. The truth of this I then doubted but its beauty needed no parchment. Impulsively, I bought it as an evening wrap for my wife. Since which time it is known in our family as "The Czar's Robe" to be brought from its cedar bag only on state occasions.

I wanted now to go to Bokhara because some trace of the fine old craftsmanship might remain in some knickknack I could buy.

After what Kirilov had said of the airfield there it looked as though I would never see Bokhara, although it lies so close to Tashkent that the old emir ruled both cities. When the curtain went up on the second act of the opera "Ulug-Beg," I got a great surprise. A flourish of Oriental trumpets announced the entrance of the Emir of Bokhara and suddenly there it was—a blaze of velvet —the same embroidery—the Czar's Robe! I learned that the actors had borrowed from the local Soviet museum for this performance, the state robes and jewels of the old emir, who died only a few years ago, an exile in Afghanistan just over the border. So, if Soviet moths ever devour this robe of state, there remains one other, in our cedar bag.

When the opera closes after this tightly scheduled day we are weary beyond words and long for bed. We are to leave early in the morning. But the handsome vice-premier is firm. After we have finished the banquet here at the opera, we must see the operetta theater where a special program has been prepared for us. Limply, we are dragged across town through the hot desert night.

This open air theater is packed to the balcony with a crowd

about nine-tenths Russian and one-tenth Uzbek. They are singing an aria from "Maritza," immensely popular in the Soviet Union. A juggler follows, and then the grand finale: chorus girls prance out in costumes made in our honor—red and white striped trunks, and blue, star-spangled brassières. Hopefully, they sing a Russian translation of "There'll be a Hot Time in the Old Town Tonight."

Because our hosts look at us expectantly, we applaud feverishly.

Zimenkov leans forward. "Typical American dance, yes? You like it?"

"Fine," I say, slipping into his lingo. "Some day you come to New York I show you typical Russian dance." He ponders this and then suddenly looks at me sharply.

And yet how hard they are working to please us!

We are now pitiably tired and wonder how the big Russian vice-premier and his cohorts have the energy to escort us back to the *dacha*. When the door opens, we understand. There, in a blaze of light, is the final banquet—our farewell to the Soviet Union—the caviar, the champagne, the roast pig. As he meets its cranberry-eyed gaze, Joyce blanches in horror, turns, flees to his room.

"Now, Bill," says Eric, "I just can't do this. You make my excuses to these fellows. Tell 'em I don't feel well. You and the correspondents have a good time. I've got to go to bed."

Puffy-eyed, we sit down. Because I can't look at food any more, I sit sidewise in my chair. But the Russians are standing.

"Where is Mr. Johnston?"

"He's gone to bed. He's very tired."

"To bed?" They don't sit down, but talk among themselves. They seem angry. Then one approaches me.

"Could it not be explained that this is in his honor, and that many important people have come?"

I weaken. "I'll see how he's feeling."

Wearily, Eric gets back into his shirt and tie.

There are the usual toasts to Stalin and Roosevelt. Eric is presented with an Uzbek robe of gold cloth, Joyce gets one of silver, while I get one of red silk. The other correspondents must settle for Uzbek skull-caps.

I talk for a while with the little Uzbek mayor, next me at the table. But the vice-premier is talking. It is his broad-shouldered driving energy which has caught the factories hurled from European Russia and planted them in the desert, which has put millions to work damming rivers, building industries and carving out the new Russia.

He is sure of himself, of the driving power of this Bolshevik system and of the new world it is opening up down here among ancient Oriental tribes. He is telling us that he is glad he had this chance to show the new Russia to Mr. Johnston and to the American press.

"But there is one thing which I ask of all correspondents," he says, "and in particular of Mr. White." Here he pauses and I sit up in alarm. "It is, that he will present the material objectively, and under no circumstances to give it to the press of Hearst."

I hope I have satisfied him. I should add that I liked him and his province.

Then the fat little Tass correspondent came up. He was pretty tight, and his German sketchier than usual. But he explained that I should take no offense at what was just said, because none was meant. "*Wir wissen das Sie waren in Finland*," he said, "*aber das ist ein kleine Sache nur*" (here he snaps his fingers)—a little, little thing and is now forgiven of me. Because it was long ago that I was in Finland, and now they will trust me to be objective.

I thank him for this compliment and their trust, assuring him that my passion for Finns is now buried under rivers of Soviet champagne, so at last I can be objective.

Then I go to bed and to sleep.

Fourteen

NEXT MORNING I follow the custom of all correspondents leaving Russia, which is to divide among my colleagues all my worldly goods (unpurchasable in Russia) except the clothes on my back. For days they have been looking covetously at my extra notebooks, spare socks, shorts, pencils, paper clips, shirts, handkerchiefs, tooth paste.

For here we leave them. Kirilov has announced that they may go by train to Bokhara and Samarkand tomorrow, while we fly on this morning to Ashkhabad, the last Russian town on the Persian border. So at last we know that we were almost as suspicious as they. All our secret forebodings that perhaps they reserve these two old Oriental towns for a special torture-ground for Poles or the Baltic middle classes dissolve before their frankness. It was only as they had said—the airfield was so bad that the big vice-premier would not take responsibility for Eric's safety.

The reporters and all the Tashkent Russians come down to the airport to see us off. In the car I ride with Nona. As we drive down a boulevard (Tashkent is very well paved) she tells us that near by is the cottage of her mother and father, a retired engineer. They live on his pension of 1,000 roubles a month, which in peacetime is decent but now is too little. But fortunately they own their house. Yes, you can now own a house in Russia and, if you like, either rent or sell it at a profit. Of course, its land belongs to the state. If they ever need it for a government store or apartment, they pay you only the cost of the house. But now you can borrow from the government without interest as much as 10,000 roubles, which will build a fair house, Nona says, and you have ten years to pay.

Eric has picked up the information that a doctor or dentist, who, of course, works in a state hospital, may have a private practice after hours, and charge what he likes—just as the peasants may sell their share of the collective's vegetables for any price, after the government has bought what it needs at the fixed low price. However, the doctor must conduct his private practice not at the hospital but in his own home, and must provide his own instruments.

Nona, swiveling her big eyes, tells me how much she liked the American pilots.

I ask her about the composer and his beautiful wife whom we met last night at the opera, but she does not know them.

"They used to live in Leningrad," I say.

"And so did I," said Nona. "It is a beautiful town."

"They were sent down here," I say, casually but slowly, "seven years ago."

"So-o?" says Nona, even more slowly. Her bedroom eyes have stopped swiveling.

"That," I say, "would be the year 1937."

She turns to look at me. Then she looks straight ahead. Nick, the NKVD man who probably doesn't speak any English, is in the front seat. We can see the back of his thick cop's neck. For quite a while nothing is said.

Then Nona begins talking of the American pilots. Such charming young boys! And when they left, several had wanted her address, so that they might write her after the war when they were in America. But at that time she had not thought it wise. She swivels her eyes on me.

"I see you know how things are with my country. You understand."

I nod.

"Only now," she continues, smiling, "with everything so good—so very, very good, with America and my country—well, you understand. Anyway, give me a pencil, so I write their names on this piece of paper, and if you ever meet them after the war, you may say to them that they may now write to Nona, if they still want to."

Just as we get in the plane I discover a forgotten can of pineapple juice and a roll of toilet paper I had cached there. It seems a shame to take them from this land of shortages, so I scramble back down the ladder and present the toilet paper to the Field Marshal and the pineapple juice, with a bow, to the little Uzbek mayor of Tashkent, who, with the big Russian vice-premier, has come down to see us off.

He was a friendly little fellow and very kind to us.

Taking off, we rise over the city, and set off southward, following the river. Below we see trails and camel caravans plodding along. While Eric, Joyce, and I may not visit Bokhara, Kirilov has arranged that we shall glimpse it. Presently the Russian co-pilot comes back with the news that we are nearing the city and that the pilot will turn so we may see all.

It slides under us—first the Oriental city, a maze of tiny alleys through yellow mud walls radiating from the central turquoise-domed mosque. We see the spacious royal palace which was once occupied by the old emir in Oriental pomp and our burnt-orange robe. Undoubtedly Commissars sit there now in white pongee suits. At one edge of the old town the new Russian city begins—wide, paved streets laid out in squares like any modern town. Taken together the two might be an air photo of any North African city—the old Arab quarter and the new French town.

Leaving Bokhara we also leave the green ribbon of irrigated river valley and enter a howling wilderness of yellow sand, as dead as the Sahara. Far out in this we spot an ancient lost city—its river dried, its walls crumbled, the dome of its mosque caved in—deserted. But there are traces of camel trails to it, left after all these decades or centuries.

Then more sun-scorched yellow sand—hours of it, until we see ahead another wandering green ribbon and know that soon we will see Ashkhabad. They tell us this desert is Turkmenistan, a Soviet republic about the size of California but 85 per cent desert. The region was once famous for its fine Oriental rugs which were called Bokhara rugs only because the tribesmen sold them in Bokhara to dealers who, under the czars, came from all over the world. But the actual weavers were these Turkoman desert tribes. Specialists in Paris and London could tell in which savage village each rug was woven, by minor differences in design.

We had planned only to stop at Ashkhabad for fuel, and push on over the near-by border to Teheran. But our start was so late that the pilot may decide to stay overnight here. The air currents in the mountain passes beyond Ashkhabad are tricky in the afternoon.

Kirilov, thank God, has promised us there is to be no schedule in Ashkhabad so if we must stay we may rest at the hotel after the banquets, ammonia plants, and operettas of Tashkent.

As we land, two surprises greet us. First a blast of desert air, oven-hot at 120 in the shade if there had been any. Second the local committee of dignitaries. It is like all the others except it is a trifle shabby, its white shantung suits faintly soiled and raveled at the cuff. In addition to looking solemn, this committee looks wistful. It is mixed Russian and Turkoman.

We look balefully at Kirilov.

Kirilov looks at his shoes.

"Now, Kirilov, see here—" begins Joyce, indignantly.

"I know," says Kirilov. Poor patient man, buffeted on both sides!

"But you promised us no schedule here!"

"Perhaps. We will see. Maybe I call Moscow."

"Call Moscow, hell. Now you tell these fellows we're tired. Got to get to bed all afternoon. Tell them what they did to us in Tashkent—"

But Kirilov is already talking with the wistful local committee.

"Now we go to hotel—to banquet," says Kirilov, and before we can interject he is off. We follow—anything—even a banquet—to get in the shade.

With the committee is a buxom Russian girl in her late twenties, the Intourist interpreter assigned to us. Her English is excellent.

The hotel of this frontier town is a dismal, ramshackle affair, but they give us their best—three rooms up three long flights of stairs. It is hot beyond words.

Joyce strips to his shorts and collapses on the bed. "I've seen everything I want to see." This time I am worried. We have watched him through lesser crises. In the past his pulse might begin to flutter, his speech to thicken, his temperature to fall and his pupils to dilate. But until now his modesty has never left him. Whenever, as constantly happens in Soviet hotels, chambermaids enter without knocking, he has always been able to scramble wildly under a blanket or at least roll off the far side of the bed onto the floor. The maid at Ashkhabad is fetchingly pretty, a quality which usually rouses in Joyce extraordinary feats of modesty. Now he only closes his eyes.

All the Moscow Russians are in complete misery. Kirilov in particular, who is big and white-skinned, with a thin layer of subcutaneous blubber which serves him well just under the Arctic Circle. Now whenever he makes the slightest effort, he sweats like a race horse. So with the buxom interpreter, a Moscow girl who isn't used to the climate although she has been here many months. We wonder what she could have done to deserve Ashkhabad.

Meanwhile, I try to organize a bath before the banquet, and manage to convey this idea by gestures to the chambermaid. She beckons me to follow. They have one, all right, and as I had guessed, it is in the basement. You first undress in your room and then, putting on whatever takes your fancy as a bathrobe, descend the three flights of stairs into the main lobby, on through the main dining room and hence into the basement.

The shower was a single pipe of sun-heated water turned on by pulling a chain. I pulled. A cupful splashed down between my shoulders; then someone turned it off. I donned my raincoat-bathrobe and went up to the main lobby to find out why. The guilty parties, it there developed, were the Municipal Soviet of Ashkhabad. There is a water shortage and it is turned on only two hours daily. I went on up to dress. On this tour I discovered that the hotel had three dining rooms, ranging from comfort down to squalor, according to which category of rationing the guest was entitled. Our banquet, however, was in none of these. Its long table was laid in the corridor on the top floor which seemed to be a private ghetto reserved for us.

Our party had now dwindled to Kirilov, Lucy the new interpreter, Nesterov, and, of course, Nick, the NKVD man. Joyce stayed in bed. The wistful local committee sat down with us. There were two Turkomans, of whom one, an alert, slender, black-eyed young man, was the mayor, and about six Russians, several of whom looked competent. The rest looked on their good behavior.

Across the table from me is Nesterov, a spare little man, who, as I have said, has been a Party member since boyhood, but who markedly resembles the late Andrew Mellon. He wears the same meticulously neat gray suits. But he has from time to time a merry twinkle in his eye. He seems a mild, conservative little man and although he doubtless had the blood of countless massacred czarist nobles on wherever a Communist keeps his conscience, we had come to like him very much. And this was our last day with our Russian hosts.

So Eric and I began deciding what political opinions these Russians would hold if they were set down in our American scheme of things. We told Nesterov that he would undoubtedly be a Republican, and he immediately wanted to know why.

Because, I explained, he was cautious, prudent, and a man of consequence in business matters. In America all such pillars of the community were not only Republicans, but heavy contributors.

Nesterov blinked but finally decided to feel flattered. Down toward the end of the table was a dumb-looking man with popping eyes, a permanently open mouth, big Adam's apple, and flaring ears, who kept leaning forward to hear.

"And that gentleman there," said Eric, designating him gravely, "would be a member of the Farmer-Labor party." It was so apt that I exploded with a laugh.

Then the Russians took up the game. I forget just what high commissariat they awarded to Eric. But Nesterov, appraising me with a grin, said that in Russia I would be a Komsomol, which is to say, a bright young man on the make, possible in line for Party membership but not yet worthy of it.

I thanked him for his carefully weighed compliment but said it was undeserved; more probably they would have me out with other political offenders, digging the Volga canal. So now, both

Kirilov and Nesterov laughed; I thought a little too heartily. And neither argued the point.

We are now hustled off to the rug factory and en route get a better look at Ashkhabad. It has, like the others, an old Oriental section, but the new Russian town is beautifully laid out and well paved. In the center is an irrigated park, an oasis of green in the yellow desert dust which blows everywhere. And in the park, under this broiling sun, is a veritable forest of Bolshevik statues, mostly Stalin. He is always striding along in his long overcoat with his ear flaps down, heavily gloved, just as he is under the Arctic Circle. It seems cruel. We want to get a can-opener and rescue him.

In this sizzling desert heat one might think he could just as easily and more appropriately sit quietly in shorts and a sun-helmet. But only one statue has been officially approved, so he must stride and sweat.

Since we have left Moscow, we have noticed that, when his name is mentioned, less and less do the Russians leap feverishly to their feet overturning furniture, although I am sure his popularity is as great. Perhaps down here they are doing a good job and know that Moscow knows it, so that even the spies and Party hacks whose duty it is to keep enthusiasm whipped up have become bored with all these surface demonstrations of loyalty.

The rug factory is most interesting. I have watched Navajo women weave, but these Turkoman girls have greater skill and a more delicate craftsmanship. They are decked out in beautiful native costumes, wearing lovely hand-hammered gold and silver jewelry, although I suspect strongly that it was borrowed for the occasion from the local museum. In weaving they squat beside the looms, using both their fingers and toes to hold the thread and tie knots. As we pass through they work feverishly but I happen to return to one room and find them relaxed, gossiping and cackling —probably at us, which is only sensible. We are now taken to a museum of their work. On the way over we are told that they turn out about a square meter of rug a week, and that their base pay for this is 350 roubles a month, although 1,500 is not uncommon among the women who can turn out the most valued rugs, which they will now show us.

The museum is filled with magnificent rugs in rich ancient patterns and colors, and I wish I could spend an hour here, instead of the allotted few minutes. But they lead us down to the end to the choicest of all. There are four rugs. Each has a narrow border of ancient design, like the others. But it encloses a woven picture of Marx, a picture of Engels, a picture of Lenin and, largest of all, a picture of Stalin.

The sad thing is that the Communist *nouveau riche* who, to demonstrate their loyalty, pay staggering prices for this beautifully woven junk, may convince the Turkoman craftsmen that Marx's bushy beard or Stalin's shaggy eyebrows are things of more breathtaking beauty than their ancient native patterns.

From the rug exhibit we go to the town's Museum of Culture, formerly a Mohammedan mosque, built in 1903 under the czars and the emirs. It is too fancy for our taste, but solidly built and kept well painted by this regime. We ask if any mosque in Ashkhabad remains open for worship, and are told that there is one, over in the native quarter, but it is small, squalid, and would not interest us.

This more stately mosque-museum is the town's art gallery, designed to elevate popular taste. On its main floor, under the great dome, carefully preserved in glass showcases, are Dresden china pieces of shepherds and shepherdesses. In another case are examples of French Sèvres dinner ware, and with this some Brittany peasant plates from Quimper. In a third they have czarist Russian china, made in the czar's porcelain works at Petrograd.

All of it is decent. None of it is remarkably good. It is the kind of solid, extremely conservative stuff which an American banker's wife in a town of 50,000 would have bought on her trip to Europe in 1913, but which her daughter-in-law would consign to the attic at the time they put in the pink bathroom fixtures and the basement rumpus room. I ask if these things came from the houses of the nobility in the province; only a few, they answer. Most of them were sent down from Moscow to raise the level of people's culture in Ashkhabad.

Free market prices seem to be lower than Moscow. Outside a woman is selling sweet soda on the street for only 10 kopeks (about 1 cent) while in Moscow it was 3 roubles (24 cents). The Intourist girl tells us that if you go out to a near-by co-operative to buy grapes, they are only 2 roubles (16 cents) a kilo, whereas in Moscow they were about 100 roubles. However, if you buy them in the Ashkhabad bazaar they must cost you 12 roubles. In general, transportation is the big price hurdle in the Soviet Union. Before they can approach our food standard, they must double or treble their rail system and build roads for trucks.

The day closes with a 12-mile trip through the blistering desert to the "horse factory." Having by now the knack for translating Kirilov's idiom into English, we had already guessed it would be a stud farm. These desert nomads, like the Arabs and the men of our own Southwest, have always been proud of their mounts. They are shrewd traders and breeders of horse-flesh. They say production goes entirely to officers in the Red Cavalry.

They are beautiful horses—well stabled, fed, and trained. As we wait in the enclosure, a couple of grinning fifteen-year-old jockeys emerge to give us a fine exhibition of fancy riding.

That night there is, as ever, the local opera. The Turkoman performance differs greatly in costumes, somewhat in music but not at all in plot. It is still the cruel khan's beautiful daughter who wants to marry the poor boy, and in the last act love finds a way. Because there is almost no rain in Ashkhabad, the theater has no roof, so we watch all this under the stars in a beautiful new building.

In the stifling heat of my hotel room, the good-natured chambermaid suggests by gestures that I would sleep better if we pulled my cot onto the balcony. The sun rises early. I look down on a courtyard of squalid tenements, windows open, and Russians sleeping everywhere, sometimes under shelter but often stretched out on the ground. The yard itself is filled with blonde, blue-eyed, flat-nosed Slav babies—two-, three-, four-, and five-year-olds toddling around, some wearing shirts and some not, beginning their early morning play before the sun is too hot.

And I marvel at this teeming, fertile, hard-working, long-suffering, indestructible race, which now spawns down here in this irrigated valley as it does under the Arctic Circle.

Properly we think of Russia's empire as a relatively empty place. There is still elbow room for this generation—but what of the next? When the collective farms are so full of people that they can no longer feed themselves or the factories—what then?

The problem is not one for our times, since today Russia, like England and America, is one of the "have" nations, with a comfortable share of the world's earth and raw materials.

Today these well-fed, blonde Slav babies play in the desert sun, reveling like all babies, in the dust of the courtyard, just under the mountains which divide the Soviet Union from Persia.

So now at the airport we say good-by to our good friends Nesterov and Kirilov, and to Nick, who has so faithfully watched over us and our contacts. As we wait for our pilot, we notice, carefully stacked by the runway, great blocks of a yellow-green substance and are told that this is raw sulphur, brought in by plane from a distant mine.

Sulphur is cheap for its weight and bulk. Under the cost system of the Western world, no one would dream of wasting valuable air-cargo space on it, even in wartime. Here, where they seem to invent their bookkeeping as they go along, block sulphur sometimes moves by plane, while war-wounded sometimes move by horse-cart.

We climb into the Douglas, for our flight back to capitalism. The pilot spirals up over Ashkhabad, getting altitude for the mountain pass. Looking down we see the old native quarter clustered around its mosque and beyond, the wide streets and parks (full of striding Stalins) of the new Soviet town. Glittering below is the cool green water of an enormous new public swimming pool. Still more significant is its placement; not in the Slav Town with the other new buildings, but on the edge of the native city, so that the Turkoman people enjoy it too. It glitters up at us like a square-cut emerald, in its snow-white concrete setting, as vivid as the sulphur blocks we still see stacked at the airport. Somehow between them they told the story of the Soviets.

The mountains were unbelievably beautiful for rain falls only on their northern slopes so this side of every foothill and knoll was Kelly green against the desert yellow of the mass. Once over the ridge, there was only tawny desolation, dropping off into flat desert until we sighted the winding green river valley of Teheran.

Within our cabin we witnessed a miracle: the Resurrection of Joyce. Behind us were the perplexities of the Soviet Union, which included both bedbugs and the NKVD. Ahead are the fleshpots of capitalism. Outstanding among which for Joyce is the American air base at Teheran where he can revel in boiled black coffee and boiled white sheets.

Even as we watch, his bubonic plague of yesterday fades like a dream, the roses are back in his cheeks, and the twinkle in his blue eye. He is wondering if maybe the American general in Teheran might not have a shot of Bourbon "To take away the taste of that damn vodka. And why wouldn't he have it? He's an Irishman, isn't he?—and with two stars. What the hell good are they if he can't get Bourbon? You speak to him, Eric."

But we were not quite through with the Soviets. At the airport they told us that the Russian Ambassador, having been informed we were on our way out, was tendering us a final dinner.

We spent the afternoon using ourselves as laboratory guinea pigs. We had just come from six rugged weeks of socialism, diluted only by Soviet champagne. What were the things which would strike us most vividly on our return to capitalism? We decided to take notes even as the Douglas was fighting the air currents in the pass.

First of all were the shops. As we had passed through Teheran en route to Moscow and fresh from America, Persia had struck us as one of the world's slum areas, as in point of fact, it is. Today our eyes feasted on the wonderful little shop windows, piled high with fruit—pink meat hanging from butchers' pegs—windows of screw drivers and saws or new clothing. This disreputable Hooverville of the capitalist world was, by contrast with the empty shops of the Soviet Union, a Dickens description of Christmas plenty. Had there been fine public buildings just over the mountains? There were finer ones here.

Now for the people; here in what we had called shabby Persia, a majority of the ones we saw on the sidewalks were much better dressed. About one-fifth approached the low Soviet average and about one in ten were in picturesque Oriental rags and tatters— worse than anything we had seen over the border. For Soviet rags are never quite that—they are always clean and neatly mended.

Another thing which slapped us in the face was that Soviet street crowds were always hurrying to get somewhere—unless they were standing in a queue. These people were taking their time. A few of them—both rich and poor, seemed to be frankly loafing and enjoying it. They had some time to kill!

Over the border life is one long frantic rush to get things done in order to stay alive, with the Communist Party feverishly prodding you on. Yet there had been no beggars, there had been no sly Oriental trickery—there had been a robust self-respect which we liked—and sometimes missed here.

Our final Soviet dinner was in the Soviet Embassy *dacha* a few kilometers out of Teheran. It was spacious like the other *dachas* in which we had been entertained. Our hosts we remembered as having met us at Teheran airport when we were entering Russia. Only where were their boiled Sears, Roebuck suits? These had not altered but our viewpoint had; after Moscow they now seemed smartly dressed.

The Soviet Ambassador was an earnestly courteous man in his late thirties with short cropped black hair—he could have been mayor of any Siberian town. But the dinner was European—gone was the great spread of fish and sausage—the lavish Oriental style. Instead there was a polished table, by contrast bare with a Spartan simplicity, at which we partook of an ordinary European meal. Soup to fish to entree to salad to dessert to coffee, with brandy at the end for toasts.

Here Eric made easily the best speech of our trip. He thanked them for their great hospitality. He told them they had not only given us their best, but that they had in every way fulfilled their promise that he might go where he liked and see what he wished. Some of the towns we had visited, he said, had not been open for foreigners since 1926. And if he had a regret, it was only that in the past there had been so much suspicion of foreigners that outsiders had seen little of Russia.

However, on our trip, he said, not only had he been taken everywhere, but had been allowed to take American correspondents with him, so that they could write something of the strong new world that was being built over the mountains and behind the Urals. And he hoped that in the future Americans could travel just as freely in Russia as Russians may travel in America.

Then the Russian Ambassador got up. He was not pleased.

He said there were good reasons why Russia in the past had been suspicious of foreigners. Even today, he said, there were reasons. There was, for instance, in Switzerland the Bank of International Settlements. An American was a member of its board, and also a German. All during the war this bank had continued to do business. Therefore, he said, the Soviet Union had good reason to be careful of foreigners.

During the last part of this speech Joyce was sitting on the edge of his chair, an Irish terrier straining at the leash, thirsty for blood. When the Soviet Ambassador sat down, Joyce was on his feet. For weeks we had been smothered both by hospitality and the ever-present attentions of the NKVD; now was his golden moment.

Fixing our host with a glittering eye, he said: "Mr. Ambassador, sometimes we have our suspicions, too. When Mr. White, here, was in Moscow, he stayed at the Hotel Metropole. His room was on the second floor. On the third floor," here Joyce paused, smiled, then continued gently, "were the Japanese." And at this point every American at the table roared with laughter. "Nevertheless, you Russians are welcome in America. You can travel, there, without permits, anywhere you like. You can send to Russia any reports about us you like, for publication in your newspapers, without any fear of American political censorship.

"I hope this will continue, Mr. Ambassador. We do not distrust Russia. I see no reason why in America we should. So my toast is to the trust between Russia and America."

Everybody drank, the Americans smiling broadly. Then the ambassador hastily said that we would now proceed to discuss economic matters because Mr. Johnston had been invited to Russia as a businessman. So we should confine our talk to matters of future trade and commerce between our two respective great nations. So we did. Presently it was time to go home. We said good-by and went.

This ends my report on the Russians and here are my conclusions. I should add that these, as well as the general viewpoint of this book, are entirely my own, and not to be charged against my good friend Eric Johnston.

Any close relations with the Soviet Union are fraught with considerable danger to us until American reporters get the same freedom to travel about Russia, talk to the people unmolested by spies, and report to their homeland with that same freedom from political censorship that Soviet representatives enjoy here, and that American reporters enjoy in England and other free countries. This must also apply to European or Asiatic territory occupied by or affiliated with the Soviet Union. Correspondents abroad are the ears and eyes of our Democracy. If we are to help build up Russia, our people are entitled to complete reports from press representatives of their own choosing on what we are helping to build.

We should remember that Russia is entitled to a Europe which is not hostile to her. We should also remember that while American aid in building back her destroyed industries is highly desirable to Russia, it is not indispensable. She will not swap it for what she considers her security in the new world.

She is, however, in a mood to accept decent compromises. But if, as our armies are in Europe while this settlement is being worked out, we find we can't get everything we want, we would be childishly stupid to get mad, pick up our toys and go home.

If we decide it is wise to do business with the Russians, we can trust them to keep their end of any financial bargain. They are a proud people, and can be counted on to pay on the nose before the tenth of the month.

But any business deals should depend on their aims in Europe and Asia. We should extend no credit to Russia until it becomes much clearer than it now is that her ultimate intentions are peaceable.

I think these intentions will turn out to be friendly. However, if we move our armies out of Europe before the continent is stabilized, and if disorder, bloodshed, and riots then ensue, the Russians will move into any such political vacuum. After all, they are not stupid. Russia for the present needs no more territory, but badly needs several decades of peace. She is, however, still plagued with suspicions of the capitalist world, and needs to be dealt with on a basis of delicately balanced firmness and friendliness. To date, the Roosevelt Administration has done an excellent job of this, in an unbelievably difficult situation.